MW00636067

Also by *Arthur Faram*

"Ancient Signposts"

ISBN-13: 978-0615814827

ISBN-10: 061-581-4824

Foundation Press
Dallas
info@foundationpress.us

LA MERICA

The first true story of the colonization of the Americas

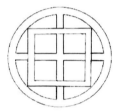

by Arthur Faram

Dedicated to my loving wife Mariko,

without whose love, support and patience, this book may have not been written.

Forward

La Merica (la mer'.e.ca) Ancient Portuguese and Templar name for America. Meaning: "The Western Star"

a Merica (a mer'.e.ca) Portuguese for "To the Western Star"

Merica (mer'.e.ca) Modern Portuguese word for America.

America (a.mer'e.ca) The name of three connected land masses, in the western hemisphere, divided into what are known as North America, Mesoamerica (Central America), and South America.

Many years before the arrival of the date of December 21, 2012, sensationalists were prophesying that the date would bring about changes in the earthly existence of man. This mass hysteria was brought about by the fact that this date was the last date recorded on the 26000 year long Aztec Calendar. This date was important for two reasons. First, it was the date of the winter solstice. The winter solstice has been held sacred in the beliefs of most ancient religions throughout the world. Secondly, December 21, 2012 represented the beginning of a new 26000 year cycle of the precession of the equinox. This precession is caused by the earth wobbling on its axis which takes 26150 years to complete. If you were to ask me how the Aztecs knew of this 26000 year cycle, I would reply that man has been on the earth studying the stars for much longer than anyone will admit. Recently man made structures have been found in Africa that are over 200,000 years old. That is ample time to compile enough information about the stars to make a calendar, or to navigate the world's oceans at will.

Every calendar has to have an end date. The Aztecs must have thought it appropriate to make the last date on the calendar the date of transition from one 26000 year cycle to another. The fact that you are reading this book proves that it was not the end of the world. Although the date was not the end of the world, it was supposed to signify a change from one era of mankind to another. Many see this as the end of a 26000 year cycle of destruction and greed, and a transition to a 26000 year period of introspection, wisdom and truth.

Since 2012 has passed many positive changes have come about in the areas of wisdom and the redistribution of knowledge and wealth. This could mean that there are great things ahead for mankind. Those good things are spiritual and philosophical and will override the physical turmoil that will be prevalent during this transition period. I trust that you will find this book one of those revealing truths.

Introduction

This story originated during the investigation of the history of the Faram family. As is customary in Celtic families, history is handed down orally from one generation to the next. Being the oldest grandson in my family, I was entrusted with the family history which was handed down through my grandfather. That history remained dormant until I retired and had the time to investigate these stories using the miracles of modern science and research methods.

During the tracing of the Faram heritage I learned that my family, and their Celtic cousins, played a major role in ancient history. That history reveals events that have been lost, distorted and hidden for millennia. I was able to trace the Faram family tree back to 43BC, during the time that the Roman Emperor Claudius was commandeering all the ships that existed along the West coast of Europe. Claudius was preparing for the second invasion of England and needed all the ships available in order to carry troops and supplies from France to England. However, this is not a story about Rome, or the Roman Empire, but a story of the forgotten Celts and Templars and Masons that fought for, and won, the territory now known as the United States.

Our story starts with a review of the history, and secrets, that were handed down to the Celts from the cultures that preceded them. This history is necessary in order to place the later actions of the Celts into their proper perspective. After establishing a base of history our story will then turn to Galicia, now a province in Spain, which was the home of the tribe that would evolve into a family known as the Farams, a family which would play a major part in molding the history of both Europe and North America.

At the time of its glory (43BC - 700AD) Galicia was the most influential Celtic country of the time. The Galician Celts and the Portuguese, previously called the Etruscans, were close allies during this period. The Portuguese, although currently a country that remains neutral in world affairs, is still a close ally with the United States. As you read the book, you will see that it was the Celts and Portuguese that settled the Pre-Columbian, American continents. Their ancient philosophies were influential in the decisions which the founding fathers made in establishing the United States.

One would have to wonder how anyone could trace their family history back to 43BC, before there were public records or even last names. The answer to that question is three fold:

First, the Faram family passed down enough information to make it possible to determine a genealogical map of their history in Europe. My grandfather, Arthur Stanley Faram, came to America, with his parents and brothers, as a young boy from England in 1901. With him he brought, and passed on to me, numerous stories of our previous history in England and Europe.

Secondly, as you will see, the Farams, previously the Farums literally left their mark down through the ages in such a manner as to be found 2000 years later. This history will be validated by monuments and geoglyphs which they left behind to tell their story.

Thirdly, the Farams existed in an area where well kept and detailed civil and church records have existed for longer than in most other parts of the world.

For the first time, this book will unveil the history of an era that has been cloaked in political and religious secrecy for centuries. You will be exposed to the European history and religious evolution pertinent to that story. You will also experience the history of the almost forgotten ancient Celts, which has been intentionally suppressed for political and religious reasons. Included will be the true history of the Vikings, the Knights Templar, and the revelation of an ancient secret handed down to the Celts from thousands of years before. This ancient secret, which I call Geoglyphology, was discovered during my research on another project. Four years of intensive research, combined with the rediscovery of ancient territorial survey markers, called geoglyphs, will reveal the true story of the colonization of regions throughout the western world, including the Americas.

In both ancient and modern times, before the invention of computers and satellites, the Celts, Portuguese, Etruscans and their predecessors marked their territories using the alignment of structures, monuments, and geoglyphs that could only be seen in their entirety from above, but could be verified from the ground. At the time that these geoglyphic structures were being built there was no expectation that computers and satellite images would be developed to reveal their secrets; or, perhaps they were left there to be found at the appropriate time.

Faram Genealogy

Once I finished researching the history of the Faram family, it came to mind that this was a story that was too incredible for most people to believe. It was then that I decided to request a DNA study on myself to either prove or disprove my findings. Contained in **Appendix A** are the data that I received back from the DNA tests. They were even better than I could have ever expected. The results proved conclusively that the migration paths of the Faram family, in the DNA tests, matched the data which I had compiled in my research. In addition, the 37 Marker testing showed, coincidentally, that our current family DNA mutation originated in Galicia, the point of origin for this story. The data also confirmed that the Farams were a close knit family which migrated together, leaving few relatives behind during their relocations. Although many families left Farum, Denmark for Ireland, there was only one family that moved to Scotland and adopted the last name Faram. Records show that others from Denmark chose different names and most moved to Ireland. The close contact, which the Faram family maintained with the other branches of the family, was demonstrated again c1600 AD when the Farams in Scotland brought the Farums that remained in Italy, to Scotland. Records indicate that, upon the Italian Farums arrival in Scotland, the new inhabitants lived with their distant cousins and immediately begin changing their name to Faram.

As you read this incredible story, please compare the physical information presented here, against the non-physical rhetoric used by some to validate past claims. Please remember that the evidence presented here is the product of first hand knowledge, research, the universal science of mathematics, and physical evidence.

My background as an analyst consists of being both the senior computer analyst for the U.S. Government at the FAA Technical Center, and the CEO and founder of the first comprehensive background check company in the US. And so it is, that I invite you to come along on an exciting and informative historical adventure which will engage you, and change the way you see the world.

© 2013

Contents

Chapter 1
Ancient European History, Relative to the Celts

Knowledge of the history of Europe is important in understanding the formation, evolution and migrations of the ancient Celts. The history that is provided here is directly related to the Celts and is necessary in order to understand the book as a whole. This is not a story which you will find in the history books, but a story that can be confirmed by bits and pieces of history that are spread around the world in various mediums. This may be the first attempt to put the pieces of the puzzle together so that the citizens of the Western Cultures will know their true history.

My heritage is Celtic. Although my ancestors had visited the Americas many times, it wasn't until c1400 that they actually moved to North America. The story you are about to read is developed from a combination of oral family history, and many years of intense research. It was my search for my family history in Europe that led me to uncover a family history and discover hidden secrets which one usually only finds in an adventure movie. My genetic DNA results are provided in "Appendix A" to verify the geographic movements of the Faram family. It is through the travels of the ancient Faram family that secrets hidden from the public, for political, monetary and religious reasons, have been learned and passed on through this book.

Through research, and the discovery of the previously secret science of Geoglyphology, I have learned that I am not alone in this knowledge. The heads of state, and many secret organizations, in every major nation in the world know this information. Before the colonization of the Americas it was kept secret so that the rich and powerful could reap the vast resources of the western hemisphere and return them to Europe, for profit, without competition.

Our history will begin in northern Italy. It is the central location of Italy, on the Mediterranean, that makes it the pivotal point for much of the history of Europe. I have attempted to provide maps and diagrams to verify the information you are about to discover.

CELTIC WARS WITH THE ROMAN REPUBLIC (c510 BC - 43 BC)

Gallic Invasions of Italy - Rome versus Gauls/Celts/Etruscans of Northern Italy - B.C. 390-121

Most of Italy's neighbors were as civilized as the early Italians themselves. The Gauls, who had settled in northern Italy, were different. They had crossed over the passes of the Alps from the unknown lands of northern Europe and were ferocious warriors. Hostilities between the two nations began in about 400 B.C. and continued for 800 years, during which time the Gauls often joined forces with Rome's other enemies. Eventually Julius Caesar suppressed the Gauls by conquering their home territories in Western Europe. The following are some of the major campaigns against Rome, between the fourth and first century B.C. in which the Gauls figured prominently.

First Invasion: the Senones - 390-283BC

The Romans first encounter with the Gauls was a terrible one. In about 400 B.C. the Senones, a tribe from Western Europe, crossed the Alps and settled in Northern Italy. There they swiftly came into conflict with Etruscan tribes in the area, who petitioned Rome for help. The Roman ambassadors sent to arbitrate with the Gauls got drawn into combat, in violation of the laws of diplomacy.

This so enraged the Gauls they marched immediately upon Rome. The Roman army, unprepared and disorganized, was routed at the Battle of Allia, and many of the citizens fled the undefended city. The Gauls burned most of the city but a garrison held the capitol until, according to Livy, the great Roman hero Camillus arrived with an army, and drove the Gauls out. The Romans rebuilt their destroyed city, but the incident left a great impression on the Romans, and July 18, the Day of Allia, was, for hundreds of years, a solemn day of remembrance on which no official business could be transacted.

Battle of Arretium - Etruscans and Gauls defeat Romans: 283BC

After this battle, the Gauls settled down in Northeast Italy, and were a constant source of threat and nuisance to the Roman Republic, later called the Roman Empire. They frequently joined with enemies of Rome, during wars of Italian unification, and were especially prominent in the Samnite Wars. In 283 B.C. they served as mercenaries in an Etruscan War, and at Arretium destroyed a Roman army with over 13,000 casualties. Revenge was soon taken.

Battle of Lake Vadimon - Romans defeat Etruscans and Gauls: 283BC

At the Battle of Lake Vadimon, the Romans defeated the Etruscans and their Gallic allies, and then marched into Gallic territory, destroyed all of the Gallic towns, killed the men and enslaved the women. The remainder of the previously mentioned Senones tribe, having no homes to return to, migrated north, into the Danube area. This is an important time in the history of the Celts. It is now known that the Etruscans were in possession of the ancient secret of Geoglyphology, which had been passed down to them from millennia before. It is also known that the Celts were in possession of these same secrets. (Chapter 5) This poses the question, until further investigation, as to whether the Etruscans shared the secrets with the Celts, did the Celts share the secrets with the Etruscans, or did they both have possession of the ancient secrets prior to their meeting.

Conquest of Cisalpine Gaul: 232-194BC

The Po valley in Northern Italy, where most of the Gallic tribes lived, was called Cisalpine Gaul, and it was the last region of Italy to come under Roman control. There was a constant inflow of Gauls coming over the mountains during the same time that the allies of Rome were expanding northward into the territory. It became clear that, by about 232 BC, it was imperative, for Roman security, to pacify the region. By 225BC, the incursions of the Romans into Gallic territory inspired the Gauls to raise an army and again march on Rome. There were several battles fought, which included disasters on both sides, but in the end Rome and her allies subdued the Gauls and made Cisapline Gaul a Roman Province.

The Punic and Macedonian Wars: 218BC

The Gauls demise, however, was short lived. The Gauls were terrific fighters, but had lacked good generals. In 218 BC, Hannibal a Carthaginian Commander and one of the greatest generals of all time, and Rome's most implacable enemy, crossed over the Alps from Spain. He joined forces with the Gauls, and for the next fifteen years, ravaged all of Italy and threatened Rome. The Gauls continued to fight Rome even after Hannibal was driven out of Italy, this time during the Roman-Macedonian War. The most significant battle during this period was Cremona, when the Romans defeated, with heavy slaughter, a Gallic army led by a Carthaginian General. Eventually, however, the Cisalphine Gaul was pacified enough so that Rome could freely move armies about in the region. This was required for its subsequent campaigns in Macedonia, Greece, and Asia Minor. Many of the remaining tribes settled peacefully under Roman control.

Third Gallic Invasion - The Averni - 121BC

During the century after the Second Punic War, Rome was engaged in a series of wars in Hispania with the object of pacifying the Celt-Iberians or Hispanic Gauls. The Rhone valley however, was home of several Gallic tribes, including the Arverni and Allobroges. When Roman armies attempted to move about in the area, they came into conflict with, and defeated the local tribes at the Battles of Isara and Vindalium. By this time Rome was secure as the dominant force in the region and was no longer threatened either by Gallic invasions, or by the danger of their enemies making harmful alliances with their Gallic neighbors.

Celtic Invasion of Rome - Celts, Gauls and Visigoths defeat Romans - 410AD

This was a time in which the Roman Empire was becoming weak and complacent. The Galician Celts (The tribe from which the Farums would evolve.), Swabians and Gauls saw an opportunity to not only reclaim Italy but to wipe out the Catholic hierarchy which they blamed for distorting the teachings of Jesus. Their conquest was successful, and complete, with the taking of the Italian Peninsula. They did however spare the clergy in their sacking of Rome. After the conquest of Italy a portion of the Farum clan remained behind while the remainder of the clan returned to their homeland in Corunna, Galicia. Italy became a centralized location for the maritime business of the Farums. As you read through the book you will discover, as I have, that both the Galician and the Italian branches of the Farums would play a part in the history of the Faram family and, indeed, world history.

Roman Influence

While the peoples of the Mediterranean Basin developed sophisticated urban societies, the peoples of western Europe were primarily agriculturalists and seaman throughout the Ancient Period. However, warfare, trade and migration brought Western Europe and the Mediterranean Basin together. The Romans incorporated much of Western Europe into its empire and the new society that developed included elements of Greco-Roman, Celtic and Germanic culture.

The Roman Empire was forever expanding in its quest for land and power. Between 55 BC and 34 BC, Julius Caesar developed plans to conquer Britain. In 34 BC, the plan was executed and the invasions of Southern Britain begin. Julius Caesar did not have sufficient resources in the way of transport and supply ships to accomplish this mission. To solve this problem he enlisted ships from around Europe to assist in the invasion. This type of enlistment later became known as privateers. Caesar left the port of what is now Boulogne France, for Britain, with over 800 ships of all designs, including troop transports, merchant ships and traders.

One of the tribes that were enlisted was a Celtic tribe that would later call themselves the Farums. The Farums, and their cousins, were expert seamen for many years and possessed ships needed by the Romans. At the time of the invasion the tribe, that would later call themselves the Farums, inhabited the area known as Corunna, Galicia on the Iberian Peninsula. The Romans armada of ships was recruited from all the shores of what are now Italy, Spain, France, Belgium, Denmark, the Netherlands and Germany. Caesar wanted to land at Dover but, on arrival, found that his ships drew too much water. Caesar opted to land further East in deeper water. During this first invasion (55 BC), the Romans met with little resistance and established colonies on the southeastern shores of Britain. However, the Romans occupation of England did not last. After the invasion, the Romans assimilated with the Britannians and things returned to normal. And so it was that, the Roman foothold in Britain was lost.

During the period between 24 AD and 43 AD, the Roman Emperors planned another invasion of Britain. The prowess of the Celtic tribes at sea had not gone unnoticed by the Romans who were again making preparations to invade Britain in 43 AD. The Romans invited Celts, who most likely assisted in the first invasion and were now pirating Roman ships, to assist in the invasion. This would put the aggressive Celtic and Germanic tribes on the Romans side. As a result the Celts were recruited to assist the Romans in the resupply of Roman troops in the second attack on Britain. The attack was planned to depart from what is now Boulogne-sur-Mer, France.

By attacking the Southern and Eastern coasts of England, the Celts were not attacking their relatives. The concentrations of Celts in England at the time were all on the western coast of England. In fact, the Celtic Danes and their Viking allies conquered all of Eastern England, the Faroe Islands, Iceland and Greenland after their move to Denmark from Galicia. This time in England's history would be known as The Period of Danelaw.

During the following decades, presumably as a result of their performance during the previous invasions of Britain, the Celtic Galicians and the Romans developed a close alliance. You might call it a symbiotic relationship. The Celts were expert seamen with a substantial fleet of merchant ships. The Romans needed the additional ships to resupply the newly established garrisons in Britain. Corunna, Galicia, located on the northwest tip of the Iberian Peninsula, became an important port on the route to resupply the Romans occupying Britain. The group, as did most Celtic tribes at the time, earned their primary living by sea trade and mining. The Galicians were content with taking a back seat to politics and the military in order to maintain their merchant trade. For example, they lived under the protection of the Romans in Galicia, and when the Romans left, c390 AD, they lived with and fought along side the Swabians.

The Swabians originated from what is now Southern Germany, at the foot of the Swiss Alps. The wealthy Celts held a prominent place in the nautical history of the world and left footprints of their presence wherever they traveled. After the Galicians later move to Denmark, they would call themselves the Farums. This name would be used until their move to Scotland at the end of the 14th century. For reasons which will be described later, it would be in Scotland that they would change their name to Faram.

THE ROMAN EMPIRE (c43BC - 410AD)
The Roman Empire in 117 AD.

The Roman Empire is the phase of the ancient Roman civilization characterized by an autocratic form of government. The Roman Empire succeeded the 500-year-old Roman Republic (510 BC-1st century BC), which had been weakened by the conflict between Gaius Marius and Sulla and the civil war of Julius Caesar against Pompey the Great. Several dates are commonly proposed to mark the transition from Roman Republic to Roman Empire, including the date of Julius Caesar's appointment as perpetual dictator (44 BC), the victory of Caesar's heir Octavian at the Battle of Actium (September 2, 31 BC), and the Roman Senate's granting to Octavian the honorific Augustus. (January 16, 27 BC). This just happens to be the time that the Galician and Romans symbiotic alliance begin to form.

From the time of Augustus to the fall of the Western Roman Empire, Rome held dominion over all of the territory depicted in the following map.

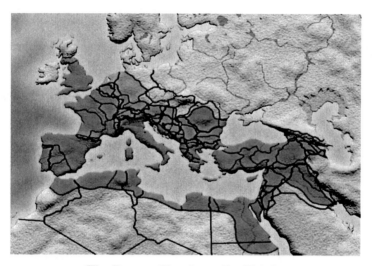

The Roman Empire at Its Height

At its territorial peak, the Roman Empire controlled so much land around the Mediterranean Sea that the Romans called it mare nostrum - "Our Sea". Rome's influence upon the language, religion, architecture, philosophy, law and government of nations around the world continues to this day.

The discipline and organization of a Roman legion made it a superb fighting machine. The Romans preferred infantry to cavalry because infantry could be trained to retain formation in combat, while cavalry tended to flee when faced with danger. But unlike a barbarian army, the legions required constant training and salaries that made them a huge expense for the empire. As agriculture and economic activity declined, taxes grew harder to collect, and the system came under strain.

Collapse of Rome (372-476 AD)

The end of the Roman Empire is sometimes placed at 4 September 476 AD, when the last emperor of the Western Roman Empire, Romulus Augustus, was deposed and not replaced. Even before this date the Empire had been divided into Western and Eastern halves, Emperor Diocletian, who retired in 305 AD, was the last Emperor of an undivided Empire. The Western Roman Empire declined and fell apart in the course of the 5th century. The Eastern Roman Empire, known as the Byzantine Empire, preserved Greco-Roman legal and cultural traditions along with Hellenic and Orthodox Christian elements for another millennium, until its eventual collapse with the conquest of Constantinople at the hands of the Ottoman Empire (Germany) in 1453.

The Alans, an Iranian people who lived north and east of the Black Sea, were Europe's only line of defense against the Asiatic Huns. Unfortunately for Rome, they had been dislocated and resettled throughout the Roman Empire. Starting in the second century, various indicators of Roman civilization began to decline, including urbanization, seaborne commerce, and population. Only 40 percent as many Mediterranean shipwrecks have been found for the third century as for the first. The population of the Roman Empire shrank from 65 million in 150AD to 50 million in 400AD, a decline of more than 20 percent.

Migrating south, the Germanic peoples reached the Black Sea early in the third century. They created confederations which proved more formidable opponents than the Sarmatians, whom the Romans had dealt with earlier. In Romania, north of the Black Sea a Germanic people, the Goths, created at least two kingdoms, one Therving, the other Greuthung.

The arrival of the Huns in 372-375AD ended the history of these kingdoms. The Huns were a confederation of central Asian tribes who founded an empire with a Turkish speaking aristocracy. They had mastered the difficult art of shooting composite re-curved bows from horseback. The Gothic people were forced to seek refuge in Roman territory in 376AD. The Goths agreed to enter the Roman Empire as unarmed settlers, but many bribed the Danube border guards into allowing them to bring their weapons with them.

In 410 AD, the Visigoths, led by Alaric I, and assisted by the Celtic Galicians and Swabians, captured the city of Rome. For three days there was fire and slaughter as bodies filled the streets, palaces were stripped of their valuables, and those thought to have hidden wealth were interrogated and tortured. The invaders respected the Roman church property. Those who found sanctuary in the religious domiciles were the fortunate few. It was during this invasion of Italy that a portion of the Galician Farum Clan decided to remain in Southern Italy and conduct part of their seagoing merchant business from the Italian port of Rossano.

Medieval European History

The Dark Age is a term used to describe nearly 1000 years of history that is often hard to understand, due to a lack of creativity and surviving documents. Western Europe was under the rule of hundreds of feudal lords and kings. Castles dominated the landscape, and entire cities were built behind protective walls.

The Romans had the power; however, the Celts carried ancient secrets of spirituality which the hedonistic Romans lacked. When Constantine begin loosing his soldiers to the new religion of the Nazarenes, the name of the Christians before the Catholic Church, he decided it was time to establish a Roman religion. This would have to be a religion that combining some of the virtues of the Nazarenes, with the other religions that existed at the time. The Roman Empire formally legalized Christianity during the 4th century, and soon afterward, the zeal and evangelism of practitioners spread this Roman Catholic faith throughout Western Europe as far west as northern Ireland, southern Ireland having been already occupied by the Celts and their Orthodox Christianity. The Catholic Church would become one of the most powerful medieval institutions through controlling the publication of books, the making

26

of laws, and participating in much of the European political world. Much of medieval Europe's art and architecture has a direct connection to the Roman Christian church. During this period, rulers of the various land holdings were required to get permission for important decisions from the Pope in Rome, through their local clerics.

Knights, soldiers, peasants and pilgrims marched along European roads and trails, as far East as Jerusalem, bringing back with them stories of differing cultures, architecture, tales of romance, and advances in medicine. Trade was both a blessing and curse. Merchants began importing silks, cottons and rare spices from all over the known world. But these ships would also bring the horror that became known as the Black Death. The disease ravaged Asia, before wiping out nearly one-third of Western Europe. The years also took their toll, from William the Conqueror's invasion of England in 1066, to the Hundred Year's War that ended in 1453 AD; there were few years that didn't see battles raging in some part of Europe. Medieval Europe saw some important developments, such as Gutenberg's moveable type printing press invented in the middle of the 15th century. This would bring printed material to the masses, and improve communication between societies. The printing press was as important to medieval society as the Internet was to 20th century society. Marco Polo would also popularize the account of his voyage to the Orient, and expose Europeans to this exotic land. Through these centuries, Europe was slowly waking from a harsh slumber, and began to sow the seeds of a Renaissance.

THE WESTERN ROMAN EMPIRE

On December 25, 800, Pope Leo III crowned Charlemagne emperor of the Western Roman Empire. By this time, the original Roman Empire had evaporated and Europe was divided into two halves, both dominated by religion and politics. In the east was the Orthodox Christian Byzantine Empire, and in the west was the Catholic influenced half of Europe. The act of crowning Charlemagne established both a precedent and a political structure that were destined to figure decisively in the affairs of western and central Europe. The precedent established the papal claim and right to select, crown, and even depose emperors. This was asserted, at least in theory, for nearly 700 years. In its primary stage, the resurrected Western Empire endured as an effective political entity for less than 25 years after the death of Charlemagne in 814. The reign of his son and successor, Louis I, was marked by feudal and fratricidal strife that climaxed in 843 AD with the partitioning of the Western Empire.

Despite the dissension within the newly created Western Empire, the Popes maintained the imperial organization and the imperial title, mainly within the dynasty, for most of the 9th century. The emperors exercised little authority beyond the confines of their dominions. After the reign of Berengar I of Friuli, who was titled the King of Italy or ruler of Lombardy, was crowned emperor by Pope John X, the imperial throne remained vacant for nearly four decades, with the Pope as the ruler of Western Europe. The Eastern Europe, the Frankish kingdom, or Germany, capably led by Henry I and Otto I, emerged as the strongest power in Europe during this period. Besides being a capable and ambitious sovereign, Otto I was an ardent friend of the Roman Catholic Church, which is revealed by his appointment of clerics to high office, and his missionary and military activities east of the Elbe River. In 962 AD, in recognition of Otto's services, Pope John XII awarded him the imperial crown and title.

THE HOLY ROMAN EMPIRE

Flag of the Holy Roman Empire

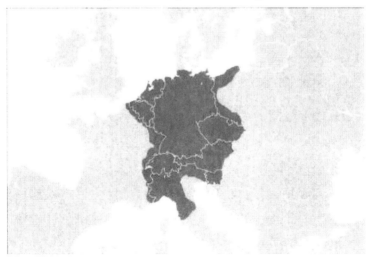

The Holy Roman Empire c1600AD

The "Holy Roman Empire" should not be confused with the "Roman Empire" which preceded it. The Roman Empire, with its final seat in Rome, fell in the 5th Century AD and predates the Holy Roman Empire by hundreds of years. "The Roman Empire" denotes the Empire of the Romans in the Mediterranean area. The "Holy Roman Empire" denotes a political entity in central Europe ,from 800 to 1806, with the Pope in Italy as its figure head. In the 11th century it was called the Roman Empire, and in the 12th century the Holy Empire. The title Holy Roman Empire was adopted in the 13th century. Although the borders of the empire shifted greatly throughout its history, its principal area was always that of the German states. From the 10th century its rulers were elected German kings, who usually sought, but did not always receive, imperial coronation by the Pope in Rome.

The Holy Roman Empire was conceived by the German nations hundreds of years after the collapse of the Roman Empire. The purpose of the Holy Roman Empire was to expand the Germanic (Holy Roman) Empire under the guise of Christendom. In 1463 AD, the divisions, both geographically and politically, of the dominions that made up the Catholic Church, precipitated one of the many Catholic schisms. The Germanic ties with Italy, on both a political and religious level, continued until after the Second World War.

Contemporaries did not quite know how to describe this entity. In his famous 1667 description *De statu imperii Germanici*, published under the alias "Severinus de Monzambano", Samuel Pufendorf wrote: "Nihil ergo aliud restat, quam ut dicamus Germaniam esse irregulare aliquod corpus et monstro simile ..." (*"We are therefore left with calling Germany a body that conforms to no rule and resembles a monster"*). In his *Essai sur l'histoire generale et sur les moeurs et l'esprit des nations*, (1756), the French essayist and philosopher

Voltaire described the Holy Roman Empire as an "*agglomeration*" which was "*neither holy, nor Roman, nor an empire*".

During this time, the dualism between the "territories" and the King/Emperor, became apparent. This practice had only changed under Otto III (King 983, Emperor 996-1002), who began to utilize Bishoprics all over the Empire as temporary seats of government. Also, his successors, Henry II, Conrad II, and Henry III, apparently managed to appoint the dukes of the territories. It is therefore no coincidence that at this time, the terminology changes and the first occurrence of a Regnum Teutonicum (German Kingdom) are found. Most importantly, the Catholic Church was clearly a player in the political system of the Empire.

Contemporary terminology for the Empire varied greatly over the centuries. Under Otto I the area of his reign was called "*Regnum Francorum Orientalium*" or "*Regnum Francorum*" meaning "*Kingdom of the East Franks*" or simply "*Kingdom of the Franks*". The term Roman Empire was used in 1034 AD to denote the lands under Conrad II, and Holy Empire in 1157 AD. Coincidently the birth of the Holy Empire coincides with the end of the Viking era. This also corresponds with the birth of the German Baltic Sea Trade Association known as "The Hansiatic League". The alliance of German kingdoms was most likely in defense of the power which the Danes and Norse had achieved over the Baltic Sea area. In order to maintain a viable relationship with Germany the Celtic Danes sent their military force, the Vikings, west to begin the colonization of Iceland.

The precise term Holy Roman Empire dates from 1254 AD; the final version called The Holy Roman Empire of German Nations appears in 1512 AD, after several variations in the late 15th century. The Holy Roman Empire was a union of territories in central Europe under a Holy Roman Emperor. The first

Holy Roman Emperor was Otto the Great in 962. The last was Francis II, who abdicated and dissolved the Empire in 1806 during the Napoleonic Wars. The Holy Roman Empire's territorial extent varied over its history, but at its peak it encompassed the Kingdom of Germany, Italy and Burgundy, territories embracing the present-day Federal Republic of Germany, Austria, Switzerland, the Netherlands, Liechtenstein, Luxembourg, the Czech Republic, Slovenia, Belgium, as well as large parts of modern France, Italy and Poland. For much of its history the Empire consisted of hundreds of smaller principalities, duchies, counties, free imperial cities, as well as several kingdoms and other domains. Despite its name, for most of its existence the Holy Roman Empire did not include Rome within its borders, but did receive guidance from the Vatican.

A UNION OF GERMANIC STATES

The empire of central Europe, at first an unstable union of Germany and northern Italy and later a loose union of Germanic states, remained in almost continuous existence for more than 800 years. During the Italian-German phase, the empire played a significant role in central European politics and ecclesiastical affairs. A central feature of this period was the mortal struggle between the Popes (notably Gregory VII) and the emperors (notably Henry IV) for control of the Roman Catholic Church. With the Concordat of Worms (1122), in an agreement between Emperor Henry V and Pope Callistus II, the ruling parties relinquished the right of spiritual investiture, or installation of Bishops into ecclesiastical office. All the ruling emperors were German kings, and because imperial duties and ambitions inevitably required their full attention, local German interests were neglected. As a result Germany, which might have been transformed into a strong centralized state, degenerated into a multiplicity of minor states under aristocratic rule.

The agreement at Worms had removed one source of friction between church and state, but through the 12th century the struggle for political ascendancy continued. In 1157 AD Frederick I, called Frederick Barbarossa and one of the greatest of emperors, first used the designation Holy Empire, ostensibly to increase the sanctity of the Crown. Frederick attempted to restore and perpetuate the ancient Roman Empire by trying to suppress both the restless nobles of Germany and the self-governing cities of Italy. His interventions in Italy were opposed by the Lombard League and severely strained his relations with the papacy. Pope Adrian IV insisted that Frederick held the empire as a papal fief, but the emperor, who had the support of the German bishops, maintained that his title to it came from God alone. During the almost two decades of sporadic warfare in Italy that followed, Frederick was defeated at Legnano in 1176 AD by the cities of the Lombard League. The cities thus established their independence from further imperial authority. Emperor Henry VI, who claimed the throne of Sicily through marriage, twice invaded Italy and the second time, in 1194 AD, conquered Sicily. Emperor Frederick II renewed imperial efforts to vanquish the Italian cities and the papacy in the 13th century, but he was unsuccessful.

The Origins of Simony

After the decline of the Roman Empire, and prior to the Investiture Controversy, the appointment of church officials, while theoretically a task of the Roman Catholic Church, was in practice performed by secular authorities. A substantial amount of wealth and land was usually associated with the office of Bishop or Abbot, therefore; the sale of Church offices (a practice known as Simony) was an important source of income for secular leaders. Bishops and Abbots were themselves usually part of the secular governments, due to their literate administrative resources or due to an outright family relationship, it was

33

beneficial for a secular ruler to appoint (or sell the office to) someone who would be loyal. The well-established institution of proprietary churches, where the founder retained the right to appoint the clergy, further blurred the boundaries between church and state. In addition, the Holy Roman Emperor claimed and had exercised the special ability to appoint the Pope, and the Pope in turn would appoint and crown the next Emperor. Thus a top-down cycle of secular investiture of Church offices was perpetuated.

The crisis began when a group within the church, members of the Gregorian Reform, decided to address the sin of Simony by restoring the power of investiture to the Church. The Gregorian reformers knew this would be impossible so long as the emperor maintained the ability to appoint the Pope, so their first step was to liberate the papacy from the control of the emperor. An opportunity came in 1056 AD when Henry IV became German king at six years of age. The reformers seized the opportunity to free the papacy while he was still a child and could not react. In 1059 AD a church council in Rome declared, with In Nomine Domini, that secular leaders would play no part in the selection of Popes and created the College of Cardinals as a body of electors made up entirely of church officials. To this day the College of Cardinals selects the pope, and once Rome regained control of the election of the Pope it was ready to attack the practice of secular investiture on a broad front.

THE REICH (The Holy Roman Empire)

The term Reich was one of the German names for Germany for much of its history. Reich was used by itself in the common German variant of the Holy Roman Empire, (*Heiliges Romisches Reich* (HRR). Wikipedia - Search word Reich)

The First Reich

Traditionally believed to have been established by Charlemagne, who was crowned emperor by Pope Leo III in 800 AD, the empire lasted until the renunciation of the imperial title by Francis II in 1806 AD. The year of establishment of the Germanic Holy Roman Empire in 800 AD is significant, in that it coincides with the movement of the wealthy Iberian Galicians to Denmark, c710 AD, and the rise of the Danish sponsored Viking era in the late 8th century. The Viking era ended c1050AD at the same time that Denmark joined the Hansiatic League, instituted by Germany. (See Chapter 4) The name Roman Empire reflected Charlemagne's claim that his empire was the successor to the Roman Empire and that this temporal power was augmented by his status as God's principal vicar in the temporal realm (parallel to the Pope's in the spiritual realm).

From the mid-11th century the emperors engaged in a great struggle with the papacy for dominance, particularly under the powerful Hohenstaufen dynasty (1138 – 1208 and 1212 – 1254 AD), they also fought with the Popes over control of Italy. In 1272 AD, Rudolf I became the first Habsburg emperor. This started a long line of Habsburg successors. Until 1356 the emperor was chosen by the German princes; thereafter he was formally elected by the electors. Outside their personal hereditary domains, emperors shared power with the imperial diet. During the Reformation the German princes largely defected to the Protestant camp, thereby opposing the Catholic emperor. At the end of the Thirty Years' War, the Peace of Westphalia (1648 AD) recognized the individual sovereignty of the empire's states. The empire thereafter became a loose federation of states and the title of emperor was principally honorific. In the 18th century, issues of imperial succession resulted in the War of the

Austrian Succession and the Seven Years' War. The greatly weakened empire was brought to an end by the victories of Napoleon.

The Second Reich

The Second Reich was a Dynasty prominent in European history, chiefly as the ruling house of Brandenburg-Prussia (1415 – 1918 AD) and of imperial Germany (1871 – 1918 AD). The first recorded ancestor, Burchard I, was count of Zollern in the 11th century. Two main branches were formed: the Franconian line (including Burgraves of Nurenberg, electors of Brandenburg, kings of Prussia, and German emperors) and the Swabian line (including counts of Zollern, princes of Hohenzollern-Sigmaringen, and princes and then kings of Romania). From 1438 AD the Habsburg dynasty held the throne for centuries. The Franconian branch became Lutheran at the Reformation but turned to Calvinism in 1613 AD, acquiring considerable territory in the 15th – 17th centuries. Both Prussian and German sovereignties were lost at the end of World War I (1914 – 1918 AD). The Swabian line remained Catholic at the Reformation and ruled in Romania until 1947. The Hohenzollern monarchs included Frederick William I, Frederick II (the Great), Frederick William II, and Frederick William III of Prussia; William I and William II of Germany; and Carol I and Carol II of Romania.

The ruling house of Brandenburg-Prussia, the House of Hohenzollern, is most famous for providing rulers of the kingdom of Prussia and later of the German empire. The ancestral home of the House of Hohenzollern is in Swabia near the sources of the Danube and Neckar Rivers, about eighty miles south of today's Stuttgart. The Hohenzollerns began their climb to dynastic fame in 1417 when Holy Roman emperor Sigismund of Luxembourg awarded the Mark of Brandenburg in what was then the far northeast to Frederick of Hohenzollern as a reward for loyal service. Although Frederick found his new land to be poor,

36

unproductive, and exposed to danger, he decided to stay. This land, in which Berlin later rose, was the foundation of the Hohenzollern dynasty, known as the Second Reich.

The Third Reich

This was the official designation for the Nazi Party's regime in Germany from January 1933 to May 1945. The name reflects Adolf Hitler's conception of his expansionist regime which he predicted would last 1,000 years. This was the successor of the Holy Roman Empire (800 – 1806 AD) and the German empire (1871 – 1918 AD). The political members of the Holy Roman Empire would eventually evolve into the Third Reich. Hitler banned all religions and declared that the Swastika was the only image allowed in the Churches. Catholics and Protestants alike were persecuted and killed if they stepped out of line. Jews were either sent to labor camps or killed. Hitler's aggression would eventually lead to the Second World War and the defeat of Germany.

It is sometimes claimed that the only surviving fragment of the Empire is the tiny, independent Principality of Liechtenstein, located between Switzerland and Austria. There is still a Habsburg claimant to the Imperial throne there; however, titles of nobility no longer have official standing in Germany or the other central European republics.

THE MUSLIM INVASION OF EUROPE. (c600-700 AD)

In the eighth century, parts of the Mediterranean and the regions now known as Spain and France fell to invading Arabs. Mohammadism was introduced and began displacing Christianity, which had existed throughout southern Europe, the Holy Lands and Egypt. Few things in history are more remarkable than the ease with which Spain, a country naturally fitted for defense, was subdued by a mere handful of invaders. The usual causes assigned are the misgovernment by the Visigoths, the excessive influence enjoyed by the clerical caste, internal factions, jealousies, and the discontent of numerous classes, especially the Jews. All of these doubtless co-operated to facilitate the conquest and to weaken the power of resistance, but the real cause is to be sought in the fact that the Visigoths had never really amalgamated with the conquered population. The mass of the inhabitants regarded their current rulers as outsiders and had no reason to resent a change of masters. This feeling was strengthened by the conduct of their new conquerors.

The Arab invasion undoubtedly brought with it considerable bloodshed and destruction of property, but it was merciful when compared with the previous inroads of the German tribes, and in the end it proved a blessing rather than a curse to the country. All who submitted to the Arabs were allowed to retain their laws and customs, and were allowed to retain their own government officials. The cultivation of the fields was left to the natives, and the overthrow of the privileged classes gave rise to a system of small holdings or properties, which was one of the causes of the flourishing condition of agriculture under Arab rule. The slaves found their lot much improved under a religion which taught that the freeing of a slave was a meritorious action.

The Jews, who had suffered most under the Visigoths, had the most to gain from a conquest which they had greatly helped to bring about. This cooperation would earn them deportation after the Muslims were defeated in 1492. But nothing was so influential in securing ready submission to the Arabs as their tolerance in religious matters. Even the most bigoted adherents of Islam found a practical check to personal ideals in their zeal for proselytism. The Christians had to pay a poll-tax, which varied according to the class to which they belonged. All property was subject to the kharaj, a tax proportioned to the produce of the soil, but converts to Mohammedanism were excused from the

38

poll-tax. A clerical chronicler of the 8th century, while bewailing the subjection of Spain to an alien race, says nothing against the conquerors as the professors of a hostile religion. His silence is an eloquent testimony to the haughty tolerance of the Arabs.

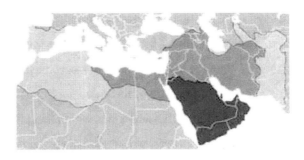

Arab Conquests 6th and 7th Centuries

⬛ Expansion under Muhammad, 622–632 AD ▨ Expansion during the Rashidun Caliphate, 632–661 AD ▨ Expansion during the Umayyad Caliphate, 661–750 AD

As time went on, and the Arabs felt more secure in their position, their rule became harsher. Many of the treaties which had secured favorable terms when the Arabs first arrived were broken, and the Christians were provoked to resistance by persecution. A notable instance of this was the edict making circumcision compulsory for Christians as well as Muslims. Greater hardships were endured by the locals, most of whom had embraced Mohammedanism from a desire for safety or for temporal gain. They found that returning to the old faith was blocked, both to themselves and to their children, by the law which punished any converting Muslim with death. At the same time their social position was intolerable, and they were excluded from all lucrative offices and from all shares in the government. Their discontent led to numerous and stubborn rebellions. It was during the Muslim Invasion of Spain c700 AD, that the Orthodox Christians in Galicia moved to the island of Zealand, Denmark.

It was fortunate for the Arabs that they succeeded at first in conciliating the natives, as otherwise their rule in the Peninsula would have been short-lived. Internal discord offered the Christians an easy opportunity for successful revolt if they had chosen to avail themselves of it. The conquerors were united by religion but not by race. When the task of conquest was achieved, and the need for unity was removed by the submission of the vast majority of the natives, quarrels arose between the various races and tribes which had taken part in the invasion. In addition to the Arabs proper, who regarded themselves as the true conquering race, there were Berbers or Moors, and converted Egyptians, and Syrians. So difficult was it to prevent their quarrels, it was found necessary to subdivide the conquered territory and to allot separate settlements to the different tribes, a measure which only tended to fragment their occupation. Matters were made worse by the constant efforts of ambitious chieftains to raise themselves to power or to ruin their more successful equals.

The first forty years of Arab rule in Spain was a period of woeful confusion, and it is difficult even to enumerate the names of the emirs who followed each other in rapid succession. The great empire of the Arabs began to fall to pieces as soon as it had reached its greatest extent. The movement, whose goal was conquest, began to fail because it ceased to conquer. The overthrow of the Omayyad dynasty by the Abbasids was a proof that disorder prevailed at the centre. The extremities inevitably displayed the same symptoms. Each new caliph sent a fresh emir to Spain; the governor of Africa claimed to interfere in the affairs of a province which had been conquered by one of his predecessors. The native chiefs were often unwilling to submit to a new ruler whose arrival was the result of a revolution in which they had no share and which they would

40

have prevented if they could. A capable and energetic governor, confronted with internal dissension and always dreading the arrival of a successor to supersede him, could only devise one way of solving the problem. The Arabs were unable to live with each other in peace, and the one means of preventing them from warring with each other was to find them new lands to conquer. Hence came the frequent invasions of Gaul (France), now ruled by the incompetent Merwings. This resulted in the conquest of the provinces of Septimania and Narbonne, and at one time threatened to subject the whole of Western Europe to the successor of Mohammed.

By 759 AD, the Arabs had been compelled to retire from all possessions beyond the Pyrenees. (The border between France and Spain) Thus thrown back upon the Iberian Peninsula, it seemed probable that their empire in Spain would also succumb to the disruptive forces which had no longer any external outlet. By the end of the 8th century, it had become evident that the Arabs had committed a great error in not devastating the whole Peninsula. The contemptuous indifference with which they had left the northern mountains, separating Spain from Galicia and Northern Portugal, to a handful of refugees was destined to bring its own punishment. Over time the will of the citizens and the in-fighting of the Arabs led to their defeat.

THE MEDIEVAL HISTORY of ITALY

Italy's geographic position, as well as its importance, as the seat of power during the Roman Empire, makes this country rich in medieval history. Rome was sacked in 410AD which brought an end to centuries of Roman rule throughout the European world. But Italy was far from vanquished, and its rise continued through religious power and its importance along trading routes. The succeeding centuries saw the development of many of Italy's most famous cities. Venice was founded in 811AD by mainlanders escaping barbarian

41

invaders. Meanwhile, the Italian Clan of the Farums maintained their seagoing merchant business, in southern Italy, until 1000 AD, when the Byzantine Empire fell to the German Ottomans. In 1060 AD, the country's first university was founded in Bologna.

Medieval Italy saw the birth of important literary works and became the cradle of Western art. In 1321 AD, Dante Alighieri finished his *La Divina Commedia* (The Divine Comedy) which formed the basis of literature in modern Italy. Artistic revolution began early in the Middle Ages as artists rebelled against the outdated Byzantine ethics that art should only have religious connotations. Soon, landscapes, floral designs, and the everyday life of common people became focal points for new works. During the 13th century, Cimabue was one of the early pioneers to portray real people in real settings. Religious art wasn't abandoned, and some of the greatest medieval masterpieces continued to portray biblical scenes.

13th century Tuscany was the focal point for tremendous political and economic growth. Not to be outdone, other cities began constructing massive buildings out of civic pride. Cathedrals were built high and were full of light to elevate the soul. Medieval Italy was an intoxicating mix of ancient Roman architecture, rising theocratic power, and artistic rebellion that would lead to the country's foundation as the heart of the Renaissance.

THE MEDIEVAL HISTORY OF SPAIN

Beginning in the 8th century AD, medieval Spain was a battlefield where Christians attempted to regain control from the Muslims who had invaded their country. The Moors were intent on conquering all of Western Europe, but they were stopped in the Pyrenees by Charles the Hammer. This defeat left the invaders settling in the lower parts of the Iberian Peninsula. The early years of

Moorish influence in medieval Spain were marked by infighting amongst the Muslim kingdoms. The Basques, who were traditionally fiercely independent, sided with French forces to expel the Moors.

The Moors' influence on Spain during the Middle Ages is still very evident. More than 4,000 words of Arabic origin are used in modern Spanish. Moorish architecture can be found throughout Spain, with its slender columns, horseshoe arches, cupolas, and airy, colorful buildings. Geometric designs and patterns can be found in surviving religious buildings, as the Koran forbade depicting human figures in places of worship.

The reconquest (Reconquista) of Spain lasted nearly 800 years. Sometime in the 14th Century, the Templars along with their longtime allies the Portuguese joined their mutual enemy, the Spanish, in vanquishing the Moors and flushing them from Spain. The Moors were defeated in Spain in 1492 AD, the same year that Columbus sailed to the Americas. The voyage of Columbus was not to discover the Americas, but to re-establish Portugal's claim to Brazil and to establish Spain and the Vatican's share of the new world. All this is clarified in later chapters.

A dark era in Spain's medieval history took place with the establishment of the Spanish Inquisition in 1480. Spanish soldiers tortured and killed those they suspected of being heretics or false converts to Christianity from the Jewish and Muslim faiths. The guilty faced imprisonment, hanging, beheading, and burning at the stake. The inquisition lasted until the 19th century, when Protestant heretics faced the same fate. This carnage, done in the name of religion, was also imported to the Caribbean and South America where millions of Native Americans were slaughtered by the Conquistadores in order to clear the way for Spain's conquest, both geographically and religiously

BREMEN, NORTH GERMANY

The first stone city walls of Bremen, Germany were built in 1032 AD. Around this time trade with Norway, England and the northern Netherlands began to grow, increasing the importance of the city. Bremen is important at this time in history since Bremen, and the German Empire, began its rise to power around the same time that the Viking era in the North Sea (c800 -1050 AD) ended. History tells us that the Vikings sudden disappearance was due to their move west to Iceland.

During this same period Charlemagne, the King of the Franks (Germans), made a new law, the Lex Saxonum. This law stated that Saxons (Germans) were not allowed to worship Odin (the god of the Saxons), but rather that they had to convert to Roman Christianity on pain of death. This period was called the Christianization. In 787 AD, Willehad was the first Bishop of Bremen. In 848 AD, the diocese of Hamburg merged with the diocese of Bremen. In the following centuries the bishops of Bremen were the driving force behind the Christianization of northern Germany. Both Bremen and Hamburg lie on the boundary between Germany and Denmark and would later become the seat of the Hansiatic League. The location of Bremen and Hamburg on the Danish/German border was not an accident. The Galicians move to Denmark c700 AD prompted a line of defense along the Danish/German border on the Jutland peninsula.

The Farums, of Farum Denmark, were able to survive as Orthodox Christians in Denmark until the last decade of the 14th century. By the 14th Century, too many things pointed to the possibility that they could lose their religion, their way of earning a living (Taxing ships entering the Baltic Sea.), or even their lives, for being Orthodox Christians in a now Catholic Denmark. This is important because the town of Farum is located only 160 miles north of the

Hansiatic coalition of Lubeck, Hamburg, and Bremen Germany. The location of Farum City is near one of only two narrow entrances to the Baltic Sea. The Hanse took control of the Baltic Sea entrance which was once the domain of Denmark and the Farums. If they remained in Denmark the Orthodox Christian Farams would have had to settle down, become Roman Christians, and adopt the Germanic policies in order to live in the Hansiatic sphere of influence.

THE HANSIATIC LEAGUE (The Hanse)

Hanse, Deutsche, a trading organization of North Sea and Baltic German towns had its beginnings in the 12th century and effectively came to an end in the 17th century. The first Hansiatic organizations were the offices set up in foreign countries, in England in1157 AD and somewhat later in Norway, by groups of German traders from Cologne and Bremen. Separate associations, based on Lubeck, newly founded in 1158, grew up in the late 12th century. One association of Gotland Merchants (Gemeinschaft der Gothlandfahrer), cultivated and protected trade in the Baltic, and achieved economic penetration into Russia. These associations grew rapidly in the 13th century under the leadership of Lubeck. More German cities, in the interior as well as near the coast, joined the Hanseatic League which, though having no formal constitution, succeeded in exercising considerable economic and political power in the Baltic area.

The town of Farum is located on the island of Zealand, Denmark near the narrowest point to one of the two entrances to the Baltic Sea. After their move from Galatia to Denmark the Farums were tasked with collecting taxes, originally for Denmark and later for the Hanse. This involved the taking of ships that would not pay a tax. The privateers were allowed to keep two thirds of any property that they acquired and were to pay the other third to the Hanse at Bremen. In all, and at different times, 164 cities belonged to the League, but the most prominent members apart from Lubeck were Hamburg, Luneburg, Bremen, Cologne, Soest, Brunswick, Stralsund, Dortmund, Stendal, Bergen (Norway), Danzig, Reval, Riga, and Wisby. The last five, though outside the boundaries of the Empire, were predominantly German cities. It should be noted that the boundary between the Jutland Peninsula, Denmark and Germany was defined by the cities of Bremen, Hamburg and Lubeck. This may have been an intentional blockade resulting from Germany's distrust of the Danes.

In Western Europe the most important transit port of the Hanse was Bruges. By the 14th century the Hanseatic League dominated European maritime trade, and its power was such that it was able to undertake a successful war against Denmark in 1367-8, and to exact stringent peace terms in the Treaty of Stralsund (1370). Records indicate that shortly after this time period the Faram clan moved to Edinburgh, Scotland. This move was shortly before Henry Sinclair's journey to North America in 1398. The majority of residents of the Danish town of Farum moved to Ireland under different names. (See Chapter 4)

The timing of the Faram's move was impeccable, and why shouldn't it be, they were clandestinely embedded in the Hanse operations. The Hanse enforced its manifesto by force in the 15th century against Denmark (1435 AD) and England (1474 AD). This is the same time frame that the first Faram name to appear in written history was recorded in the government records at Edinburgh, Scotland. This is also the same time period that the Templars Rosslyn Chapel was constructed. The first record of the Faram name was found in the records of Edinburg officials in 1488 AD. Circumstances surrounding later church records in Fishlake, England would confirm that the Farums name had been changed to Faram when they moved to Scotland. A name change would be a logical move since the Farums had been influential members of the Hanse in Denmark. During the Farams early years in Scotland their ties with

Germany became a valuable asset. In 1454, shortly after the Farams return to Scotland to construct Rosslyn Chapel (See Chapter 8), Scotland was able to formulate a maritime treaty with the Germans when no other country was able to do so.

Bremen, Hamburg and later Lubeck were the eyes through which medieval Saxony viewed the North Sea. The cities were not only the joint centers of a metropolitan archbishopric whose jurisdiction originally stretched across Scandinavia and northern Germany; they were also great commercial centers. Hamburg was to play a leading role in that federation of merchants and towns which came to dominate the medieval trade of the Baltic and North Sea worlds. Initially commercial pre-eminence lay with the more westerly of the two towns. Indeed, as early as the eleventh century, the chronicler Adam of Bremen claimed that the merchants of the whole world congregated in Bremen. Although such a comment was laced more with local pride than statistical rigor, the city did develop into a bustling port, internationally famous from the thirteenth century for its manufacture of beer, with a population of perhaps 15,000 on the eve of the Black Plague. Like many ancient, inland Baltic ports both Bremen and the City of Faram lost their river access due to what is called Glacial Rebound. This is caused by land that was depressed by the weight of ancient glaciers slowly rising again after the Glaciers melted. This process has been ongoing for thousands of years and continues, at a slower rate, to this day. Bremen simply moved their port to the mouth of the river that served the city. Access to the city of Farum eventually became unnavigatable.

By the thirteenth century, Bremen's Hansiatic commercial connections extended southwards, towards England and the Netherlands, and northwards, into the Scandinavian world, as well as into the city's Saxon hinterland. Whether or not they extended westwards, to Scotland, is less certain. Scottish chronicles, meanwhile, are stonily silent about Bremen. This was most likely the result of religious differences than any other factors. Records indicate that by the later thirteenth century Bremen merchants did not play a discernible part in Scottish trade. Only from the fifteenth century, after the Orthodox Christians departure from the Baltic, does concrete evidence of their commercial activity in Scotland emerge and even then, compared to the trading activities of other Hanseatic merchants in Scotland, the role of Bremen merchants in Scottish trade seems to have been of a comparatively small scale and irregular nature. This is not surprising. Bremen produced little which Scottish merchants could not obtain elsewhere and, despite the fame of its breweries, it was the rival beers of Hamburg and Stralsund that seem to have supplied the Scottish market with what, in any case, remained something of a luxury product for most Scotts. By the same token, there was only a limited market in Bremen for Scottish exports. Demand for wool, Scotland's chief export throughout the Middle Ages, was restricted since Bremen was not a town renowned for its cloth consumption. Instead, its cloth imports were more readily furnished from England and the Low Countries. Although, given medieval religious customs and dietary conventions, there was a prodigious demand for fish in both Bremen itself and in neighboring Westphalian towns, such as Osnabruck and Herford, this was supplied largely from Scandinavian sources, among which Shetland, at least until its annexation by the Scottish crown in 1469, ought to be included. Bremen and Scotland were not, then, close trading partners in the Middle Ages.

While these two semi-detached North Sea neighbors pursued their commerce largely independent of one another, by the early fifteenth century, they did so against a common background of a strained economy and a restructured political landscape. The effect of the Black Death and subsequent population loss had been to reduce the overall demand for goods.

THE MEDIEVAL HISTORY of SCOTLAND

The Middle Ages saw the birth of Scotland. This land had been under constant attack from Norsemen, Picts, Britons, Celts, and Anglos, but Kenneth Macalpine, King of Scotts, in 843 AD united clans and declared himself ruler of Scotia. He took the Stone of Destiny to Scone to be used in his coronation. This stone is traditionally regarded as the pillow of Jacob in his dream of a ladder carrying angels between heaven and earth. Generations of Scottish kings were crowned on a throne that housed this stone.

William the Lion's ill-fated expedition to capture Northumberland in 1174 AD led to the humiliating "Treaty of Falaise" that placed Scotland under English rule. This rule was increasingly severe through the time of Edward I, who named himself overlord of Scotland. The Scotts patriot William Wallace, whose exploits were later immortalized in the movie Braveheart, resisted Edward and was later executed for this. Robert the Bruce went to Scone castle in 1306 AD and had himself named King. Robert went on to defeat Edward II's forces at Bannockburn in 1314 AD to win back Scottish independence. Scotland's new found independence may have contributed to the Farums decision to move there.

END CHAPTER

Chapter 2

The Ancient Celts

The Celts 600 BC.

The Celts, through their actions and migrations, had a profound effect on the history of the Ancient and Middle Ages. Not much is written about Celtic culture because, due to their secrecy and practice of passing information orally, their identity became lost in the hierarchy of the times. It is not widely known that Celtic tribes populated most of Europe prior to establishing their final kingdoms in Galicia, Portugal, Scotland, Ireland, The Isle of Man, Wales, Cornwall, and Brittany. There were many events, scattered over time, in which the Celts interacted to shape the history of the world in which we live. A world that was, to a large degree, shaped by a forgotten Celtic culture that played a major role in the history of the Western Hemisphere.

Genetic studies indicate that early Celtic tribes had their origins from the near East. Early population expansions, according to the respected Roman historian Livy, occurred about 600 BC, ushering in successive waves of Celts moving in all directions, tending to dilute their Eastern heritage the further West and North that they moved.

Confirmation of migrations have been found in three genetic studies from France, Italy, Switzerland, Southern Germany, Norway, and the East Anglians who are perhaps descendants of the first migration to the area around Jutland (Denmark) and Fyn (Finland). Ultimately the major expansion began at the beginning of the 4th Century BC. Soon the La Tene Celtic culture was found from Greece and Turkey in the East to Spain in the West. This Celtic genetic marker is not observed in Northern Germany, but is found in restricted areas of Scandinavia. After the initial migration the "heartland" of the early Celtic culture appears to have ranged from Eastern France to the Alps and from Switzerland to Bavaria and Austria. Three foci relating to centers of power or rich material culture of the La Tene include the Champagne-Marne area in France, the Hunsruck-Eifel area of the Mosel Valley in Germany, and Bohemia. The maximum extent of the Celts geographic influence is quite vast and covered areas no longer thought of as "Celtic". Celtic expansion was quite successful, early on, primarily because of their iron weapon technology and fierceness in battle.

ANCIENT CELTIC ORIGINS

Norway and Sweden were not originally considered part of the Celtic culture. The Celts move to Denmark c700 AD, from Celtic Galicia, and the close association of Denmark and Norway since then, has blurred those lines. These cultural differences would later play a part in the treatment of the Vikings, by the Celts, after the Vikings move to Iceland c950 AD.

Many times Norsemen is used to refer to the group of people, as a whole, who speak one of the North Germanic languages as their native language. ("Norse", in particular, refers to the Old Norse language belonging to the Early North Germanic branch of Indo-European languages, especially Norwegian, Icelandic, Swedish and Danish in their earlier forms.) The meaning of Norseman was *people from the North*" and was applied primarily to Nordic people originating from Scandinavia. The term "Normans" was later primarily associated with the people of Norse origin in Normandy, France who later assimilated into French culture and language. The term Norse-Gaels was used concerning the people of Norse descent in Ireland and Scotland, who assimilated into the Gaelic culture. Although the Celts lived and fought along side the Norse for over 300 years, the Celts that moved to Denmark from Galicia never considered themselves Norse.

Northern Celtic origins can, however, be traced back to the Scandinavian Countries. The original German language branches developed in modern Scandinavia, giving birth to the Germanic "Nations" (ethno group). The Early German Nordics became the ancestors of all Scandinavians (except Finnish). Later, what we now know as Germanic peoples, would migrate to the mainland (modern Germany), becoming a separate ethno group from their Scandinavian relatives to the north. The Northern European Celts would become known as the Hallstatt Celts and would occupy primarily the areas now known as Germany and Southeast England. The Near East Celts, evidently ardent mariners, would become known as the La Tene Culture and would migrate to all the shores of Europe, the British Isles, and eventually North and South America. These Mediterranean and Western European Celts would develop their own identity. During this time period the European and the German Celts became two separate cultures altogether.

During these migrations, one group stands out. This culture was called the La Tene Celts. In concert with the indigenous Celts, and later the Swabians, this group became the Galicians and formed the first country in Europe. The country of Galicia is now incorporated into the northwest section of Spain and still bears its original name as a province of Spain. Galicia is where we will later pick up the history of the clan that would later call themselves the Farams.

ETURIA AND THE ETRUSCANS (Northern Italy - 650 BC)

You are being introduced to the Etruscans early in this book to set the stage for the geoglyphic history that will follow. The diagram of the Etruscan cemetery, which follows, is one of the most descriptive examples of ancient Geoglyphology yet encountered (Explained in Chapter 5). Geoglyphology will be the origin of much of the information which you will encounter throughout this book.

Keep in mind that this science is not unique to the Etruscans or the Celts. The leaders of countries as far back as 10,000 BC have used these same geometric protocols to mark their territories. As a result, they have unwittingly left a permanent record of their movements for us to discover and use to rewrite history.

The area covered by the Etruscan civilization.

Etruria, usually referred to in Greek and Latin source texts as Tyrrhenia, was a region of Central Italy located in an area that covered parts of what are now known as Tuscany, Latium, Emilia-Romagna, and Umbria. A particularly noteworthy work dealing with Etruscan locations is D. H. Lawrence's "Sketches of Etruscan Places" and other Italian essays. The ancient people of Etruria are labeled Etruscans. Their complex culture was centered on numerous city-states that rose during the Villanovan period in the ninth century BC. The Etruscans were very powerful during the archaic periods. The Etruscans were a dominant culture in Italy by 650 BC, surpassing other ancient Italic peoples such as the Ligures. Their influence can be seen beyond Etruria's confines through their contact with the Greek colonies in Southern Italy (including Sicily). Indeed, at some Etruscan tombs, such as those of the Tumulus di Montefortini at Comeana (Google: Carmignano) in Tuscany, physical evidence of trade has been found in the form of grave goods. Such trade occurred directly with Egypt and other Mediterranean and Atlantic Coast cities. A mound identical to the Etruscan mounds can be found on Scilly Island, the southernmost point in the England.

The Etruscans, even further back than the 9th Century, were traveling to the Americas. The Etruscans, as had their predecessors and successors, inherited geometric secrets, which they included in their monuments, buildings and gravesites. These architectural secrets produced a survey of the lands which they had visited and claimed as their own. These ancient, immoveable and well documented structures prove, to the angst of many scientists and historians, the extent of their travels and territories. The following picture of the Etruscan graves, at the Banditaccia Necropolis in Northern Italy, clearly indicates the extent of the travels of the Etruscans in the 9th Century BC. The precision with which these lines were laid out is unbelievable. Some are as accurate as today's GPS. There have been hundreds of similar geoglyphs collected and documented from all over the world, some older than 10,000 years. They all use the same protocols, which indicate that the knowledge required to lay them out has been handed down for at least 10,000 years.

The Etruscan Cemetery at Banditaccia, Italy - 9th Century BC.

The Etruscan Cemetery at Banditaccia, with Magnetic Bearings Plotted.

The Extended Radials of the Banditaccia, Italy Cemetery Bearings.

Endpoints of the Banditaccia extended radials

(Please take note of these endpoints, as you will see them many times in future geoglyphs throughout the book.)

098 Degree Radial - Easternmost Tip of the Mediterranean
156 Degree Radial - Southeast Tip of Sicily
218 Degree Radial - Southern Tip of South America
227 Degree Radial - Geoglyphs on the NE Tip of Carlforte Island, SE Sardinia
231 Degree Radial -Westernmost Point in Africa
234 Degree Radial - Easternmost Point in South America
241 Degree Radial - Eastern Tip of Canary Islands
244 Degree Radial - Northern Island of Cape Verde
251 Degree Radial - Western Tip of Canary Islands
257 Degree Radial - Island of Medeira in the Atlantic
265 Degree Radial - Lisbon, Portugal
275 Degree Radial - Southern Point of the Original North American Territory
276 Degree Radial - Border Between Portugal and Galicia. Oldest Border in

Europe.

270 Degree Radial - Orientation Radial

289 Degree Radial - Geoglyphs at Sentier du Litoral Point, Corsica.

310 Degree Radial - Southern Tip of Ireland

317 Degree Radial - The Croagaun Monolith on the Keel Peninsula, West Ireland

318 Degree Radial - Geoglyphs on Small Island on the NW Corner of Ireland. (Geoglyphs present on the Island and at Kilgalligan on the Mainland.)

319 Degree Radial - The Knocknarea Monolith at Lecarrow, Ireland.

337 Degree Radial - Orkney Island, North Tip of UK.

342 Degree Radial - Shetland Islands. Northern tip, of the northern most Island in the British Isles.

350 Degree Radial - Southern Tip of Norway.

It would be impossible for the Etruscans to know the North, Midpoint and Southern tip of South America, unless they, or their predecessors, had been there. In addition, if the Etruscans, and other privileged civilizations, were able to calculate the mathematics to achieve such a fete, it proves that they had the ability to navigate anywhere in the world with pinpoint accuracy.

Rome was influenced strongly by the Etruscans, with a series of Etruscan kings ruling at Rome until 509 BC when the last Etruscan king Lucius Tarquinius Superbus was removed from power and the Roman Republic was established. The Etruscans are credited with influencing Rome's architecture and ritual practices; it was under the Etruscan kings that important structures such as the Capitolium, Cloaca Maxima, and Via Sacra were constructed.

The Etruscan civilization was responsible for much of the Greek culture imported into early Republican Rome, including the twelve Olympian gods, the growing of olives and grapes, the Latin alphabet (adapted from the Greek alphabet), and architecture like the arch, sewerage and drainage systems. The classical name Etruria was revived in the early 19th century, applied to the

Kingdom of Etruria, a creation of Napoleon I of France. This kingdom existed only from 1801 to 1807.

It is not difficult from the preceding photos to see that the Etruscans, who later evolved into Portuguese Celts knew of and were traveling to the Americas in the 9th Century BC. The Etruscans, whose major operations were originally conducted from Italy, were eventually pushed to the west coast of Europe and occupied the country of Portugal. The oldest continuous boundary in Europe is the boundary between Galicia, the historical origin of the Farams, and Portugal. Geoglyphs and structures around the world prove that the Galicians, the Portuguese, and their predecessors, sailed the seas of the Western Hemisphere for thousands of years.

THE CELTS

The Celts, as we know them, first appeared in history around 600 BC. At that time they had spread over much of the Alpine region and the areas in France, and Spain. These Celts are associated with the Hallstatt culture of the European Iron Age. Excavations have revealed rich tombs of the chieftains or royal classes. Evidence discovered in these tombs point to trade with all the classical Mediterranean civilizations. The Hallstatt culture eventually contracted into what basically became Germany.

Beginning in the fifth and fourth centuries BC, the La Tene Celts spread to France and the British Isles. Decorated metalwork from the La Tene culture was found in these areas; however, recent evidence reveals that the La Tene Celts may have been occupying these areas in an earlier time period. It is the La Tene culture that we will be examining in this book.

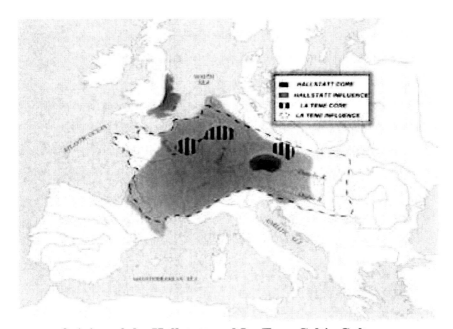

Origins of the Hallstatt and La Tene Celtic Cultures.

The striped areas are the La Tene Culture which would eventually occupy from western Britain to Russia.

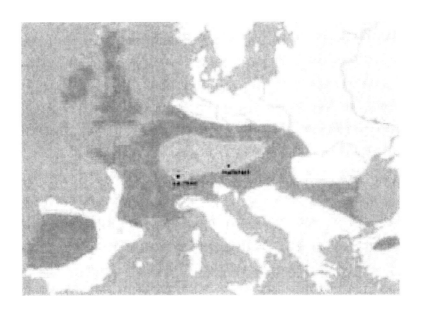

Celtic Distribution c500 BC

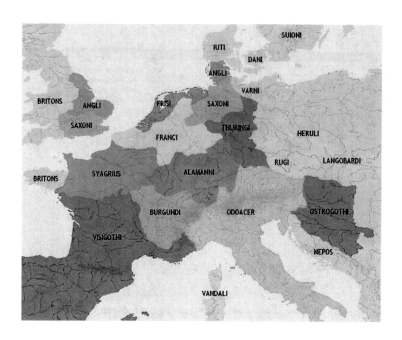

Celtic Distribution - c400 AD

Notice, in the previous map, the areas labeled Britons, Varni, Suiani, Dani and Iuti. These are the areas where the La Tene Galician Celts eventually settled, this includes Galicia, which is not shown. Also notice the Island of Zealand, labeled Dani. This is where the Farums settled after their move from Galicia. It is on this Island of Zealand where the towns of Farum and Copenhagen, the capital of Denmark, reside. The areas labeled Angli and Saxoni, on the European mainland, later evolved in to the territory controlled by German Hallstatt Celts.

By the third century BC, isolated Celtic tribes stretched from Ireland to Turkey. However, during the later third and second centuries BC, Celtic lands in the Mediterranean were beginning to come under pressure from the Germans and falling under the rule of the Roman Empire. In Turkey, the Romans crushed the power of the Galatians. (That is the Celtic tribes in Galatia, Turkey, not to be confused with the Celts on the Iberian Peninsula in Galicia.) They were almost annihilated by the kingdom of Pontus c80 BC. Recent research gives reason to believe that a red haired tribe of defeated Turkish Galatians moved to Scotland. The greatest blow to the Celts was the conquest of Gaul c50 BC. This left Northern Portugal, Galicia, Ireland and the other islands West of Mainland Europe as the only Celtic strongholds. In 43AD, the Roman Emperor Claudius invaded southeastern Britain and by 80AD, the Romans had conquered as far north as the border of Scotland (Caledonia). The Roman legions were unable to invade Scotland, and basically ignored the Western Peninsula of Cornwall, which remained a free zone of Celtic people.

Although there were seven Celtic nations, (See the following illustration. Iberian Galicia is the missing seventh territory.) It is generally understood that the Celtic people lived in smaller, looser formations known as tribes. Throughout Celtic history, these tribes have been known to move across the territories in pursuit of better lands to settle and better opportunities, such as less tribal warfare and the increasing need for more space. They also moved to escape famine, disease and war. It becomes evident that the Celts were more interested in trade than war. However, they were well equipped to do both. To date there have been fourteen different Celtic tribes identified by Roman writers.

Six of Seven Celtic nations.

 Scotland Ireland Isle of Man Wales Cornwall Brittany

Britain is a word that had Celtic roots. The Greek author Pytheas called them the Pretanic Isles, which was derived from Pritani, the name the inhabitants gave themselves. This word was mistranslated into Latin as Brittani. The peninsula on the west coast of France, where the Celts moved when the Saxons invaded southeast Britain, still retains the name Brittany. From the Iberian Peninsula a number of Celts migrated to Ireland. This migration settled the southern tip of Ireland. Ireland was never invaded by the Romans and as such, probably has a language that is the closest to the original Celtic language.

The Scotts, however, clashed with the Romans around the River Clyde, where they came into prominence. The Scotti later moved to establish the

Kingdom of Dalriada in Argyll which was on the west coast of Scotland. The Scotts then expanded and usurped the Picts, another Celtic race that had arrived in Scotland earlier.

The Galli tribe settled in France and the region and people became known as the Gauls. The Gauls were an aggressive people and they were constantly involved in invasions of Northern Italy. When the Roman Empire expanded, many of the Gaullish tribes were forced to flee or become Romanized, thereby loosing their Etruscan Heritage, including their language. Even later, the area was invaded by the Franks who were a Germanic tribe. The Franks gave the area their name, but adopted the language and customs of the people living there. So France became a region peopled by Celts, speaking a Roman language in a country that held a Germanic name.

It is noteworthy that the most impressive Celtic finds come not from the European regions, but Denmark. Almost all archeological finds originate specifically in the Jutland Peninsula and the associated islands. It has been noted that some of the very finest of Celtic artistry, anywhere, has been found in archaeological assemblages associated with the Cimbri Tribe of Celts in what is now Denmark. The earliest item is from Hjortspring on the Island of Als off the Eastern side of Jutland. Here in a peat bog were found long wooden shields of the Celtic type with spears and their wooden shafts along with a boat. This votive offering is dated to the late 3rd Century BC, which suggests that the Cimbri may have been established there from at least that date.

Contemporaneous is the bronze cauldron at Bra near Horsens in Eastern Jutland (Denmark). This vessel has the capacity of 130 gallons. The ornamentation is spectacular; and this object has been associated with similar items from the Bohemian - Moravian Region. Closer in time (1st Century AD) is the pair of four wheeled carts and the Celtic face masks found in Western Jutland at Dejdjerg. The decoration points to the items having been manufactured in Gaul. One of the richest La Tene finds to ever be found is the elaborately decorated Gundestrup silver cauldron, found within the area where the Cimbri resided in historic times in what is today Himmerland (the county named after the Cimbri). It is believed that it may have been manufactured in the region of Thrace or Middle Danube by a Celtic tribe known as the Scordistae. These non-indigenous finds support the idea of sporadic Celtic migration from the west coast of Europe to Denmark, over a sustained period of time. The Farums would also follow this trend, and relocate from western Spain (Galicia) c700 AD, and from Italy c1000 AD, and make the island of Zealand, Denmark their new home.

This brings a clear focus on the La Tene Celts retaining their early culture, regardless of their location. Their exploration took them to Northern Portugal, Galicia, and South and East to the Adriatic in repeated military campaigns. Ptolemy, in the 2nd Century AD, called one tribe the Kimbroi and traced them to the most northerly part of the Jutland, Denmark peninsula. It appears that this may have been part of the group to invade, in concert with Galicia and other North Sea ports, Kent and the Isle of Wight. These regions would later become the Anglian Kingdoms in England during the Anglo-Saxon (German) incursions of the 5th Century AD.

The Greeks encountered the Celts around the sixth century BC and called them Keltoi. When Julius Caesar encountered the Gauls (French) around 58 BC, he said they called themselves Celts. One suggestion is that the word is derived from the Indo-European root 'kel,' which means 'hidden.' The Celts were the hidden people. The term 'Celt' or "Kelt" applies to any of the European peoples who spoke a Celtic language. The historical Celts were a diverse group of tribal societies in Iron Age Europe. They left their legacy behind in Britain, Ireland, Spain, France, southern Germany and the Alpine lands. They also had influence in Bohemia, Italy, the Balkans and even central Turkey. Maintaining these ties required loyalty and expert seamanship.

Greeks and Romans portray them as barbaric. Unfortunately, there are no written Celtic texts to defend this accusation. Archaeology has proved that these people were not the barbarians they were accused of being, but that their society was a superior one, especially in the areas of metalworking. Many of their lands were well populated and farmed, dotted with settlements and gathering places. Forts and shrines were often found at these sites. The Celts were wealthy and intelligent and played a pivotal role in the formation of Europe. There were many tribes, some in Eastern Britain incorrectly labeled as Celts by the Romans. The advanced societies of Celts tended to exist on the West coast of England, Scotland, Western Europe and Denmark. The Celts were the first Trans-Alpine people to emerge into recorded history, originating, according to ancient chroniclers, from the region around the Lower Danube. They, along with their Etruscan cousins, invaded and settled in Italy at the beginning of the third century BC and sacked Rome, in 387-386 BC. The Romans remained under Celtic domination until 349 BC when they rose against their conquerors, and by 355 BC the Celtic conquest had been turned back. However, the Celts remained in Italy, as settlers, down to imperial times. Evidence of their settlement is shown in such place names in northern Italy as Trevi, Treviso, Treviglio, and the River Trebia. A comparison with some Cornish place names develops an interesting connection.

Rome was sacked again by the Celts in 410 AD. After a successful takeover of Italy, part of the Farum tribe would remain in Italy for over 1000 years as part of the Byzantine (Orthodox Christian) Empire, until displaced by the

Ottoman (Catholic) Empire. After the Ottoman takeover, most of the Italian Farums would move to Farum, Denmark to join their cousins. The few Italian Farums that remained in Italy c410 AD would reunite with their cousins again, c1600 AD, after the Farams moved to Scotland. This reuniting of families, after such a long period of time, shows the unity and communication which both the Farums and other Celts maintained. To further emphasize this unity, and passion for secrecy, both the Scottish and Italian Faram families begin intermarrying. The Italians also changed their last names from Farum to Faram. (It should be noted that the Scotish Faram and Italian Farum families had been genetically separated for over 400 years when this took place.)

In the next century the Celts turned towards Greece, and in a spectacular campaign destroyed the armies of Macedonia, Haemos and Thessaly. Finally, they defeated an Athenian army at Thermopylae before flooding through the gorges of Parnassos to sack the great temples of Delphi in 279 BC. Although the Greeks finally turned back the Celtic invasion, Thrace remained a Celtic kingdom until 193 BC. Some Celts pushed into Asia Minor and established a state called Galatia. (Not to be confused with the Iberian Galicia.) Ancient Galatia was an area in the highlands of central Anatolia in modern Turkey. Galatia was named for the immigrant Gauls from Thrace, who settled here and became its ruling caste in the 3rd century BC, following the Gallic invasion of the Balkans in 279 BC. It has been called the "Gallia" of the East, Roman writers calling its inhabitants Galli (Gaul or Celt). The Galatians remained a Celtic speaking country up to the fifth century AD. These Celtic Galatians are the object of the Apostle Paul's "*Epistle to the Galatians*" the ninth book in the New Testament of the Christian Bible. The importance of the Apostle's continued association with the Celts became evident when several of the Apostles moved to Iberian Galicia after the death of Jesus.

The early Celts were exponents of the Druid religion who taught the doctrine of immortality; that death is only a changing of place and their souls would return to earth again. Julius Caesar observed that this religious outlook could have accounted for the reckless bravery of the Celts in battle, with their apparent complete lack of any fear of death.

The Druids were great natural scientists who possessed the knowledge of physics and astronomy. The earliest known Celtic calendar dates from the first century AD and is far more elaborate than the Julian calendar. A Celtic calendar is now in the Palais des Arts in Lyons and is the oldest document in a Celtic language. This was the civilization from which the Cornish emerged.

The Celts began to settle Britain in the first millennium BC and at the time of the Roman Conquest, in 43 AD; Britain was Brythonic, or British speaking. In the fifth and sixth centuries, in the face of fierce invasion by the Saxons (Germans), a large group of Brythonic Celts migrated to Europe, taking with them the name of their country, which is known today as Brittany, France. Their language at the time of migration was exactly the same as Cornish and Welsh.

The remaining Brythonic Celts occupied Western Britain, from Cornwall and Dover, their settlements extended from Wales to Cumberland, and into Scotland, where they mixed with Goidelic Celts. Faced with the onslaught of the Saxons, the Celts formed an alliance with the Scots, but after nearly two centuries the Celts were defeated by the English at the Battle of Winwaed Field in 655AD. This was the last time the western Celts seriously contended with the Saxons for supremacy in Britain. This was not the case however, after the Danish Celts joined their forces with the Vikings in Denmark in the 9th century AD. During this time the Danish Celts and Norse Vikings, working in concert, invaded Britain with great success. The Danish domination of England lasted from approximately 800 AD to 1050 AD. This coincides exactly with the appearance and then the disappearance of the Viking era. This period of Danish rule in England is known as the period of Danelaw.

During this period, the western Celts became split into three groups and separated from each other. The main bodies were driven into the mountainous western peninsula that became Wales. In the eleventh century, a country called Cymru was formed in Northern Britain and became part of the Celtic kingdom of Scotland. The following century, the Scotts were defeated by the English but they retained the ancient name of Cymru in the Anglicized form of Cambria and Cumberland. Unfortunately, the Celtic language soon ceased to be spoken, though Cumberland is still full of Celtic place names.

In the south-west of Britain the Celts of Devon and Cornwall united into the kingdom of Dumnonia, but its eastern border was weak and the Saxons (Germans) began to move into Devon. Within a few years, Dumnonia had fallen and the Celts were confined in the southwestern peninsula of Kernow which the English now call Cornwall.

The geographical separation, imposed upon the various groups of Britionic Celts, caused differentiations in their languages to emerge. Until the reign of Henry VIII there is no reliable knowledge of the state of the Cornish language; by this time it had become transformed from harsh Old Cornish into a softer sounding tongue, today called Middle Cornish. The fact that the language was reaching its highest development may be seen from the amount of literature left to us from fifteenth and sixteenth century manuscripts.

By the start of the seventeenth century only a few Cornish speakers were left, and they were mostly in the extreme west of Cornwall. Most of eastern

Cornwall spoke only English, while the rest of the Duchy was bilingual. The seventeenth century saw a rapid deterioration of the language as an everyday form of speech and by the end of the century; Cornish speakers remained only from Land's End to the Mount, towards St Ives, and Redruth and again from Lizard towards Helston and Falmouth.

The eighteenth century was the last in which the Cornish language was in general use. How it had survived 800 years after Cornwall's conquest, is a fact to be wondered at. It is claimed that by 1722 AD, only St. Ives fishermen and miners used the language, though later in the century a Dr. Edward Lhuyd, a scholar from Wales, while visiting Cornwall to study the language, found Cornish spoken in twenty five parishes as a first language.

(Source of information: "*The Story of the Cornish Language*" printed in Cornwall by H.E. Warne Ltd. of St. Austell for the publishers, Lor Mark Press.)

ROMAN INFLUENCE ON THE CELTS

Roman rule appeared to have wiped out the Celtic culture. However, many Celts were content with maintaining an underground culture while appearing to conform to their conquerors customs. After Rome fell in the fifth century AD, the old Celtic lands came under Germanic rule, even the name of Gaul was replaced by the name France (derived from the Germanic tribe of the Franks).

Following the appearance in Britain of the proto-Welsh and other British kingdoms, there was resurgence in Celtic culture. Ireland retained much of its Celtic history because it had not been romanized like the British Isles. The story of the Celts, in Western Europe during the later Middle Ages, is one of gradual absorption and partial assimilation by France.

The Celtic Empire

Before recorded history, the Celtic Empire stretched from Portugal to Turkey. This changed as warring tribes pushed the Celts to the West Coast of Europe and the British Isles. One of the indications of the early extent of Celtic influence, is found in the ancient geoglyphs placed atop the newly discovered Bosnian Pyramids. The Pyramids themselves, although not Celtic, have been carbon dated as being over 10,000 years old. The geoglyphs, which were later placed atop the original pyramids by the Celts, refined and reduced the original territorial boundaries defined by the geoglyphic pyramids themselves. The geoglyphs that were added atop the pyramids later describe the Celtic empire as covering the whole of Europe. It is an accepted historical fact that the Celtic Culture once extended from the Baltic Sea to Scotland. Pressure from Eastern and German tribes pushed the Celts westward until they occupied what is currently thought of as the only territories previously occupied by the Celtic Cultures. The territorial markers, placed atop the Ancient Bosnian Pyramids indicate the greater extent of the Celtic Empire at some point.

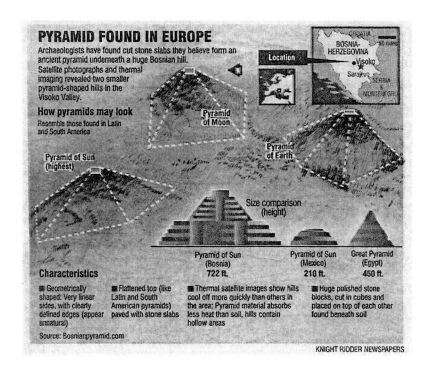

PYRAMID FOUND IN EUROPE

Archaeologists have found cut stone slabs they believe form an ancient pyramid underneath a huge Bosnian hill. Satellite photographs and thermal imaging revealed two smaller pyramid-shaped hills in the Visoko Valley.

Location

CROATIA
BOSNIA-HERZEGOVINA
•Visoko
Sarajevo
SERBIA & MONTENEGRO

How pyramids may look
Resemble those found in Latin and South America

Pyramid of Moon

Pyramid of Earth

Pyramid of Sun (highest)

Size comparison (height)

	Pyramid of Sun (Bosnia)	Pyramid of Sun (Mexico)	Great Pyramid (Egypt)
	722 ft.	210 ft.	450 ft.

Characteristics

- Geometrically shaped: Very linear sides, with clearly defined edges (appear unnatural)
- Flattened top (like Latin and South American pyramids) paved with stone slabs
- Thermal satellite images show hills cool off more quickly than others in the area: Pyramid material absorbs less heat than soil, hills contain hollow areas
- Huge polished stone blocks, cut in cubes and placed on top of each other found beneath soil

Source: Bosnianpyramid.com

KNIGHT RIDDER NEWSPAPERS

The Bosnian Pyramid Complex

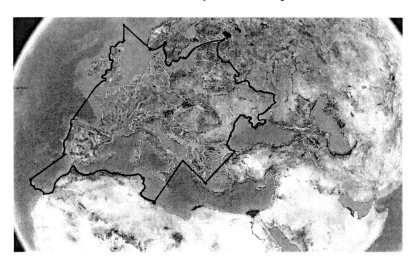

The Territory outlined by the Celtic Geoglyphs Located on the Top of the Bosnian Pyramids

In the 3rd Century BC, the Celtic culture expanded until it reached its greatest extent, with Celts living in Ireland and Spain in the West, and as far as Galatia (Turkey) and Asia Minor in the East. This was due to cultural exchange and peaceful transmission of ideas combined with massive military campaigns like that in northern Italy.

From then on, however, the Celts began to lose ground. Starting even in the 3rd century BC, the Romans began to conquer the Celtic lands from the south and only a little later, Germanic pressure from the northeast forced the Celts to the western Coast of Europe. By the end of the 1st century BC, all the Celtic lands but the British Isles were conquered either by the Romans or had become Germanized. Most of Britain comes under Roman control less than a century later, leaving what are now Scotland, Ireland, and Denmark as sovereign Celtic territory. Although Norway and Sweden were not considered Celtic, their alliance with Denmark leads many to the false assumption that they were of the Celtic culture.

Since the Celtic clans were ruled by a Chieftain, it was originally thought that the Celts had little in the way of any central government. Slowly, one by one, the Celtic clans were absorbed by the conquering Romans. Between 250 BC and 400 AD the only Celts not absorbed by the Roman culture were the Irish, Scots and the Danes. That is not to say that there were no more Celts in Europe. Many groups appear to have allowed themselves to be assimilated into the Roman Empire while maintaining their Celtic culture in secret.

Much of what we know about the Celts comes from Roman and Greek sources. And many of these are either biased, such as the "Gallic War" by Caesar or from second and third hand sources such as the Greeks Strabo and Diodoros. Although we know the Celts were not ignorant of writing, some Druids were able to read and write both Latin and Greek, they chose not to document their histories or culture. They instead relied on highly trained lore masters and musicians called "Bards" to record and recite their histories, feats, battles and deeds, in song and verse. It wasn't until the Christian monks started transcribing the songs and verse, many times with Roman Catholic modifications, that we had any clue as to the nature of the Celtic mythology, heroes and history. From these sources we can learn something of their society, religion and warriors. Unfortunately for history, their government and secrets were kept in the heads of their upper class, as is suggested in the following Celtic verse:

"The Triads of Britain"

"The three principal endeavors of a Bard:
One is to learn and collect sciences.
The second is to teach.
And the third is to make peace
and to put an end to all injury;
For to do contrary to these things
Is not usual or becoming to a Bard."

Celtic Druid Priests

The greatest asset of the Celts was their wisdom. Secrets and information had been accumulated and handed down by the Celts since a time before the Pharoes. The wise man of each tribe was known as a Druid. Down through time many people, to suit their own agenda, have attempted to discredit the Druids by calling them magicians and other, not so flattering, names. In reality the Druids, of Stonehenge fame, were the wise men and scientists of their day. It is said that Jesus, seeking wisdom, visited the Druids during the missing time between his twelfth and twenty eighth birthdays.

According to Caesar, the Druids were a highly organized intertribal brotherhood, which met annually in the territory of the Carnutes in Gaul to confer and elect a Chief Druid. The word 'Druid' is connected with the Celtic term for oak. Trees and sacred groves undoubtedly loomed large in Celtic religious life. Their gathering places were in sacred groves called 'Drunemeton' or 'oak sanctuary'. These were not pious priests who abstained from violence or sex; however, they were very spiritual leaders who retained knowledge which had been passed down for millennia. It is not known whether each tribe had its own specific group of Druids, but later Irish tales record that kings were served by a personal Druid.

Druids were guardians of the tribe's traditions and administered tribal law. As privileged members of a learned class, the Druids were exempt from military service and taxation. They were involved in politics and diplomacy and even though the chieftain or king ruled the tribe, the Druids had the final say in these matters. This was the reason why the Romans attacked the Druidical center in the territory of the Carnutes and later the Isle of Mona. The Druids were instrumental in deterring Rome's progress.

In some accounts, there was a different task associated with each Druid. One might be a healer and one might be musically skilled (Bard). The Druids passed on their teachings to novices for initiation into the Druidical order. Novices were expected to memorize a great number of verses, laws, histories, spiritual knowledge, and traditions. It could take as long as twenty years for a Druid to complete their studies. With the ancient knowledge that had been passed down through the ages, and the new knowledge that was required to be assimilated by the Druid priests, it would seem difficult to label them simply as barbarians. Druids usually wore white hooded robes and carried an oak staff. Some accounts say they shaved their forehead from ear to ear. There was an air of mystery surrounding the Druids and they were well respected and possibly even feared by other members of the tribe. Shrines that were used by Druids were often situated close to the powers of nature on hilltops or in grottoes. Some were in sacred groves, holy lakes, pools and springs, as well as formal religious temples.

Celtic Christianity

The early introduction of the teachings of Jesus to the Celts is a matter of extreme controversy; however, this controversy is put to rest by documents of the Catholic Church itself. The Celts adopted Christianity 300 years before the Latin version was conceived. After the Roman Catholic Church was formed, (c326 AD) Catholicism was spread rapidly throughout Europe by the Roman Soldiers. In order to survive it was necessary for the Orthodox Christian Celts to practice their religion in secrecy. Some even assumed the role of Catholic priests in order to survive. Through this intermingling of ideas the Celtic concept, although retaining its core values, absorbed some Catholic rituals and practices.

Although Orthodox Christianity was adopted by most Celts, it was not until Roman Christianity began to gain ground in Denmark, with the baptism of Harald 'Bluetooth' Gorsem around 960 AD, that Catholicism begin inroads into the Celtic Culture. A popular legand has it that the king was converted by a Frisian monk who held a heated piece of iron in his hand without apparent injury. Impressed by the display, Harald allowed his son and daughter to be baptized, clearing the way for Roman Christian succession. Although the reasons for Harald's conversion remain ubiquitous, there is little doubt that the decision was based on practicalities as well. Beside him at the time of his baptism was Emperor Otto I, a powerful German Catholic ruler on whom Harald would rely upon in future years, would later overthrow the Orthodox Byzantine Empire of Western Europe.

By the 11th century, Christianity was accepted as the major religion by the majority of the population; however, the version of Christianity being practiced by the Celts was not in line with what the Pope had in mind. Celtic Christian ideas were blended with Latin rituals and some Celtic beliefs remained. Sacred groves and springs, along with other natural sights believed sacred, were incorporated with Celtic Christian beliefs, often leading to the building of chapels at set locations. Sacred pools of water would be associated with certain saints, becoming desired places for baptism.

By the 12th century, Catholicism had taken root in Denmark. With eager encouragement from the Pope, Danish saints began to be canonized and an archbishop appointed to oversee Denmark and Scandinavia. Catholicism would be linked to the Danish monarchy and embraced by the population until the turbulent time of the Reformation, at which time the Danes again found themselves choosing a different system of beliefs.

(*How Christianity portrayed Jesus as a warrior to woo the Vikings*. Rugg, Andy - The Copenhagen Post, November 6, 2011)

Assimilation Not Annihilation

Another contributor to the demise of Celtic Culture was their habit of blending into the culture of their host country. Although the Celts maintained a tight knit society within their own ranks, they sought to work behind the scenes, mostly as mariners, within the culture in which they lived. This was beneficial for two reasons. First their society would not have to fund a standing military force, drafting a military would be the responsibility of their host country. Another benefit would be that they would not have to physically participate in political matters. Their only involvement would be influencing their hosts to operate in a manner favorable to their needs. Examples of this are exemplified by their use of government contracts and military protection while participating in the Roman Empire, and again with their recruitment of their neighbors, the Nordic Vikings, as their military force after the Gilicians migration to Denmark in c700 AD.

The Celts' volatile relationship with the powerful Roman Catholic Church, which continued for over a thousand years, almost eliminated their place in the history books. Celtic stories persist that tell of Jesus visiting Cornwall England, as well as India, during the time that he was absent from Palestine, and that the Church of Jesus was founded in Cornwall, England. This belief was maintained even after the Romans, who put Christ to death, claimed the origin of Christianity 300 years later. Since the Celts were a secretive society, and passed their history down orally, the Roman Church had a distinct historical advantage as they translated Celtic folklore and wrote the history of the Celtic/Roman relationship.

The Nazarenes, as they were called prior to the establishment of the Roman Catholic Church in 326 AD, were eventually absorbed in name, if not spirit, into the overwhelming power of the Catholic Church. Even then they continued practicing their beliefs through the Cistercian Order of the Catholic Church.

JESUS IN CELTIC BRITIAN
Jesus and Joseph of Arimathea in Britain

For centuries, stories have circulated about Jesus visiting England. Establishing this point is important in that it explains much of the future history of the Celtic religious beliefs and actions. According to author, Glyn Lewis' book "Did Jesus Come to Britain" Christ did indeed pay England a visit and returned to Judea just a few years before his crucifixion by the Romans. Lewis' conclusion that Jesus sailed to England on a trading ship is based on stories from local legends, architectural evidence from two ancient churches and letters from the earliest historians. The key, he says, lies in Christ's family. More specifically his uncle Joseph of Arimathea, who as a metal trader, traveled between Britain and Judea. "*Joseph of Arimathea almost certainly came here to buy tin in Cornwall and copper and lead in Somerset. In the Bible Joseph of Arimathea approached Pontius Pilate to retrieve Jesus' body after the crucifixion.*" Lewis points out that this establishes the closeness between the two according to the law at the time. By law, only a close relative could have claimed the body, which shows that Joseph and Jesus knew each other well. Pilate also gave Joseph time in a meeting, which showed that Joseph wasn't just 'anybody' but a respected member of the community.

Lewis points out the fact that Cornwall and Somerset, the two places in Britain where the Virgin Mary's uncle Joseph of Arimathea traded, have legends saying that another man, namely Jesus, was once there. "*Britain is one of the very few countries that have songs and hymns about Jesus being there. There are so many that it just seems strange they would all be fictional.*" By collating stories from local legends, architectural evidence from two ancient churches and analyzing letters from our earliest historians, author Glyn Lewis believes the tale of Jesus' visit to Britain is true. There also exists documented evidence that Jesus visited India during his time away from the Holy land. India was a favorite trading place for Egyptians and their predecessors, and the center for ancient religious knowledge. In Indian religious history, Jesus is held in high esteem as a prophet.

The fact that Joseph was a trustworthy businessman is born out in Mark 15:43 where he is described as an "honorable counselor". It is interesting that both places in Britain where Joseph traded have legends saying that "*another man*", namely Jesus, was once there. Joseph of Arimathea was here for tin", said Lewis. Lewis estimates that Jesus was in Britain between the ages of 12 and 28 years old. He was crucified by the Romans at age 30. Jesus would have needed transportation from the holy land to England and India. As will be explained later, the Celts were sailing these same routes at the time of Jesus.

Writer, Dr. Strachan, claimed Jesus could have come to England to further his education. *"He needed to visit a group that could teach him about ancient wisdom. The wisdom of the Druids in Britain went back hundreds if not thousands of years. He probably came here to meet the Druids (Wisemen), to share his wisdom and gain theirs."* Among the places Jesus is said to have visited are Penzance, Falmouth, St-Just-in-Roseland and Looe, which are all in Cornwall, as well as Glastonbury in Somerset, which still has particular legends about Jesus. *"St Augustine wrote to the Pope to say he'd discovered a church in Glastonbury built by followers of Jesus. St Gildas (a 6th-Century British cleric) said it was built by Jesus himself. It's a very ancient church which went back perhaps to AD 37."*

Miners' songs in Cornwall mention Joseph and Jesus and folk songs from Somerset also tell of the days where Jesus walked among the people of Glastonbury. *"We have no written history until about the 6th century when famed historian Gildas started writing. In his writings Gildas does refer to Jesus' time in Britain".* According to Lewis, Jesus either set off from the Palestinian ports of Tyre or Sidon, sailed through the Mediterranean and Straits of Gibraltar, then to the north through the Straits of Biscay, before sailing across the English Channel and to the Cornish coast on his journey with his uncle.

Another piece of evidence of the journey are the hieroglyphic carvings around the 1,000 year-old arched south door of Roseland church in St. Anthony. The hieroglyphics were first interpreted by an archaeologist in the Seventies. Says Lewis: *"He interpreted the pictographs as telling of Jesus' birth and his visit to Cornwall. The lamb and the cross face the rising sun, meaning that he was here in his early life. Because it is on the left of the centre line it indicates he was here just before the turn of the year, probably December. The hieroglyphics also reveal that Jesus and Joseph had a little trouble while sailing, and were most likely shipwrecked."* Lewis thinks that if this is the case, then the two men would *"erected a shrine to give thanks for their deliverance from the sea"* and this shrine is where St Anthony's church is today. Lewis says that if the inscription is indeed real, then *"this arch is one of the few ancient records that exist to support the legend that Jesus visited Britain".* Roseland, not to be confused with Rosslyn, is located in Cornwall, the area that Joseph would have visited in his mining ventures.

From Cornwall, it seems most likely that Jesus and Joseph would have travelled to another well-established route for metal traders, Somerset. Lewis also believes that Jesus stayed in Glastonbury. *"Jesus had links to the Druids. I believe he stayed awhile in Glastonbury to study for his ministry. While Joseph was trading I think Jesus found in Glastonbury, a seat of Druid learning, people who thought much like he did."* According to Lewis, the Druids believed in one God and the Holy Trinity. More importantly, they searched for a savior, whom they called Yesu. *"I think he stayed there for a while to study. I certainly think he was away from Nazareth for some time because in the gospel when he returns people don't recognize him. Upon his return he is far wiser and they ask him where he obtained his wisdom."*

After the crucifixion of Jesus, Joseph of Arimathea came to Britain in fear for his life because he had retrieved Jesus' body and made it known he was a family member. He built a chapel on the site of Jesus' Glastonbury home, which is today a church bearing the name of St. Joseph.

Lewis says: *"The facts do come together and I've come to the conclusion that, yes, He did come here. It doesn't conflict at all with the gospel stories, ancient documents or local history."*

Further Proof of Jesus in Britain

The Catholic priest Polydore Vergil, who was born in Italy in 1470, studied at Bologna and Padua. He was so renowned for his literary talents that the Catholic King Henry VII asked him to write an English history. As an Italian and a Catholic proxy Bishop, Prebendary and Archdeacon, he became Chamberlain to Pope Alexander VII, having no axe to grind on behalf of Britain or the British Church. It would no doubt have suited him much better if he could have written of Catholicism as being the first Christian church, but he could not and did not.

He wrote:

"Britain, partly through Joseph of Arimathea, partly through Fugatus and Damianus, was, of all kingdoms, first to receive the Gospel." (Even before Palestine).

The antiquity of the British church has been challenged before by the ambassadors of Spain and France before the Roman Catholic Council of Pisa (A.D. 1417). The British delegates Robert Hallam, Bishop of Salisbury, Henry Chichele, a former Archbishop of Canterbury and Thomas Chillendon, won the day, the council affirmed that the Keltic church (Not the Church of England and not the Catholic Church.) was the first Christian church community. The ambassadors appealed to the Roman Catholic Council of Constance, also in A.D. 1417, and that council confirmed the findings of the Council of Pisa.

A third decision by the Roman Catholic Council at Sienna 1424 again confirmed the antiquity of the British church and, finally at the Council at Basle in 1434 it was laid down that the churches of Spain and France had to accept the precedence of the Keltic Church, which it affirmed, was founded by Joseph of Arimathea (Mary's uncle) *"immediately after the passion of Christ."*

A Vatican manuscript quoted by Baronius in *his "Ecclesiastical Annals A.D. 35",* (the same year in which the Acts of the Apostles state that all, except the Apostles, were scattered abroad from Judaea) records that in this year Lazarus, Maria Magdalene, Martha, her handmaiden Marcella, Maximin a disciple, Joseph the Decurion of Arimathea (Roman Minister for Mines), were exposed to the sea in a vessel without sails or oars. It is widely accepted that the passengers eventually came to France and then to Britain. It is inconceivable that the boat drifted to France. It is this writer's opinion that Joseph of Arimathea, using his shipping contacts, arranged for a vessel to be waiting offshore to pick up his passengers and take them to Marseilles. From Marseilles Joseph and his company passed into Britain then Scotland. Other sources report that there were a total of 14 people in the vessel.

Jesus, from the cross, had made John the guardian of Mary. However, John became a fugitive and so passed the guardianship over to Mary's uncle Joseph of Arimathea who, being the Roman Minister of Mines, was the least vulnerable member of the family and therefore Mary could not be any safer than she was with him.

The fact that Mary was not with John is proved by his second letter. The letter was written to Mary saying that he hoped to be able to visit her; but that he became exiled on the Island of Patmos. There he was inspired to write the Book of Revelation/Apocalypse. So, Mary went with Joseph of Arimathea to England. This story used to be taught by the early Catholic Church. Britain was the only place they could go to, that was safe from Roman persecution, because the Romans had already conquered and subjugated everywhere, except for Western and Northern Britain.

It is necessary to know the Celts in order to understand the profound effect they had on the Celtic Faram family, the shaping of Europe and the Americas, both politically and religiously. The Celts have the distinction of having formed one of the largest empires in the history of Europe, while on the surface it would seem that they have faded into obscurity. This is far from the truth. The Celts, after their initial conquests, reverted to a philosophy of planned assimilation rather than confrontation against governments. This philosophy has been passed down under various societies since Roman times, and exists to this day.

Far from the barbarians, with which they were often identified, the Celts had a highly developed society. During the period covered in this book, the basic structure of Celtic society was divided into three classes: the Royal Clan (headed by the Sinclairs), the Warrior Aristocracy (headed by the Farams), and the remainder of the Celts, often referred to as Freemen, the origin of the term Freemasons.

Although slaves did constitute a small percentage of the population, slavery was generally frowned upon in Celtic society. However, though Celtic social structure appeared loose and primitive to the Romans and Greeks, the Celts were by no means the "savage race or pagans", a title which the Roman Catholic scholars often bestowed upon them. Archeological evidence has shown the Celts to be an advanced race for their era. They made use of chain mail in battle and utilized machines for reaping grain. There is also evidence that the Celts had begun extended roadways across Europe centuries prior to the Roman Empire's much-lauded road system, and it is widely believed by historians that it was from the Celts that the Romans and Greeks first learned the use of soap.

Regardless of their apparent advancements, the Celts were not an urbanized people, and their tastes ran to simple rather than extravagant. The Celts non-materialistic spiritual existence showed in the original teachings of Jesus. This explains their disdain for the Christianity of Rome, which they found spiritually corrupt when compared to the teachings of Jesus. Certain themes appear repetitively in reference to Celtic culture, including the predominance of rural settlements, the traditions governing hospitable feasts, and the evidence of fellowship drinking. Pork tended to be a primary item of diet, and clothing often followed a plaid design. This design can still be found in Scotland where the distinctive patterns identify the various clans. However, though rural themes dominated their society, and many settlements were merely farming communities, the Celts were far from uneducated. Contrary to popular belief, historians have concluded that the Celts had a written language as early as the third century BC, but made little use of it except on coinage and memorials, placing a higher value on the ability to remember vast quantities of information correctly. Their oral traditions would allow their goals to prevail throughout the ages without being discovered by the outside world.

Celtic society declined in the face of Rome's advancing power, however. As the Roman culture begin to dominate the face of world politics and trade, the Celts soon found themselves with no choice but to accept Roman rule. And, as Roman culture began dominating the Celtic tribes, the tribal culture was replaced by a racial identity. By the withdrawal of Roman troops from Britain in approximately 340 AD, Celtic culture had waned nearly into oblivion. It would enjoy a brief period of renewal between 700AD and 1400AD with the fall of Rome, and Celtic migrations to Denmark, Ireland, Scotland and eventually North America.

And so, the proud people who had once dominated the European continent would seem to be lost in history, except for the enduring footprints they left behind to be discovered later. It is from these historic footprints that the history of the Celts, and their prodigy, is revealed in this book.

END CHAPTER

Chapter 3

The Farums in Corunna, Galicia

CELTIC GALICIA

Galicia is located on the Northwestern tip of the Iberian Peninsula in what is now Spain. The area was settled by indigenous Celts which were later joined by Low Land Celts that migrated from Northwest Europe about 50 BC. The match up must have been amicable since the two tribes built the first recognized country in Europe (Galicia) and went on to accomplish great things together. Until this time Europe, and most of the world, consisted of families and tribes competing, through war, for land and resources. Later, the Celts were responsible for settling most of the English speaking nations west of Europe. In Europe, the oldest existing boundary between two established countries is the boundary between Galicia and Portugal. As will become apparent, Portugal was a major ally of the Galician Celts. The reason Galicia is important in this story is that, this is where we first find the group that would eventually call themselves the Farams. At the time people did not use last names and were usually named with reference to their trade or some unusual characteristic that they possessed.

Modern scholars have clearly proven that Celtic presence and influences were most substantial in Iberia (with perhaps the highest settlement saturation in Western Europe), particularly in the Western and Northern regions. Galicia is the most forgotten of the seven Celtic countries. Most likely because Galicia is not listed as one of the major Celtic locations. This is strange because it is from Galicia that the colonization of many of the other nations sprang. Even so, Galicia has the most pure and the oldest Celtic tradition, going back more that 2000 years without medieval influence. The Galicians were known for their expertise in architectural work with stone and for their expert seamanship. Galicians have equals only in their Celtic brothers of Eire and Breizh. The similarities of tradition, the costumes, and philosophy of life between Galicians, Irish and Scotts are what characterized the Galician people. These Celtic people had little contact with the Visigoth, now Spanish, way of life, from which Galicians separated themselves.

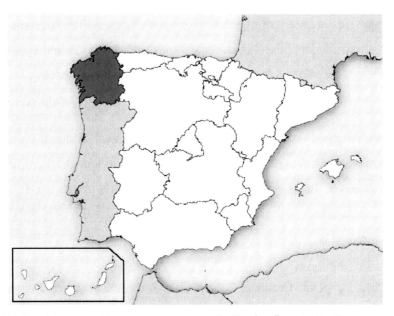

Galicia is located on the Northwest corner of the Iberian Peninsula. It covers an area of 29,575 square kilometers. Its geography is irregular and the coast is jagged, forming many rivers.

At the end of the 19th century, traditional scholars acknowledged the Celts of the Iberian Peninsula as a culture relatable to the La Tene Celts. Three divisions of the Celts of the Iberian Peninsula were assumed to have existed: the Celtiberians in the mountains near the center of the peninsula, the Celtici in the southwest, and the Celts in the northwest (Galicia).

In their role as civic leaders, and expert seafarers, the Galicians saw the need for, and conceived the idea of, a lighthouse at the highest point in what is now the town of Corunna Spain. The lighthouse was named the Farum Brigantium. The area was blessed with a protected deep water harbor, which not only served the Galicians but also was the midpoint between Gibraltar and Boulogne, the main trading route for resupply of the Roman garrisons in Britain. The Galicians were not only profiting from their own trading routes, but were also profiting from servicing the Roman trade routes between Rome and Britain. This arrangement allowed the Galicians to become wealthy without interference from the dominant force in the area, the Roman Empire.

The port at what is now Corunna was a busy one. Travel during this era was unpredictable and it was common for ships to arrive during night time. The Atlantic is one of the most inhospitable areas in the world in which to sail. In addition, the entrance to the harbor at Corunna is curved and rocky. Although the Romans had built beacons to guide their ships in preparation for their landings in Britain, they were very crude when compared to the lighthouse at Alexandria, Egypt and Corunna, Galicia. Caligula built a beacon at Boulogne in 43 BC, in preparation for the second invasion of Britain. In 24 BC Claudius, Caligula's successor, built a beacon at Dover, the planned landing site for his 24 BC invasion of Britain. Augustus Caesar followed Claudius as Emperor and was the leader of the second, and most successful, Roman invasion of Britain. By improving upon the crude beacons used by the Romans during their invasions of Britain, and by imitating the celebrated "Lighthouse at Alexandria" Egypt, the Galicians designed and built a lighthouse known for 2000 years as the "Farum Brigantium". The Roman beacons built prior to the lighthouse at Galicia were simply markers and did not come close to the technical features and functionality of the Galician lighthouse. The Galician lighthouse is what prompted the Farums to adopt the last name of Farum, 700 years after their clan constructed the lighthouse.

During the evolution of Galicia, the Celts developed a business strategy that would serve them, and their successors, well for the next sixteen centuries. They learned that if they could integrate their merchant and shipping business into the infrastructure of the Roman Empire, and later other host governments, they could gain total control of the sea trade in the area. Without fail, the Celts would infiltrate the local government that controlled an area and, as a result, would become the dominant sea merchants. They were careful to maintain a low profile within the government, so that any attempts at revolution would be directed at the heads of government and not at them. Their low profile and practice of passing information orally is most likely one of the reasons why, after the 8th century, the Celts "seem" to have faded from history.

Galicia is now a district in Spain, subject to the rule of the central government. Galicia was the first, and the oldest, independent kingdom of Europe. Its beginnings can be placed in the Old Kingdom of Galicia, created by the Iberian Celtic people prior to the coming of the Romans in the 1st century BC. By 409 AD, the Galicians put out all that was left of the Roman presence. The government helped unify the different Galician tribes to form the first kingdom of Europe, under King Hermerico. This marked the beginning of the fall of the Roman Empire. In 410 AD, the Celtic tribes joined with the Visigoths to overthrow Rome and the sack the Italian Peninsula. It was during this period that a portion of the tribe, that later called themselves the Farums, settled in, and occupied, the port of Rossano near Naples.

THE SOUTHERN ITALIAN TOWN of ROSSANO

The town of Rossano is the port that a small group of Galatians (Farums) picked to expand their sea trade after the Galician invasion of Italy in 410 AD. Rossano is located in Southern Italy in the province of Cosenza (Calabria). The city is situated on a bluff two miles from the Gulf of Taranto.

Under the Roman Empire, the town of Rossano was named Roscianum. In the 2nd century AD Emperor Hadrian built a port here which could accommodate up to 300 ships. It was mentioned in the Antonine itineraries, as one of the important fortresses of Calabria. Emperor Hadrian is famous for the stone wall he built across central Britain to keep the Scotts out of Roman occupied Southern Britain. In the following century the Goths of Alaric I laid siege to the fortress at Rossano but were unable to take it.

The Rossanesi showed great attachment to the Byzantine Empire, whose officials, represented by the Farums, had their seat in Rossano. In the Arab invasions of the Eighth Century the Saracens failed to conquer the port; however, in 982 AD Otto II captured it from the Byzantines. This is precisely the time that most of the Italian Farums moved to Denmark, to join their Galician cousins, in the town of Farum, Denmark. It must have been an ordeal for the Farums to leave Italy. They had built two Orthodox Christian churches in the area, which are now Italian national treasures. Their fondness for building churches would be demonstrated at least three more times. The Farums/Farams would also construct a church in Farum Denmark in 1100 AD, Rosslyn Chapel in Scotland in the 15th Century AD, and the church at Astbury (Now Congleton) Staffordshire England in the 19th Century AD.

The Byzantine Styled "Calibria Catolica" Rosano, Italy

Built by the Farums Circa 500 AD.

The Virgin at Rosano

The Byzantian Styled "Calibria Catolica" Stilo, Italy

Built by the Farams c500AD

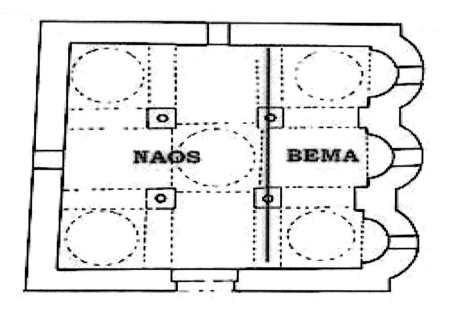

Floor plan of Calibria Catolica, Italy

The floor plan of the church at Calibria represents the Byzantine symbol of a cross within a square. In Chapter 4, you will see this Byzantine symbol come together with the Celtic symbol, to create the Faram logo of a cross within a square, within a circle. This symbol is known in only three places in the world: in the city of Faram, Denmark, in the main window of Rosslyn Chapel in Edinburgh, Scotland, and in a "henge geoglyph" in the USA. The Byzantine cross also appears in the floor plan of the first Cistercian Monastery over 500 years later. This monastery was built by Bernard de Clairvaux, one of the founding fathers of the Knights Templar.

The churches Byzantine Greek character was preserved long after its conquest by the Ottomans, as noted by its long retention of the Greek Rite (Orthodox Christian) over the Latin Rite. The city in fact maintained notable privileges under the subsequent Hohenstaufen and Angevine dominations, but this subsequently decayed after the feudalization in 1417 AD.

Rossano was the birthplace of Pope John VII and Pope Urban VII. Rossano is also the birthplace of Saint Nilus the Younger, who founded the Abbey of Grottaferrata, and whose life is a valuable source of information about southern Italy in the tenth century.

The Cathedral is the main monument of Rossano. It has a nave with two aisles, and three apses. The bell tower and the baptismal font are from the 14th century, while the remaining decorations are from the 17th and 18th centuries. The church is famous for the ancient image of the Madonna Acheropita, now located in the Diocesan Museum, probably dating between 580 AD and the first half of the eighth century. In 1879, the famous Codex Rossanensis was discovered in the sacristy of the church. It is a Greek parchment manuscript of Matthew and Mark, written in silver on purple-stained parchment, and is one of the oldest pictorial Gospels known. Scholars date the codex from the end of the fifth to the eighth or ninth century; it is probably of Alexandrian origin. This discovery is further evidence of the Orthodox Christian influence of the Farums in the 6th Century AD.

It should be remembered that by the time the Celts Invaded Italy, in 410 AD, Celtic Christianity was four centuries old and the Catholic Church was but a century old. The Papal seat for Catholicism was in Constantinople. The Papal seat was later moved to France and then to Rome. The advent of the politically based Catholic Church, and their actions, would be a point of contention that would continue right through to the conflict between Northern and Southern Ireland in the 20th century.

In the high Middle age period and thereafter, the kingdom of Galicia stands alone. In time royal heritages, and the marriages of kings and queens, brought together a coalition known as Galicia. But through it all, Galicia has always conserved its own language, costumes and differentiated culture. The inaccessibility, by land, of the West side of the Celto-Iberian peninsula is the result of a natural mountain chain formation that isolated Galicia and also Portugal from Spain.

Geography has helped to maintain the purity of the Celtic tradition of Galicia. They have the same Celtic spirituality as 20 centuries ago, today the names have changed, no more names of Celtic gods and goddesses. The names today have references only to the Christian influence. However, it can be said that Galicians occasionally pursue their Celtic religion under Christian names. This was especially true during Medieval Times when the Catholic Church, aligned with the power of Rome, did not allow the pursuit of other religions.

The Farum Brigantium

The Second Century AD saw the building of, what is today, the oldest working lighthouse in Europe. The lighthouse in Galicia, known for 2000 years as the "Farum Brigantium", is now known as "The Tower of Hercules", Hercules being a mythical Spanish caricature. This lighthouse bore the name which the Farums adopted after their move to Denmark. The name was most likely taken by the Farum family as a last name after their move to Denmark, in remembrance of their residence in Corunna, Galicia.

The Galician lighthouse was no doubt inspired by the first lighthouse in the known world which was built at Alexandria, Egypt (247BC - 1323 AD). The Egyptian lighthouse remained a daytime navigation marker until the First Century BC, at which time reflective mirrors were added and facilities to accommodate a fire for nighttime navigation. As the Galician lighthouse was built in the second century AD, it would be safe to assume that it was an idea whose time had come. The lighthouse at Alexandria inspired the generic name for lighthouse throughout the ancient world. The name for lighthouse originated from the name of the Alexandrian lighthouse, which was Pharos. The name Pharos became the etymological origin of the word 'lighthouse'. The word was translated into Greek, Bulgarian and many Romance languages, such as French (phare), Italian (faro), Portuguese (farol), Spanish (faro), Romanian (far), and Catalan (far).

The meaning of the lighthouse name **Farum Brigantium** can be broken into its main parts:

Farum = **"Far"**, the Roman name for lighthouse and **"um"**, the Roman suffix for enclosure. **Brigantium** =**"Brig"** - The Celtic word for high, or holy, **"anti"** - is Latin for against, **"um"**- roman suffix reserved for enclosures of people, such as stadium and coliseum. The term Farum Brigantium literally means **"Enclosed Lighthouse for persons who are against the Roman Empire"** or, **Lighthouse Prison.** This may have been the origin of the slang nautical term for jail known as *"...thrown into the Brig"*.

The Farum Brigantium was built by Caius Servius Lupus, an architect from Aeminium (Coimbra) in Lusitania (Portugal). This would be expected since Galicia and Portugal were allies and the dominant sea forces of the time. The architect left a carving on a rock at the foot of the tower. The tower had three floors, and an indoor ramp leading to the beacon. The building was square and had windows and a door built into the outside wall. The building was double walled, which served a purpose. The distance between the inside wall and the outside wall was the width of the staircase leading to the top. This prevented any unplanned access to the stairs by the prisoners which were housed within the inner walls. The genius of the design is that the lighthouse was most likely maintained by the prisoners which it housed. That would have reduced the paid workforce to just a few guards. If food and water were supplied for the prisoners and oil for the burning beacon, the lighthouse would be self contained and operate continuously. The original foundations of the building were revealed in excavations conducted in the 1990s. Many legends from the Middle Ages to the 19th century surround the unique "Farum Brigantium" as it is the only lighthouse of Greco-Roman antiquity to have retained a measure of structural integrity and functional continuity for 2000 years.

The Tower, built on a 57-meter-high rock, rises another 55 meters. Immediately adjacent to the base of the Tower is a small rectangular Roman building. The site also features the Monte dos Bicos rock carvings from the Iron Age and a Muslim cemetery. In the early eighth century, multiple Arab tribes invaded Europe and Galicia. It was during this period that the Orthodox Christian Galicians, later to call themselves Farums, after their lighthouse, moved from Galiza (Galicia) to their home in Denmark. In the Middle Ages the lighthouse

was still known by the name Farum Brigantium. In the 20th century a modern lighthouse was constructed around the remains of the old lighthouse and the name was changed to "The Tower of Hercules".

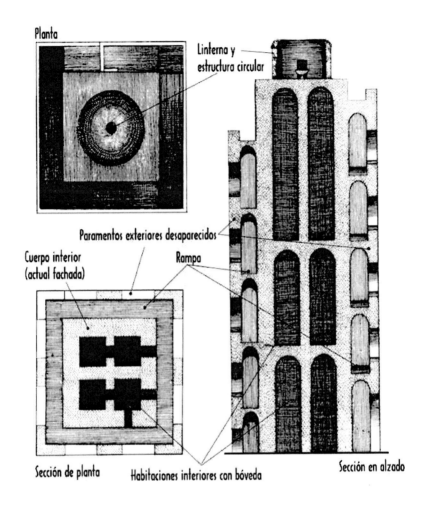

Planta

Linterna y
estructura circular

Paramentos exteriores desaparecidos

Cuerpo interior
(actual fachada)

Rampa

Sección de planta

Habitaciones interiores con bóveda

Sección en alzado

Original Farum Brigantium Design

The Existing Lighthouse

In 407 AD, the Roman armies departed Galicia for Rome, and Galicia became the first country to emerge in medieval Europe, prior to the fall of the Roman Empire. Galician historian Paulus Orosius, who lived during the first years of the new Galician kingdom, mentioned the Tower of Brigantia in his *Historia adversum Paganos:* "Brigantia, city of Gallaecia, where a lighthouse stands very high looking towards Britannia".

Many scholars have noticed the fact that the lighthouse beacon could only be seen from the West and Southwest. This would be in keeping with the fact that the most dangerous coasts are North and South of Galicia. Research shows that the Celts, in particular the tribe that would later call themselves the Farums, were in the mining business from ancient times. Upon their move from Galicia to Denmark (c700 AD), the Farams expanded their mining operations to both

Sweden and Denmark. The vast mining areas controlled by the Celts, while they were in Galicia, were in Cornwall, Britain. The directions from which the lighthouse can be seen is in line with a route from the west, both from Cornwall and, as some believe, North America.

The Swabian Royal Dynasty

The first Swabian king Hermeric became the first feudal king of Medieval Europe after unifying all the Celtic tribes of the province. That kingdom was known in Europe with the names of *Galliciense Regnum* (Kingdom of Gallaecia) or *Regnum Suevorum* (Kingdom of the Swabians).

For almost 200 years, the Swabian Royal Dynasty governed the Kingdom of Gallaecia, establishing a foreign policy of alliances with Burgundy and Constantinople. The Swabian Dynasty also conquered and expanded the territorial borders of Gallaecia out to Hispania Betica (southern Spain). Generally, it is understood that there are seven separate, though related, Celtic nations and tribes. All of these are connected to each other by not only common history, but also culture. Many of these nations are settlements of Celtic tribes. The seven nations are Aba (Scotland), Cymru (Wales) Kernow (Cornwall), Mannin (Isle of Man), Galicia (Spain) Briezh (Brittany) and Eire (Ireland). The Swabian Dynasty was credited for unifying and bringing together all the Celtic tribes of Galicia into a kingdom that was known thereafter as "The Kingdom of Galicia". It should be mentioned that some of the Galicians that departed Iberian Galicia c700 AD moved to the area now known as Poland. It was there that one of the regions was renamed Galicia and eventually evolved into another territory called the "Empire of Galicia". This area was the last northern European country to adopt, by force, Catholicism.

Europe by 476 AD

The Swabian Dynasty was dethroned after King Andeca of Gallaecia was defeated in battle by Hispanic-Visigothic king Leovigild in 585 AD. The Visigothic dynasty became the new ruling house of the Kingdom of Gallaecia and king Leovigild took the title of king of "*Gallaecia, Hispania et Narbonensis*". Years later, his successor, King Recaredus, was still addressed by Pope Gregorius Magnus as "*King of the Goths and of the Swabians*". In about 700 AD the Arab invasion caused the Celtic Galicians to depart Galicia and move to Denmark. The Farum clan moved to the eastern island of Zealand, Denmark, the location of the current Danish capital of Copenhagen.

The Arab Invasion of Spain. (c700 AD)

After the departure of the Farums to Denmark, Arabs swept over the Eastern and Southern Mediterranean, France and Spain. Needless to say the Catholic Church was in disarray. The Arabs required the populace to accept Islam or pay extra taxes. The Farums in Calibria, Italy successfully defended their seaport against the Muslims, but were overrun, 300 years later in the 10th century, by the Ottomans, from Germany.

By 759 AD the Arabs had been compelled, by local combatants, to retire from all possessions beyond the Pyrenees, the boundary between France and Spain. The Arabs were also forced out of Galicia and Northern Portugal. Thus thrown back upon the peninsula, it seemed inevitable that the Arab empire in Spain would also succumb to the disruptive forces which had no longer any external outlet. By the end of the 8th century it had become evident that the Arabs had committed a great error in not devastating the whole Peninsula. The contemptuous indifference, with which they had left the northern mountains to a handful of refugees, was destined to bring its own punishment. Over time, the will of the citizens and the in-fighting of the Arabs led to their retreat.

The story of the Galicians is but one of many colorful bits of history that is Europe. What makes the Galicians special is that, they had a profound effect on the English speaking peoples of the western world. The Celts were responsible for settling most of the English speaking nations west of Europe, including North America.

END CHAPTER

Chapter 4

The Farums in Denmark

Galicians to Danes

It is now early in the 8th century. The Arabs and Islam have taken over the Eastern and Southern Mediterranean, France and Spain. Rome has fallen and the Roman Christian Church is in disarray. The Arabs are forcing Islam on the European Christians and were about to conquer the West coast of Spain. The Celtic Galicians see their trade in the Mediterranean drying up and are forced to make a decision to stay and fight or return to their Scandinavian roots. They choose the later. The Celts depart for Denmark and their allies, the Swabians, return to Swabia (Central Europe North of Switzerland).

The Galician Celts have a difficult time establishing themselves on their return to their Germanic homeland. Archeological findings indicate that the Galicians found a home on the peninsula and surrounding islands of Jutland (Denmark). Although their roots are Germanic they are viewed with suspicion. They are of the La Tene Celtic culture and are not inclined to join the Hallstatt Celtic culture, which existed in what is now Germany. The Galicians were seasoned traders and had many contacts in the North Sea and Mediterranean. After moving to Denmark, the Galicians no longer enjoyed the protection previously afforded by the Romans and the Swabians. The Galicians no longer have the umbrella of protection under which they operated for centuries with impunity.

History seems to paint a picture of a group that was not readily accepted by the Germans. However, the Celts returning to Denmark had the numbers, equipment and a strategic location which made them a force to deal with. Although rocky at times, the Celtic Galicians (Danes) and mainland Germans learned to tolerate one another.

During the eighth century, the Arab tribes were encroaching on the Germanic tribes from the South and also had the geographical capability to attack Celtic Denmark from the East, through the Baltic Sea. It was at this precise time that the Vikings came into being. Research points to the Galician Danes, fearing attacks from outsiders, creating their own sea going force. It would have been expedient to approach the nearby tribes located in Norway with a proposition that would benefit both parties. Had the Galician Danes agreed to supply the Norse with ships and equipment, the arrangement would have benefited everyone. The Danes would have had protection and dominance over the entire North and Baltic Sea area, and the Norsemen would enrich them selves beyond anything up to that time.

The Celtic tribes would then have protected trade routes throughout the area. The monetary agreement would most likely have been the same as dictated after the "Hansiatic League" which was initiated later around 1000 AD. The Hanse agreement stated that the privateer would keep two thirds of any property that they might capture and one third would go to the League. The "Hansiatic League" (The Hanse) was a group of German states that later joined together to protect their trade interests in the Baltic area. Only Baltic ships would be free from taxation and priveteering. The Farums, as they now called themselves, had a strategic location at the entrance to the Baltic Sea and later played a major part in enforcing the "Hanse" policies and collecting taxes for Denmark.

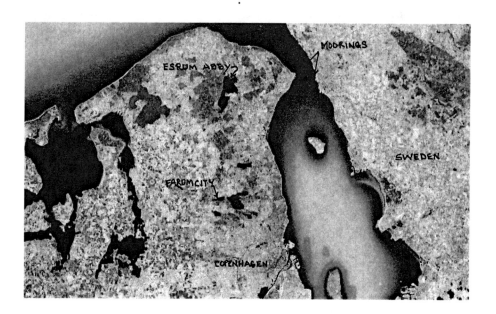

North Zealand, Denmark

(On this map can be seen the locations of Esrum Abby, the Farum mooring spots on Oresund Sound, The City of Farum, Farum Sound, and Copenhagen. These locations will become important later in the chapter.)

When the Galicians moved to Denmark, they settled an area that extended from the Jutland Peninsula, in the west, to Prussia in the east. It was the Farum clan, which settled in the west central portion of the Danish island of Zealand. The Farums, being merchants, and the initial Navy of the Galicians after their move to Denmark, required a secure port from which to conduct their business. That protected port became Farum Sound. This location was the perfect spot from which to conduct their most important duty to the Danish community. That duty consisted of intercepting and taxing ships sailing in, or out of the Bearing Sea through Oresund Sound. This task was made easier by the fact that the Farum's port city, Farum Sound, was only a few miles from the entrance to the Baltic Sea. The distance from Denmark to the other side of the entrance, at the time owned by Denmark but now owned by Sweden, was less than 4 miles. Since visibility to the horizon on the open sea is 12 miles, it meant that no one could pass without being seen.

In 982 AD, the Farums that had occupied Rossano, Italy, since its defeat by the Galicians in 410 AD, were defeated by the Ottoman Empire and forced to leave their beloved port. Soon thereafter, circa 1000 AD, many Italian Farums moved to the island of Zealand Denmark and joined their cousins in the town of Farum City. The move of the Farums Italian branch, to Denmark, also coincided with Denmark becoming a country, the formation of the German Hansiatic League, and the disappearance of the Vikings. If the Hansiatic league were to be successful in promoting peaceful trade in the Baltic, the Vikings would now be a liability to the idea of peaceful trade in the North Sea and Baltic areas. In addition, the Farums, in their strategic location on Oresund Sound could now, in peacetime, serve as Denmark's navel force if necessary. As you will discover later, by the end of the 10th century the Farums had, what would later be called, the Templars aboard their ships. This gives credence to the idea that the Danes were using the Vikings as their navy, prior to the Templars being formed.

At the same time that the Vikings disappeared, the Danes obviously had some non-aggression pact with the Hansiatic League of Northern Germany. This is evidenced by the fact that they co-existed, without major difficulties, for about 400 years. No one has ever explained why the Viking era was so short, and where they went after such an abrupt end. I'm sure that you are beginning to formulate an answer by now. The answer is covered in detail later in the chapter on the Vikings.

Farum City and Farum Sound.

Farum Sound was once connected to the sea.
Notice the Farum crest near the sound

THE DANISH INVASION of ENGLAND - The rise of Danelaw

Beginning in 800 AD, the Danes, aided by the Vikings, led a series of sea attacks on the poorly defended English coast and gradually captured parts of

England. In 865 AD, Danish settlers began arriving and laying claim to English land. The Danes first took control of East Anglia in 867 AD. Securing a hold on East Anglia, they launched a surprise attack on Northumbria. The Danes defeated Northumbria's splintered defenses, which were caught fighting a civil war over the Northumbrian throne. The Danish King Gunthrum ignored the claims of both the deposed king, and his usurper, and placed an English puppet king on the Northumbrian throne. By 871 AD, the Danes controlled East Anglia, Northumbria and Mercia. Anglo Saxon England, the southeast German held territory, began to refer to the areas under Danish rule as **Danelaw.** Only Wessex and few small independent kingdoms remained unconquered. The fact that both the Vikings and the Danes were attacking Britain at the same time, confirms that they were working together.

The year 865 AD heralded disaster for Anglo-Saxon England. Anglo-Saxon England was the Southeast portion of England, including London, which the Germans had colonized prior to the Danes arriving. This was the year of full scale invasion by the Great Army of the Danes. The Anglo Saxon Chronicle said: "*And the same year a great raiding army came to the land of the English and took winter quarters in East Anglia where they were provided with horses, and made peace with them*". According to Aethelweard writing 100 years later, the leader of the Danes was Igwar or Ivar, one of the two sons of Ragnar Lothbrok. Ragnar had two sons involved in these raids. One was called Ubba, and the other was known as Ivar the Boneless. The chronicle implies that the Saxon King Edmund paid them off in money and supplies to keep the peace in East Anglia.

In 866 AD, the Viking force marched north from East Anglia, took York and thus conquered Northumbria. The brilliant cultural life of the north, the schools, libraries, churches and ministries were all destroyed. "*An immense slaughter was made of the Northumbrians there"*. In 867 AD, the Vikings moved on Nottingham and the Mercians surrendered.

"The Danes rode across Mercia into East Anglia and took winter quarters in Thetford. That same year King Edmund fought against them, with the Danes winning the victory. They slew the Catholic King and overran the entire kingdom". That description came from the Anglo-Saxon Chronicle, version A, written between 877 and 899 AD, and is the first record of the death of King Edmund, later to be called St. Edmund, King and Martyr. A note to Version F adds that the Danish head men who slew the King were Ingware (Ivar) and Ubba. Version B, copied at Peterborough in 1103 AD also added that they destroyed all the Catholic monasteries to which they came, one of which was Peterborough itself.

Later stories were to tell how King Edmund was captured in battle, and was offered his life, to share his kingdom and renounce his Roman inspired Christian faith. This he refused to do and was killed. According to Abbo of Fleury, writing in 985 AD, the death of St Edmund occurred at Haegelisdun Wood. According to Herman of Bury writing in 1095 AD, *"The saint was then buried nearby at Sutton"*. Aeldorman Aethelweard, writing at the end of the 10th century said *"...and his body lies entombed in the place which is called Beadoriceswyrthe"*. For the next fifty years, East Anglia was under Viking control.

After 871 AD, part of the Viking army settled at York and took to farming. King Godrum led another party to Cambridge and in 876 AD, they launched another assault on Wessex. They lost 5,000 men at sea, and were forced to retreat. In 878 AD, the Vikings surprised the English army at Chippenham. Much of Wessex was taken and the Danish territory was expanded to its greatest extent ever.

By May, the English rallied their army and won a decisive battle over King Guthrum. Under the Treaty, the borders of Danish rule were rolled back and established east of Watling Street, along a line from London to Chester. Essex was ceded to the Danes. Godrum converted to Celtic Christianity and changed his name to Athelstan, his new Christian name. He also agreed to pull his army back into East Anglia. Various ranks of Danish and Saxon citizens and their values were set out in this Peace, and the country was now officially partitioned. The Danish held area was to be called the Danelaw. As Athelstan, Godrum would start to issue coins in his new name, based upon the coinage of Alfred. For a Viking, this was an adoption of English ways, as the traditional Viking medium of exchange had always been raw silver, exchanged by weight.

Danish settlement began in earnest following the invasion. Here the raiding army went from Cirencester into East Anglia, and settled that land and divided it up. In many ways the Danelaw, including East Anglia, now became like a Danish province. Old allegiances to local lords were weakened. Before the Danes, land could only be transferred by the King's charter. Viking law allowed it to be bought and sold in front of witnesses, at least in the chief towns of Cambridge, Thetford, Ipswich and Norwich. Streets like Colgate and Fishergate in Norwich took their names from the Danish 'gata', meaning street. York became a Viking capital, and it's well known Coppergate derives from this time. 'Viking' objects are increasingly found at Ipswich from this period through to the early 10th Century. The abrupt termination of Viking artifacts after this time period coincides with the Viking move to Iceland and Greenland.

By 885 AD, the Vikings had largely converted to Celtic Christianity, and within only twenty years of Edmund's death, they themselves were issuing coinage in his memory. Viking coinage of Danish East Anglia was issued from 885 to 915 AD. St Edmund memorial coinage was produced, as was coinage in memory of St Martin of Lincoln.

In 886 AD, King Alfred occupied London Fort and all the English race turned to him, except that territory that was held by Denmark. By 890 AD, Alfred had held Mercia and Wessex and established a balance of power with the invaders. Alfred found time to translate Latin texts into English and had these distributed throughout his lands. Coins were minted naming Alfred King of the English; of course this excluded the Danelaw, north and east of a line from London to Chester.

The Cuerdale Hoarde

In 892 AD, the Vikings landed in Devon and raided for more than a year. King Alfred constructed defensive strongholds along his borders, following the Danish example. He also designed new ships meant for naval battles. In 893 AD, the Danes, including those from East Anglia, continued to attack in the west, at the Severn and north to Chester. Asser wrote of the Life of King Alfred in which he refers to the death of King Edmund, the East Anglian King, in battle. Meanwhile, the coinage known as St Edmunds memorial coinage continued to circulate in East Anglia even as official Danish currency, testifying to the rapid acceptance of him as a Christian Martyr.

In 970 AD, a new set of regulations, based on Benedictine practice for monastic life in England, was drawn up by Dunstan, the Bishop of Winchester. This led to a well trained body of monks that made monastic life their obsession. King Edgar supported all these church reforms, removing secular monks and replacing them by celibate monks with allegiance to St Benedict's rule, rather than to local landlords. In East Anglia, these church reforms were supported by Elderman Athelstan, 'Half-King', who helped found the monastic houses of Peterborough, Thorney and Ely. The Catholic Monasteries had been demolished by the Danish and Viking invasions, but at Ramsey, a great new religious house was set up. This must have started to put pressure on the clergy who were in control of St Edmund's shrine. They may have had wives, and did not follow the, restored, Benedictine strict codes of subjugation to the rule of a monastic order. Dunstan delayed Edgar's coronation until the king was 30, the age for ordination of priests. The kingship ceremony was made intensely religious at this time, and the King became Christ's' appointed, a religious power as well as a secular one.

The secular priests who had been in charge of St Edmund's shrine for most of the century, had been overtaken by new ideas of what was a suitable devout religious practice. The rule of St Benedict was being adopted in the new monasteries. In the late 10th Century, a second wave of Danish attacks assailed East Anglia. In 991 AD, a large, well organized army led by Olaf, later King of Norway, defeated the English at Sandwich, then attacked and ravaged Ipswich. Olaf Tryggvason of Norway seems to have masterminded this attack along with Svein Forkbeard of Denmark. This led finally to the famous Battle of Maldon, commemorated in an epic poem. Olaf had 93 ships and having over-run Ipswich defeated Elderman Brihtnoth of Essex at Maldon.

In 994 AD, Olaf of Norway, and Swain of Denmark, came to London to attack it and ravaged Essex, Kent, Sussex and Hampshire. They were given 16,000 pieces of silver to desist. From 997 to 1014 AD, Viking raids occurred every year. By this time Norwich had probably outstripped Thetford as the main city of the Norfolk area. It had better access to the sea than Thetford and could handle more trade more cheaply because of this advantage.

In 1002 AD, King Ethelred ordered a general massacre of all the Danes in England on St Brice's day, November 13th. His orders were unlikely to have been carried out in the Anglo-Danish area of East Anglia, but elsewhere, one victim turned out to be the sister of King Swein of Denmark. In 1003 AD, King Swein invaded South West England seeking revenge for his sister. In 1004 AD, he sailed to East Anglia. Norwich was sacked and three weeks later the force reached Thetford and burnt it down. Ulfketel Snilling was the local Anglo-

Danish Elderman, and he raised a force to confront the invaders. Ulfketel, also known as Ulfcytel, took heavy casualties the next day and lost the most senior of his East Anglian troops. However, although the invaders won the day, they too took heavy losses, and they ran for their ships and left the country. Ulfcytel had anticipated this and had sent orders to destroy the ships, but this order was never carried out. A Danegeld (A payment for peace.) was paid by the English of 36,000 pieces of silver.

In 1009 AD, King Swein attacked England again. By the following year, he was moving on East Anglia. In 1010 AD, a large Danish force under Thurkill the Tall landed at Ipswich and sacked the town in the spring. The force then moved towards Thetford. They marched to meet the Anglo-Saxon forces, led by the Earl of East Anglia, Ulfcytel, at Ringmere Heath. The battle was described as a 'bed of death', and despite help from Cambridgeshire, the English were defeated. The Vikings ravaged at will for three months, burning Thetford, Ipswich and Cambridge. The village of Balsham was destroyed by the raiders.

The remains of St Edmund were taken to London for safekeeping out of harm's way by a monk called Egelwin or Ailwin. In London, the body was lodged at the church of St Gregory the Great. There are some accounts, reported by Yates, in his 1805 book on Bury, wrote that Turchill, one of the Danish leaders under Sweign, having harassed and devastated the whole of East Anglia, burnt and plundered Bury. Ailwin, presumably, got away before this happened. The Danes proceeded to the Thames Valley and into Oxfordshire and back to Bedford burning as they went. They returned to their ships with much plunder.

In 1011 AD, Canterbury was besieged and taken by the Danes and the Archbishop was murdered. The Danes left, only to return with King Swein the next year. The Danegeld (Ransom) paid to save the city was 48,000 pieces of silver, a massive sum, the biggest ever recorded. By 1013 AD, Ethelred had lost his grip and King Swein of Denmark landed to be accepted as King of Northumbria and eastern England. By the end of the year Ethelred fled to Normandy and Swein became King of all England. England was again under Danish rule.

By now it was judged safe to return the remains of St Edmund to the monastery at Bury. On the journey back, the body passed through Stapleford, and miraculously cured the local Lord. The manor of Stapleford was given to St Edmund in gratitude. This journey was said to pass through Edmunton, Chipping Ongar, Greenstead, Chelmsford, Braintree, and Clare. An overnight stay took place at the wooden church at Greenstead, which remarkably survives today with many wooden features still in evidence. At the time it was probably entirely made of wood, as were most Saxon buildings.

In 1014 AD, King Swein Forkbeard died suddenly. He was said to have been struck dead while threatening to sack St Edmund's town or extract a heavy ransom from it. Pictures of this event were to be painted over Edmund's shrine centuries later. The local people of Bedericsworth were said to have been so pleased to be spared King Swein's extortions, that they voluntarily agreed to pay a carucagium, or local land tax, to the monastery. The levy was four pence on every piece of land. In later centuries no doubt, this story was produced to answer local critics who questioned why this tax should be paid.

After King Swain's demise, his son Cnut (or Canute) took over, but Ethelred returned and drove him out. Cnut returned to try some inconclusive campaigning. In 1016 AD, Ethelred the Unready died and his son, Edmund Ironside, was proclaimed King in London, but Canute was also crowned at Southampton. After fierce fighting at Ashingdon in Essex in which Ulfcytel, Earl of East Anglia was killed, Edmund kept the land south of the Thames, and the rest went to Canute. King Edmund Ironside died within a month of the

Battle of Ashingdon, and so Cnut received the entire kingdom. He was the first Danish King of all England, while only 23 years old. King Canute built a church dedicated to St Edmund at the site of his victory at Ashingdon, in Essex. This act of Canute may indicate an existing interest in St. Edmund, which was to help the development of St Edmund's shrine and Sainthood in the near future.

Suffolk, and indeed all England, was now once more under Danish rule and was to remain part of a large Scandinavian empire until 1042 AD. When King Ethelred the Unready had died, he left a widow, Queen Emma. Canute now married Emma and gave her West Suffolk as a wedding present. Emma was the daughter of Duke Richard of Normandy, and by this act Cnut perpetuated the Norman claim to the English throne. The gift of West Suffolk may imply that it already existed as a unit of land holding, or administration, of Denmark.

In 1017 AD, King Canute created four new earldoms of Wessex, East Anglia, Mercia and Northumbria, killed several leaders of the old regime and took firm control. Thurkil the Tall was made Earl of East Anglia, for his part in the invasion. Godwin was made Earl of Wessex.

In 1018 AD, Canute levied a tribute of 11,000 pieces of silver in London, and 72,000 pieces of silver from the rest of the country, using this to pay off part of his army. King Canute sat at Oxford to draw up laws governing both Danish men and Englishmen. This was based on Edgar's law and Christian teaching. In 1018 AD, Canute also became King of Denmark, and overlord of Norway. This coronation highlights the relationship between Norway and Denmark.

King Canute was interested in religion and had already supported the order of St Edmund. In 1020 AD, he made a pilgrimage to the shrine at Bedericsworth. At Bury, King Canute had to settle a dispute between the shrines' priests and the Bishop of Elmham, whose diocese included Bedericsworth. The priests refused to turn over the normal tithes that were due to the Bishop, believing that St Edmund was exempt from such dues. Possibly in consultation with his new wife, Queen Emma, who owned the jurisdiction of West Suffolk, King Canute tried to sort out the situation. To appease the Bishop, the dozen secular priests were fired, but the Bishop did not get control. Perhaps to atone for his father, King Cnut arranged for the building of a rotunda to the church of St Mary at Bury. Bishop Ailfric of Elmham then granted the monastery freedom from Episcopal control, and replaced the secular priests guarding the shrine by 20 Benedictine monks from St Benet Hulme near Horning and from Ely. The Benedictines were now financially and spiritually independent of the Bishop.

The exact organization of local government at this time is extremely vague to us today; however, we need to remember that Anglo-Saxon England was a highly structured and organized society. Administration seems to have been very efficient by the standards of the time. We know that by 1097 AD, the rents for burgage tenants, called hadgovel, had to be paid to the Reeve. This office later became what is now called the Bailiff. By 1097 AD, the Reeve was appointed by the abbot, and so the rents accrued to the abbey. It is likely that a Reeve was appointed as part of the setting up of a town, just as a Shire Reeve (later to evolve into the word Sheriff) was appointed to control the Shire. He was there to make sure local dues were paid to the King, and that the royal writ was obeyed locally. These new dues may have included Hadgovel, or the rent of one penny for each measure of land inside the town, probably for the right to occupy a tenement or dwelling. This land could be inherited by its occupier's kin, but only on payment of a lump sum.

In 1026 AD, King Canute had to defend Denmark against Swedish attack and incurred heavy losses. At the time Denmark claimed ownership of both sides of Orsund Sound, the entrance to the Baltic Sea. One side of the entrance was on the Swedish Peninsula, but was owned by the Danes. This did not sit well with the Swedes, and they eventually gained ownership of the land on their side of this important seaway.

In 1027 AD, Cnut paid a courtesy visit to the Pope and various shrines, and was an enthusiastic Christian and patron of the arts, giving many splendid gifts to other religious houses, as well as to Bury. In 1028 AD, Cnut returned to Norway to secure his claim by expelling Olaf. In 1032 AD, the new round church of stone was consecrated at Bury, situated to the north of where the Chancel of the Norman Abbey would later be built. In 1035 AD, King Cnut died and was buried at Winchester. Cnut declared Harold Harefoot his successor despite severe opposition from Wessex. Harold was the son of Cnut and his first wife, Elgifu of Mercia. Emma herself wanted her own son, fathered by Cnut, called Harthacnut, to be king.

Although Viking influence lingered on, the Viking Age in England really died with Canute. In 1040 AD, King Harold Harefoot died and was succeeded by Harthacnut who was condemned by the Anglo-Saxon Chroniclers for increasing taxes and saying *"he never did anything kingly."* He was apparently prone to illness. In 1042 AD, Danish rule finally ended when Harthacnut collapsed and died and was succeeded by King Edward the Confessor.

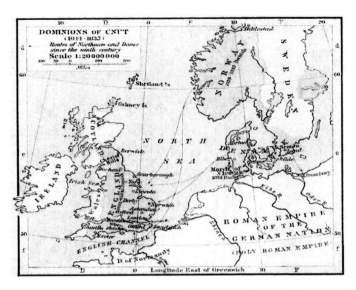

A Map of the Danish Empire in 1014 AD, just before the Vikings disappeared. Also notice the "Holy Roman Empire" that eventually became Germany.

The Fall of Danelaw

The failure to capture Wessex led to the eventual fall of Danelaw. The Danes honored the peace treaty signed by Gunthrum for ten years. During that time, King Alfred established control over all parts of England not under Danish rule and strengthened the army. The unification of England, the strong defenses and organized army prevented the Danes from capturing more English lands. Gradually the English took back control of the Danelaw lands. By 954 AD ,when Edward the Elder forced Eric Bloodaxe out of Northumbria, Danelaw was no more.

Various petty kingdoms existed throughout the area now known as Denmark for many years. Around 980 AD, Harold Bluetooth appears to have established the unified kingdom of Denmark. Around the same time, he received a visit from a German missionary who, according to legend, survived an ordeal by fire. This convinced Harold to convert to Roman Christianity which replaced the Old Norse religious practices and gained many advantages for the king. Christianity brought with it some support from the Holy Roman Empire (Catholic Germany). It also allowed the king to dismiss many of his opponents who adhered to the old religious practices. The Church would bring to his lands a stable administration that he could hopefully use to exercise control. After the death of King Canute the Great in 1035 AD, England broke away from Danish control and Denmark fell into disarray for some time. Vikings from Norway raided the now Catholic, Denmark sporadically. Canute's nephew Sweyn Estridson (1020–1074 AD) re-established strong royal Danish authority, and built a good relationship with the archbishop of the German City of Bremen, at that time the Archbishop of all of Scandinavia. It is precisely at this period in history that Denmark became an independent country, the Vikings disappeared, the Hansiatic League was established to reduce piracy and monopolize trade in the Baltic, and the Farums from Italy moved to Denmark. Through all of this, the Farums remained Orthodox Christians.

Establishment of the Kingdom of Denmark

Often regarded as Denmark's "birth certificate", the large carved Jelling Stone announces the unification of Denmark by Harald Bluetooth c980 AD.

Harald "Bluetooth" Gormsson (probably born c935 AD) was the son of King Gorm the Old and of Thyra Dannebod. He died in 985 or 986 AD, having ruled as King of Denmark from c958 AD, and King of Norway for a few years probably around 970 AD. Some sources state that his son Sweyn forcibly deposed him as King. Harald caused the Jelling stones to be erected to honor his parents. The Encyclopedia Britannica considers the runic inscriptions as the most well known in Denmark. The biography of Harald Bluetooth is summed up by this runic inscription from the Jelling stones:

"King Harald bade these memorials to be made after Gorm, his father, and Thyra, his mother. The Harald who won the whole of Denmark and Norway and turned the Danes to (Latin) Christianity."

Denmark After Danelaw

In the early 12th century, Denmark became the seat of an independent church province of Scandinavia. Not long after that, Sweden and Norway established their own archbishoprics, free of Catholic Danish control. The mid-12th century proved a difficult time for the Kingdom of Denmark. Violent civil wars rocked the land. Eventually, Valdemar the Great (1131–1182 AD), gained control of the kingdom, stabilizing it and reorganizing the administration. King Valdemar and Absalon (1128–1201 AD), the bishop of Roskilde, rebuilt the country. During Valdemar's reign construction began of a castle in the village of Havn, leading eventually to the foundation of Copenhagen, the modern capital of Denmark. Valdemar and Absalon built Denmark into a major power in the Baltic Sea, a power which later competed with the Hanseatic League, the counts of Holstein, and the Catholic Teutonic Knights for trade, territory, and influence throughout the Baltic. In 1168 AD, King Valdemar and Bishop Absalon gained a foothold on the southern shore of the Baltic, when they subdued the Principality of Rugen.

The history of Copenhagen dates back to the first settlement at the site in the 11th century. From the middle of the 12th century, after coming under the control of Bishop Absalon, Copenhagen grew in importance. The city was fortified with a stone wall during the 13th century. The harbor and the excellent possibilities for herring fishing contributed to Copenhagen's growth and development into an important trading centre. It was repeatedly attacked by the Hanseatic League as the Germans became aware of its expansion and were threatened by their influence and nautical power in the Baltic Sea. In 1254 AD, Copenhagen received its charter as a city under Bishop Jakob Erlandsen.

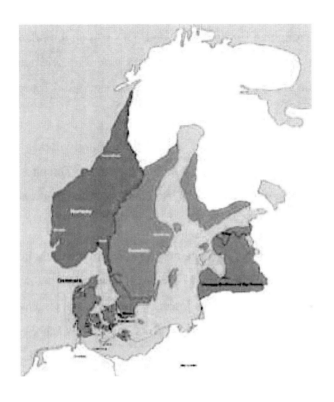

Scandinavia in 1219

■ Norway ■ Sweden ■ Denmark ■ Sword Brethren ░ Saaremaa (Osel) claimed by Denmark but conquered by the Sword Brethren in 1227 along with the territories conquered by Denmark in northern Germany.

The Cistercian Monks

While the Farums were living in Denmark, they were not just busy taxing ships that entered and exited Orsund Sound. As the Farum Crest, prominently displayed in the city of Farum, and on Rosslyn Chapel, attests they were busy at another history making adventure. They were associated with the ordination and indoctrination of new Templars who would join, be indoctrinated, and then be dispersed throughout Europe, as needed. This was an important task as ninety percent of Templars who went to battle were slain or wounded. There were three main players in the implementation of the initial Templar organization.

The first of the main influences was the Sinclair family in Scotland. The Sinclairs had family ties in France, the birthplace of the Templars, and were sympathetic to the newly organized Cistercian Order and their conservative Benedictine beliefs.

Secondly, the Cistercians were attempting to return the Catholic Church to the original, conservative teachings of Jesus. It is believed that the Sinclair family, of both France and Scotland, were responsible for sending Bernard de Clairvaux who, along with 35 of his relatives, joined the Catholic monastery at Cîteaux, France. This voluntary act was not so much to serve the church, as it was to revise the order from within. Whether or not it was in the initial plan, this introduction of Orthodox Benedictine Celts into the order would eventually lead to a validation of a group of monks, called the Templars, by the Pope. The Templar charter, obtained by Bernard de Clairvaux, led to the expansion of the Templars into one of the most powerful organizations in Europe.

The third element of the success of the Templars was the training provided at Esrum Abby, just north of Farum Denmark. It is not well known that the Templars were required to be ordained monks. Esrum Abby was constructed under the direction of Bernard de Clairvaux, one of the founders of the Templars. The Farums, with their fleet of ships, not only provided a secluded place for the training of the Templars, but with their fleet of ships they were able to transport them anywhere in Europe. Later, the Templars were instrumental in ridding the Iberian Peninsula of the Muslims and in the colonization of North America.

Esrum Abby Zealand, Denmark

Esrum Abby was the main Danish headquarters for the Farum, Templar, and Cistercian movement while the Farums were in Denmark. The abbey was built in 1151 AD by Bernard de Clairvaux of Templar fame. The building was destroyed and the timbers were used to build Kronborg Castle, when the Farums and Cistercians left Denmark for Scotland c1397. Kronborg Castle then became the fortress which was responsible for collecting the Sound Dues after the Farums, who had been collecting the taxes, left Denmark in the late 14th Century. A new abbey was built in 1996; however, the foundation of the old abbey still exists nearby. It is very close to the size of Bernard's abbey in Clairveux, France.

The keynote of Cistercian life was a return to literal observance of the Rule of St Benedict, while rejecting the liberal changes the Benedictines of the Catholic

Church had undergone. The monks tried to replicate monastic life, exactly as it had been in Saint Benedict's time. The most striking feature in the reform was the return to manual labor, especially field-work, a special characteristic of Cistercian life. In relation to fields such as agriculture, hydraulic engineering and metallurgy, the Cistercians became the main force of technological diffusion in medieval Europe. These skills played a major part in their roles as Crusaders and later as Templars.

Benedict of Nursia, Italy, (Italian: San Benedetto da Norcia) (c.480–547), wrote seventy-three short chapters comprising the rules of being a monk. Its wisdom is of two kinds: spiritual (*how to live a Christocentric life on earth*) and administrative (*how to run a monastery efficiently*). More than half the chapters describe how to be obedient and humble, and what to do when a member of the community is not. About one-fourth regulate the work of God (the Opus Dei). One-tenth outlined how, and by whom, the monastery should be managed. And two chapters specifically describe the abbot's pastoral duties.

A supremely eloquent and strong-willed mystic (*Transcendentalist*), Bernard de Clairvaux was to become the most admired churchman of his age. In 1115 AD, Count Hugh of Champagne gave a tract of wild, forested land known as a refuge for robbers, and located forty miles east of Troyes, to the order. Bernard led twelve other monks to found the Abbey of Clairvaux, and began clearing the ground and building a church and dwelling.

When Bernard de Clairvaux arrived at Cîteaux, with 35 relatives, it was not by fate, but was a carefully orchestrated movement to restore the church back to its original morality and standards, standards which had been kept alive by the Orthodox Celts for over 1000 years. In addition, the movement would restore the Celts control over much of Western Europe from where they had

126

been both religiously and physically removed. You will read in the Chapter on the Templars that their plan was so successful, and they became so powerful, that in 1312 AD, the Pope authorized the leaders of the Templars killed and the order disbanded.

The abbey soon attracted a strong flow of zealous young men. At this point, Cîteaux had four other abbeys: Pontigny, Morimond, La Ferté and Clairvaux. Other French abbeys of Cîteaux would include Preuilly, La Cour-Dieu and Bouras. Bernard de Clairvaux's entry into the monastery helped the rapid proliferation of the order. By the end of the 12th century, the order had spread throughout France and into England, Wales, Scotland, Ireland, Galicia, Portugal, Italy, and Eastern Europe, which are all Celtic strongholds. Bernard's benefactor, Count Hugh de Champagne, is known to have gone to the Holy Land with the Templars in some of their Crusades.

Clairvaux Monastery Floor plan

Notice the square with the Benedictine Cross. This pattern was also in the floor plan of the Farum's Chapel at Rossano over 500 years earlier. Also, note that the Alter is against the East wall, as is the custom with Orthodox Christian Churches. This monastery was built just a few years after the Farums, who were officials in the Byzantine Empire, were defeated in Italy by the Ottoman Empire.

In the year 1128 AD, Bernard de Clairvaux assisted at the Council of Troyes, which had been convened by Pope Honorius II, and was presided over by Cardinal Matthew, Bishop of Albano. The purpose of this council was to settle certain disputes of the bishops of Paris, and regulate other matters of the Church of France. This is also the Council in which the Latin Order of the

Knights Templar was adopted. The bishops made Bernard secretary of the council, and charged him with drawing up the synodal statutes.

Map of Cistercian Influence c1250

Kronborg Castle

The story of Kronborg Castle, previously called Krogan Castle, dates back to the 1420s. The Castle was ordered built by the Danish king, Eric of Pomerania to collect taxes, called "Sound Dues", from ships passing through Oresund Sound. In 1426 AD, after the Farums departure from Denmark c1397 AD, Kronborg Castle was built to collect the Sound Dues previously collected by the Farums. The fortress was built at the narrowest point in the Sound. Prior to this time, the territory of the Kingdom of Denmark existed on both sides of Orsund Sound. Just before the Farums departed for Scotland the land was awarded to Sweden. This was just one more of the reasons, which are listed later in the chapter, for the Farums departure from Denmark. On the eastern shore, in Sweden, the Helsingborg Castle had been in existence since the Middle Ages. With the two castles, and guard ships, it was possible to control all navigation passing through the narrowest point between, what is now, Denmark and Sweden.

Kronborg Castle was built on Orekrog, a sandy tongue of land stretching into the sea from the Northeast coast of Zealand, Denmark and towards the coast of what is now Sweden. The castle consisted of a square curtain wall with a number of stone buildings inside. The stone building in the northeastern corner contained the king's residence. The building in the southwestern corner contained a large arched banquet hall. The building in the southeastern corner possibly served as the chapel. Large portions of the walls of Krogen, the original Castle, are contained within the present-day Kronborg Castle. King Christian III had the corners of the curtain wall supplemented with bastions in 1558-59 AD.

Kronborg Castle

Notice that the Fort is itself a geoglyph. This is common for Forts of this era.

The Greek Cross

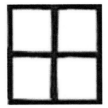

The Greek cross within a square is usually taken to represent earthly affairs or the temporal authority of the Greek and Byzantine Churches. The development of the Byzantine Empire, Eastern Europe, arose from the Greek Church's, and others, choice to remain Orthodox Christians rather than converting to Catholicism. They were joined by the Russian, Syrian, Egyptian Orthodox Christian Churches.

Just as the Galician Celts had brought the traditional Celtic Cross to Zealand Denmark c700 AD, when the Italian Farums moved to Denmark c1000 AD, they brought the Byzantine Greek Cross to Denmark. Both these spiritual symbols were united to form the Faram Crest.

The Greek Cross was also adopted as the symbol of the Templars, when their organization was commissioned c1126 AD. As is demonstrated in the following photo, the true Templar Cross exemplified a cross with an invisible, stylized square cross surrounding it. This deception was necessary because the Templars, being Orthodox Christians, were fighting in a Catholic Order.

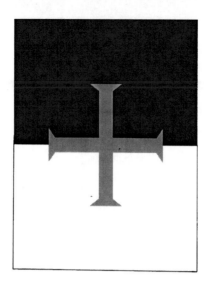

Templar Flag Showing the True Templar Cross

The Farum Crest
Farum City, Denmark

The Faram Crest developed from the combining of the Celtic Cross and the Greek (Byzantine) Cross. Both symbols were important, to both sides, of the Farum Clan. There are only three places where this crest is known to exist. One is in the city of Farum, Denmark, another is in the main window of Rosslyn Chapel in Edinburgh Scotland, and the third is in a Scottish henge in the USA. All three places were known Templar sanctuaries, and all three icons were constructed by the Faram family. Rosslyn Chapel was commissioned by the grandson of Henry Sinclair I, and the construction supervised by Robert Faram.

Robert, who was most likely the grandson of the Farams that accompanied Henry Sinclair to America, would have returned from North America, in order to assist in the construction of the Rosslyn Chapel. Robert Faram is listed as a Scottish official in the records of Edinburgh in 1488 AD, the date of the completion of Rosslyn Chapel. The Faram crest evolved into a symbol unique to the Farum Family who supported the Templars, while living in Farum, Denmark.

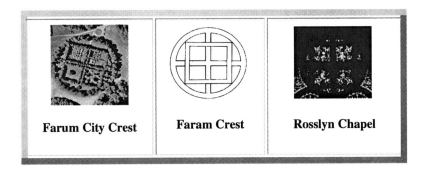

| Farum City Crest | Faram Crest | Rosslyn Chapel |

THE KALMAR UNION 1397–1523

The Kalmar Union is a historiographical term meaning a series of personal unions (1397–1523) that united the three kingdoms of Denmark, Norway, Iceland, Greenland, and the Faroe Islands. On 2 August 1379, at Marstrand, near Tønsberg, Norway, King Haakon VI of Norway invested and confirmed Henry Sinclair as the Norwegian Earl of Orkney over a rival claim by his cousin Malise Sparre. Later Scotland joined the union as well as Shetland, Orkney, and Sweden under a single monarch. For a period before this Denmark colonized and claimed the West coast of Sweden as belonging to Denmark. This fact was an important part of the Farum story with regards to the method in which they collected taxes for Denmark.

The Kalmar Union countries had, in theory, not given up their sovereignty or even their independence, but in reality they were not autonomous and shared a common monarch holding sovereignty and, in practice, leading foreign policy. Diverging interests, especially the Swedish nobility's dissatisfaction over the dominant role played by Denmark and Holstein, gave rise to a conflict that would hamper the union in several intervals from the 1430s until its breakup in 1523 AD, when Gustav Vasa became king of Sweden.

Kalmar Union Capital - Copenhagen, Denmark
The Kalmar Union was comprised of:
Denmark
Faroe Islands
Scotland
Orkney
Greenland
Iceland
Norway
Sweden
United Kingdom (in part)
Finland

The Kalmar Union was established through the work of Queen Margaret I of Denmark (1353–1412), a daughter of King Valdemar IV of Denmark. At the age of ten, she married King Haakon VI of Norway and Sweden, who was the son of King Magnus IV of Norway and Sweden. Margaret succeeded in having her son Olav recognized as heir to the throne of Denmark. In 1376 AD, Olav inherited the crown of Denmark from his maternal grandfather as King Oluf III, with his mother as guardian. When Haakon VI died in 1380, Olav also inherited the crown of Norway. The two kingdoms were united in a personal union under a child king, with the king's mother as his guardian.

Olav died in 1387, before he came of age and could take over the government. Margaret was successful in getting the Danish Council of the Realm to elect her as regent of Denmark, but, at the time, she did not attempt to assume the title of queen. On February 2 the next year (1388 AD), she was also recognized as regent of Norway. She adopted her sister's grandson Bogislav, a son of prince Vartislav of Pomerania, and gave him the more Nordic name Erik. Margaret successfully maneuvered to have the Norwegian Council recognize him as heir to the throne of Norway, and in spite of his not being first in the line of succession; he was installed as king of Norway in 1389, with Margaret still as his guardian.

In Sweden, this was a time of conflict between King Albrecht of Mecklenburg and leaders of the nobility. Albrecht's enemies, in 1388 AD, elected Margaret as regent to the western part of Sweden, which Denmark controlled, promising to assist her in conquering the rest of the country. Their common enemy was the Hanseatic League and the growing German influence over the Scandinavian economy. After Danish and Swedish troops in 1389 defeated the Swedish king, Albert of Mecklenburg failed to pay the required tribute of 60,000 silver marks within three years after his release and

Margaret's position in Sweden was secured. The three Nordic kingdoms were united under a common regent. Margaret promised to protect the political influence and privileges of the nobility under the union. Her grandnephew Erik, already king of Norway since 1389, succeeded to the thrones of Denmark and Sweden in 1396. This government turmoil, in addition to other factors, would prompt the entire Farum clan to desert their beloved town of Farum, Denmark and move to Scotland and Ireland in preparation for the Celtic colonization of North America.

The Nordic union was somewhat formalized on June 17, 1397 by the Treaty of Kalmar, signed in the Swedish castle of Kalmar, on Sweden's south-east coast. In medieval times this was close to the Danish border of what is now the west coast of Sweden. The treaty stipulated an eternal union of the three realms under one king, who was to be chosen among the sons of the deceased king. They were to be governed separately, with the respective councils, and according to their ancient laws, but foreign policy was to be conducted by the king.

THE DENMARK - NORWAY ALLIANCE

Capital - Copenhagen, Denmark
Countries in the Alliance
Denmark
Faroe Islands
Greenland
Iceland
Norway
Schleswig-Holstein

Origins of the Union

The Denmark–Norway Alliance is the historiographical name for a former political entity consisting of the kingdoms of Denmark and Norway, including the originally Norwegian dependencies of Iceland, Greenland and the Faroe

Islands. Following the strife surrounding the break-up of its predecessor, the Kalmar Union, the two kingdoms entered into another personal union in 1536 AD which lasted until 1814 AD. The corresponding adjective is Dano-Norwegian. The term Kingdom of Denmark is sometimes used to include both countries in the period 1536–1814 AD, since the political and economic power emanated from Copenhagen, Denmark. The term covers the "royal part" of the Oldenburgs as it was in 1460 AD, excluding the "ducal part" of Schleswig and Holstein. The administration used two official languages, Danish and German, and for several centuries both a Danish and German Chancery existed.

Conflict

In 1814, in the Treaty of Kiel, the king of the Denmark–Norway alliance was forced to cede mainland Norway to the king of Sweden, Charles XIII. Norway, led by the viceroy prince Christian Frederick, objected to the terms of the treaty. A constitutional assembly declared Norwegian independence, adopted a liberal constitution, and elected Christian Frederick king. After a brief war with Sweden, the peace terms of the Convention of Moss recognized Norwegian independence, but forced Norway to accept a personal union with Sweden.

In the middle of the 19th century, many intellectuals joined the Scandinavist movement, which promoted closer contacts between the three countries. At the time, the union between Sweden and Norway under one monarch, together with the fact that King Frederick VII of Denmark had no male heir, gave rise to the idea of reuniting the countries of the Kalmar Union, except for Finland.

The Move to Scotland

Around the end of the 14th century, the Orthodox Christian Farums decided it was time to depart their predominantly Roman Catholic Country of Denmark. Scotland had just won its war against England and was finally independent.

The surname Faram does not appear in Scottish records until 1488 AD. This can be explained by the fact that the Farams were in North America from 1398 AD until Robert Faram returned to build Rosslyn Chapel for the Sinclairs, in the middle of the 15th Century. The first recording of the name Faram was as a city official in Edinburgh Scotland in 1488 AD, the same year Rosslyn Chapel was completed. The Scotts tend to be a little more reluctant to release civil records than England, so there may be more recordings of the Faram name that are not yet accessible. The next record of the Faram name appears in England in 1567 AD, living near the current border with Scotland. From 1567 AD forward, a continuous genealogical record can be found on the Faram name. In the 17th century, the remainder of the Farum clan, from southern Italy, joined the Farams in Howden and Fishlake, England. They too changed their name to Faram.

Reasons for the Farums to leave Denmark - In descending order:
1. Norse Colonization

In 1362 AD, the King of Portugal ceded the land now known as the United States to the Templars for their assistance in eliminating the Muslims from the Iberian Peninsula. The Farams and Sinclairs became aware that the Greenlanders and Icelanders, previously known as the Vikings, were now migrating to North America. The Norse migration to North America was the result of dire climactic changes that had not been unforeseen when the Vikings were given Greenland and Iceland to settle. Since the Icelandic descendants were not Celts, and had been disowned by all the countries of Europe, they were not welcome in the new Celtic Templar Territory. This situation became even more critical when the Norwegian Norse begin colonizing the territory just west of the Mississippi River, from Minnesota to Texas. If this were allowed to continue their colonization, and eventual claiming of the territory, would have blocked access from the East coast to the West coast.

It was in 1398 that the Sinclairs, along with ships most likely owned by the family now called the Farams, sailed to Druid Hill Park, in what is now Baltimore Maryland to establish what would later be called the United States. (See Chapter 11.)

Shortly after, in 1415 AD, a Portuguese Nobleman, named Henry the Navigator, started a school to train navigators in Sevres, Portugal. The Portuguese had been sailing the world in secret for hundreds of years. Why would they pick this particular time to open the world to other ships? The answer is simple. The Portuguese had already settled the east coast of South America, now their allies, the Celts, were colonizing the east coast of North America. The secret was out. What was the point in having all those resources in Brazil, if you had no one to buy them? The selling of resources from North and South America would make both Portugal, and what is now the United States, two of the richest countries in the world during this period in history.

2. The Little Ice Age

Two great natural disasters struck Europe in the 14th Century. One was the climatic "Little Ice Age". This term is used in wildly varied ways by different authors, and there actually seems to have been two cooling episodes: an earlier one from the late 1200's to 1600 or so, and a later one in the 1700's and 1800's. During the earlier freeze, in 1303, 1306 and 1307 AD, the Baltic Sea froze over, something never before recorded. Alpine glaciers advanced. The Norse settlements in Greenland were cut off and grain cultivation ceased in Iceland. The last ship sailed from Iceland to Greenland in the early 1400's. Can there be any doubt that the Vikings of Greenland and Iceland moved further south to the warmth of North America? In 1315 AD, crops failed after heavy rains in France. This period was marked by widespread famine, reports of cannibalism and epidemics. When contact was resumed with Iceland, in the 1700's, the settlements were long abandoned.

3. The Black Death

If the Little Ice Age weakened Europe's agricultural productivity and made life uncomfortable, the Bubonic Plague brought life to a virtual standstill. In October 1347 AD, two months after the fall of Calais, Genoese trading ships put into the harbor of Messina in Sicily with dead and dying men at the oars. The ships had come from the Black Sea port of Caffa (now Feodosiya), in the Crimea, where the Genoese maintained a trading post. The diseased sailors showed strange black swellings about the size of an egg or an apple in the armpits and groin. The sick suffered severe pain and died quickly within five days of the first symptoms. As the disease spread, other symptoms of continuous fever and spitting of blood appeared instead of the swellings or buboes. These victims coughed and sweated heavily and died even more quickly, within three days or less, sometimes in 24 hours.

In 1349 AD, it resumed in Paris, spread to Picardy, Flanders, and the Low Countries, and from England to Scotland and Ireland as well as to Norway. There a ghost ship with a cargo of wool and a dead crew drifted offshore until it ran aground near Bergen. From there the plague passed into Sweden, Denmark, Prussia, Iceland, and as far west as Greenland. Leaving a strange pocket of immunity in Bohemia, and Russia until 1351, it had passed through most of Europe by mid-1350. Although the mortality rate was erratic, ranging from one fifth in some places to nine tenths to almost total elimination in others. The overall range of the disease, figured by modern demographers, has calculated the affected area as extending from India to Iceland. Around the same figure is expressed in Froissart's casual words: *"a third of the world died."*

4. The Kalmar Union

Margaret I, (1353-1412 AD) tried to join the three kingdoms of Denmark, Norway, and Sweden (including the Faroe Islands, as well as Iceland, Greenland, and present-day Finland) under her rule. This relationship became known as the Kalmar Union, made official in 1397 AD. This destroyed the autonomy of both the Farams and the Sinclairs. It was in 1398 AD that both families departed for the new world. Henry Sinclair's motivation, by his own statement, was *"To baptize the Indians"*.

END CHAPTER

Chapter 5

Ancient Secrets

Discovery

During my research for this book, I discovered that down through time civilizations have passed down a secret science which I have named Geoglyphology. There currently exists a legacy of geoglyphs, "geo" meaning earth and "glyph" meaning writing, on the shores and highlands of land masses around the world. A well known example of a geoglyphic survey marker is the Stonehenge monolith in England. Stonehenge has been known for centuries, as have earlier monoliths, for the many astrological alignments that were designed into its construction. This phenomenon of astrological alignment is present in most ancient megalithic and geoglyphic structures around the world, and has been accepted as a scientific fact. Until now, the other attributes of these structures and geoglyphs have been known only to a few people in societies which have guarded and handed down the secrets for millennia.

A prudent person would ask; why information of this magnitude would be kept secret for so long and how do you prove it? The answer to the second part of the question is the subject of this book. The answer to the first part of the question as to why this would be kept secret requires a complicated answer. You see, the practice of marking territories with geoglyphs has been passed down secretly for millennia. Given that the practice of Geoglyphology is to mark a claimed territory, the practice would inherently require some degree of secrecy. Most of these survey markers are so large, and so spread out that they remain hidden unless someone that knows of their existence points them out. By being so large they are, for the most part, immune to tampering and remain hidden, unless the builder needs to prove their prior claim to a given territory.

Another reason for hiding the Geoglyphs is that, since they are survey markers, they reveal the history of the people that placed them. This is no more evident than in the establishment of the United States itself. Contrary to popular belief, most of the men and women who originally colonized the United States were from somewhere other than the British Empire. Celtic descendents, in the form of the Portuguese, Danes, Scotts, Irish, Norse, Templars and Freemasons, established colonies in North America in order to escape the tribulations of Europe, with its wars, plagues, religious persecution and the mixing of church and state.

Geoglyphology

Until now, the majority of the information which has been available to the Archeologist has been gleaned from information recovered at a dig site. During my research, I realized that a great majority of the ancient architectural, monolithic and geoglyphic structures built around the world had something more to offer. There exists a commonality in that the structures, and associated geoglyphs, were aligned in such a manner that the study of their linear alignment unveils a much larger story and immensely expands the data available to the archeologist, historian, and the related disciplines.

Extensive research on these geoglyphs, which exist on every continent and many islands around the world, have shown that no matter when or where they were constructed they all tie into a worldwide network of civilizations that have progressed, prospered and suffered setbacks for millennia. These geoglyphs range in age from before the 10,000 year old Yonaguni Pyramid in Japan, to geoglyphs constructed as late as 250 years ago.

Data recovered from these studies reveal the geographical range of the culture being studied, the level of sophistication that existed in relation to their understanding of mathematics and geometry, their knowledge of world geography, and the discovery of other archeological sites that were unknown prior to the studies. In addition, the dating of the culture at the dig site can be verified by the data collected at the offsite locations.

What are Glyphs and Geoglyphs?

Glyph - A glyph can be any design that is used to convey a message.

Geoglyph - A geoglyph is a glyph that occurs on the ground.

Bearing - A bearing refers to the direction that any line, formed by a geoglyph, points in relation to "Magnetic North". Magnetic North can be used at the geoglyph site because it has not been distorted by deviations that exist between the starting point and the destination. A "True" or direct line is used once you depart the origination point. This is necessary because as soon as you begin tracing a line away from the source, magnetic deviation becomes a factor. Magnetic Deviation exists all over the world, and renders the magnetic heading of a compass useless over long distances, because of the error occurring naturally from the magnetism of the earth. A true heading is the shortest distance between two points without having to consider magnetic deviation. True headings can be scribed on a globe, derived from Celestial Navigation, GPS, and computer software. These methods only produce True Headings which are not distorted by Magnetic Deviation. It was learned, through the efforts of Google Earth, that all the bearings used in Ancient Geoglyphs proved to be true radials emanating from the source.

Radials - Radials are bearings after they leave the source. At the source,

Magnetic Bearings and True Headings are the same, because no magnetic distortion has taken place by traveling away from the source. Once a direction away from the source is plotted it must be plotted on a true course, not a magnetic course, in order to avoid magnetic deviation.

Geoglyphs, for the most part, are so large that they can only be recognized from the air or satellites. The civilizations that placed these geoglyphs must have had mathematical capabilities well beyond anything we give them credit for. I have visited some sites on the ground and even knowing they are there, I find them difficult to locate. The glyphs take on several forms. Some take the form of a triangle, another might be one or more circles, and another may be one or more lines touching or crossing each other. No matter what shape a glyph takes, any line can be a pointer to a place important to the creator of that glyph.

What follows are a few examples of how bearings are derived from various geoglyphic patterns.

Symbol	Directions

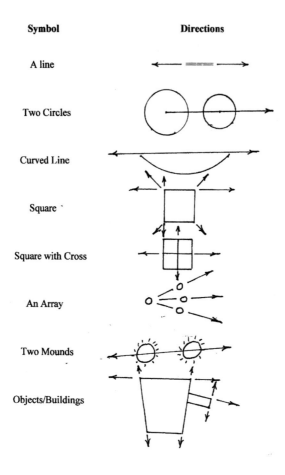

Symbol
A line
Two Circles
Curved Line
Square
Square with Cross
An Array
Two Mounds
Objects/Buildings

After applying the previous criteria to a geoglyph it is then necessary to apply certain secret protocols which have been passed down for millennia from one civilization to another. These protocols allow the user to determine the destination and termination point of the bearings which emanate from the geoglyph.

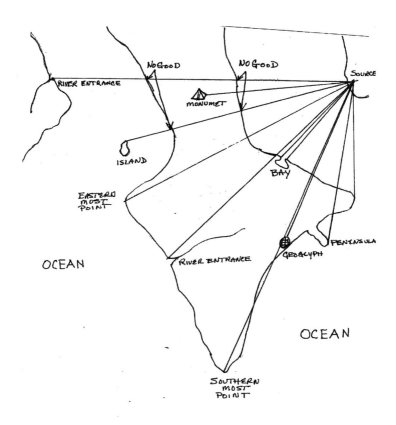

Examples of the criteria used to verify the intended termination point of a Geoglyph radial, and at the same time, to locate other geoglyphs.

Once the bearings are established for a geoglyph, at the point of origin, the bearings are extended in the form of radials (True headings) to determine if, and where, they intersect with an object that meets the protocols which were established millennia ago. In order for an extended radial to be considered legitimate, it must intersect at one of the following points: the mouth of a river, another geoglyph, a monument, a location sacred to the culture that built the

147

geoglyph and validated by being identified by another geoglyph, the entrance to a bay, a significant protrusion on a land mass such as the corner or tip of a continent, the tip of a peninsula, or an island.

After some study, it was discovered, that many mediums were used to construct geoglyphs. These included the arrangement of stones, the planting of different colors of flora, and the sterilizing of the ground, the scraping of the earth to reveal a different color underneath (Nazca), the changing of natural geological features with the features modified or supplemented, the wall alignment of structures (Caral, Peru), the alignment of Monoliths (Stonehenge), the alignment of Pyramids (Worldwide), the creation of stone and earth mounds, and more. For instance, the edges of the mounds of the, so called, Mississippian Indians, in the central United States have been proven to be geoglyphic territorial pointers.

Ancient archeological locations, many previously unknown, have been identified through Geoglyphology. The accuracy of the calculations of the ancient peoples is incredible. The GPS accuracy of the modern software program is seldom more accurate than the orientations of the ancients. By calculating the bearing at the source one can follow the extended radial for sometimes thousands of miles and locate a related geoglyph with little or no error.

The percentage of success in locating a verifiable glyph or ancient location, using each of the extended radials of any one glyph, was variable but ran in the range of 90% to 100%. Much of the lack of success was attributed to urbanization, overgrowth, vandalism, etc. Surprisingly, based on the glyphs that were found, there seems to be an incredible amount of durability built into the geoglyphs. It appears that the meteorological conditions at any given site were considered in determining the materials used. At sites where rain and wind are seldom seen, most glyphs were made of earth. At locations that encountered rain and wind, stones and rock were used.

Research results indicate, that Geoglyphology holds great promise in expanding our understanding of the civilizations that have preceded us. Through the tireless efforts of many devoted archaeologists, and new methods of discovery, the world is on the cusp of a new awakening. To some this new paradigm change will be quite uncomfortable.

SOME GEOGLYPH EXAMPLES

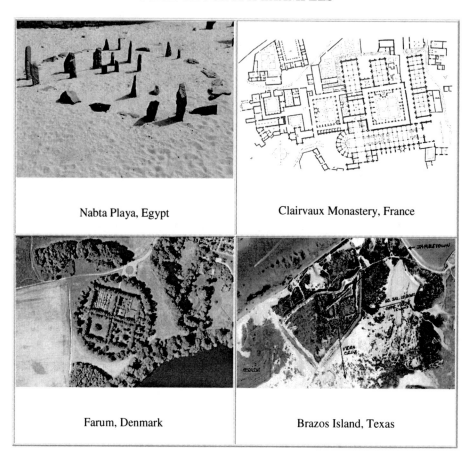

Nabta Playa, Egypt	Clairvaux Monastery, France
Farum, Denmark	Brazos Island, Texas

Note: The calculations performed during the writing of this book required the use of a special software called *"Google Earth"*. Google's software is able to calculate true spherical bearings on the curved surface of the earth and then display them correctly on a flat plane.

Spherical Geometry

In Spherical Geometry there are no parallel lines. It is difficult to grasp the concept that two bearings of the same value can cross. That is because we are used to thinking in terms of Plane Geometry on a flat plane. However, all this changes when you draw lines on a sphere. In dealing with a sphere you enter the realm of Spherical Geometry.

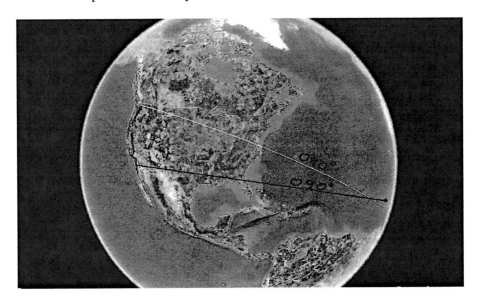

Example of how parallel lines of the same value always cross on a sphere.

Spherical Geometry is the study of figures on the surface of a sphere, as opposed to the type of geometry studied in plane geometry or solid geometry. In spherical geometry, straight lines are great circles; therefore, any two lines will always cross in two places somewhere on the sphere. An accomplished mathematician, as were the ancients, can use a line to point to a distant object, or use two lines to come together at a distant point to highlight an important place, or three lines to make a triangle.

In the field of Geoglyphology, we are plotting lines in a spherical world and then displaying the results on a flat plane. It is difficult to grasp the concept of combining Spherical Geometry with Plane Geometry. That is why the new field of modern Geoglyphology could not have been proposed without the advent of the "Google Earth" software that computes using Spherical Geometry, and then displays the results on a flat plane. This type of precise mapping precludes the plotting of these bearings on a flat map. Maps become distorted when converted from a sphere to a flat map. Any lines that are depicted in this article on a flat, non-satellite map were first plotted using the software and then drawn on the flat map after the end points were determined. Even then, the proper curvature is missing. The compelling question is; what knowledge did the ancients possess, 12,000 years ago, that allowed them to do these calculations. The most likely answer is their accumulated knowledge of the earth, inherited mathematics, and their obsession with astronomy.

The Stonehenge Geoglyph, Salisbury Plains, UK - c3100BC

I thought we would begin by using a structure with which most people are familiar. Stonehenge will also play an important role with other geoglyphs later in the book. Stonehenge is located in the South Central portion of England and is centrally located in the eastern Celtic geographic arena. Stonehenge has been accurately dated by renowned scientists as being approximately 5100 years old. For Millennia, visitors have speculated about the purpose of Stonehenge. Up to this point, the purpose has generally been speculated to be some type of celestial calendar. There is no doubt that the monolith is some form of celestial device, however, new evidence resulting from our research suggests that it is much more than that. Stonehenge in addition to being a celestial calendar, is also a world class survey marker. (See the following Plates.)

Stonehenge - Ground Level View

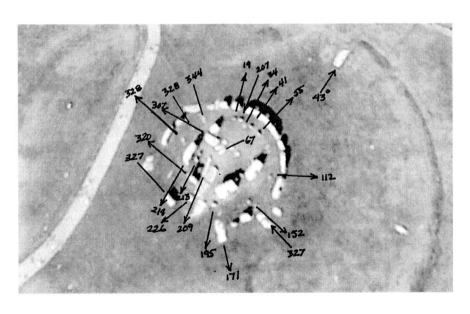

Stonehenge - With Geoglyphic Bearings Plotted

153

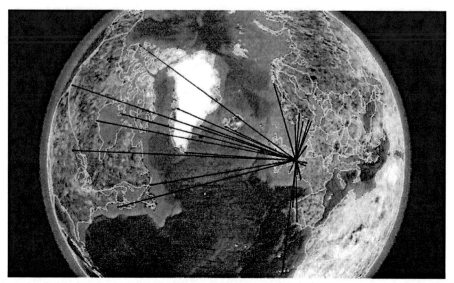

**STONEHENGE - With extended radials outlining the Celtic Territory
established c3100BC**

The preceding three photos show the method of calculating the territory that
any particular geoglyph may outline. In this case, of course, the subject is the
famous Stonehenge monolith. This sequence of processing a geoglyph is used
in most cases. First, the geoglyph must be located so that an accurate
measurement of the bearings which emanate from the geoglyph can be
measured accurately. In the case of Stonehenge, as well as many of the older
geoglyphs, there is an orientation line (The Stonehenge orientation line is
nearby, but not shown here.) that tells the person reading the geoglyph how
many degrees to add or subtract from the bearings found at the source. This
adjustment is necessary in order for the geoglyph to be aligned correctly. In the
case of Stonehenge, that correction factor is minus two degrees. That simply
means that two degrees must be subtracted from the bearings found at the site,
in order for it to be aligned correctly. These correction factors are common in
older geoglyphs, but are rarely used in later geoglyphs.

Once the bearings are determined the bearings are extended using the Google Earth "Ruler" function. As each radial is created, the radial line is inspected along its length until a point is observed that meets one of the ancient protocols previously mentioned. One would initially think that this could be very time consuming. They would be right; however, after much study it was learned that the geoglyphs follow certain patterns, which make them easier to locate for an experienced researcher. Once all the radials are plotted, the territory which is associated with the geoglyph can be roughly determined by connecting the termination points of all the radials.

There are some exceptions. In the case of Stonehenge, as in a few other territorial geoglyphs, there is one radial which points to the location of the geoglyph that describes the starting point of the territory next to the one you are working on. In the case of Stonehenge that radial is the one that terminates at Inspiration Peak in Minnesota, USA. In the Caral, Peru geoglyph, which follows later, there is one exterior radial which points to the origination point of the territorial geoglyph north of the South American Territory. That adjoining geoglyph is the pyramid at Chichin Itza, Mexico.

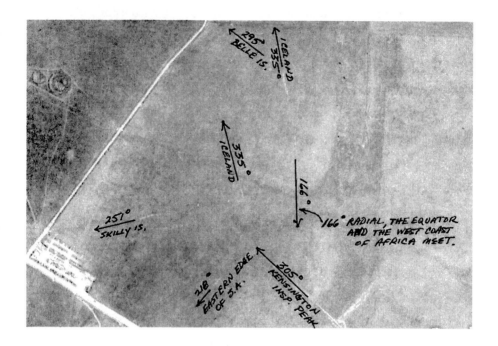

This plate shows just a few geoglyphic lines and their associated pointers in the field north of the Stonehenge Monument.

The above plates show Stonehenge and a portion of the area north of the Monument. The entire surrounding area is covered with glyphs of various symbols and lines. All symbols point to what research has shown to be geographical landmarks significant in the history of the Celts, their descendents, and allies. These particular markers may be part of a burial process. This is deduced from the fact that the Celtic graves in the Americas have at least one pointer that points to a Celtic occupied place in Europe, while the pointers in the fields around Stonehenge point to locations outside Britain. Whether these indicate the place the subject was born, visited or died will require further research.

THE NORTH AMERICAN GEOGLYPHS

As shown previously, the Stonehenge geoglyph outlines a Celtic Territory claimed by the Celts c3100 BC. There is also a geoglyph in Tiniteqilaq, Greenland which outlines a slightly modified Celtic territory claimed c1100 AD. It will become clear, in the following chapters, that the Portuguese, and their predecessors, had been traveling the world for centuries and claimed all of the Americas as now belonging to Portugal.

The following three geoglyphs, The Newport Tower, The Kensington Runestone, and Inspiration Peak, MN USA, combine together to modify an ancient North American territory once defined by Inspiration Peak alone. That ancient North American Territory once extended from the equator to the North Pole. When Stonehenge was built, the part now known as Canada was claimed by the Celtic culture in Britain. When the Tiniteqilaq Geoglyph was constructed it moved the boundaries, outlined by Stonehenge, west.

The Tiniteqilaq Geoglyph – Greenland's Stonehenge

Scholars have been debating for centuries as to how far south, in North America, the Celts of Europe traveled. After you finish this book you will be convinced that the Egyptians, the Etruscans, the Portuguese, the Danes Scotland and Ireland, visited most of North and South America long before and after Columbus.

As has been the case with every major culture, which we have researched, the Celts have also left us geoglyphic signposts which outline the territory which they intended to colonize after their departure from Western Europe. There is one indisputable geoglyph which the Celts left behind that should answer everyone's question as to the territory that they claimed to replace the Celtic Territory outlined by Stonehenge. That is the Tiniteqilaq, Greenland geoglyph depicted below. The glyph is well hidden in the Sermilk fjord in Eastern Greenland and is a prime example of the value of this rediscovered science called Geoglyphology.

The Tiniteqilaq Geoglyph (65 53 23.72N 37 46 24.91W), located on the Sermilk fjord, Greenland

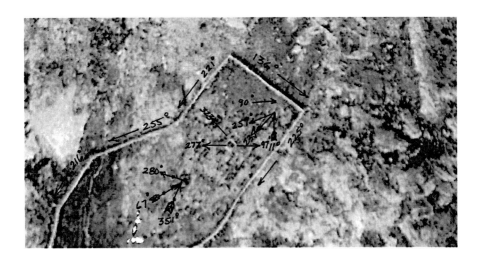

Bearings generated by the North half of the Tiniteqilaq geoglyph.

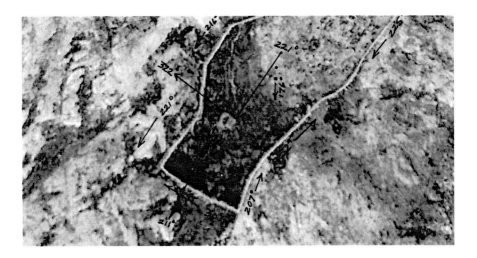

Bearings generated by the South half of the Tiniteqilaq geoglyph.

(Please be aware that the readings for the bearings shown in these photos were taken at a much higher magnification.)

159

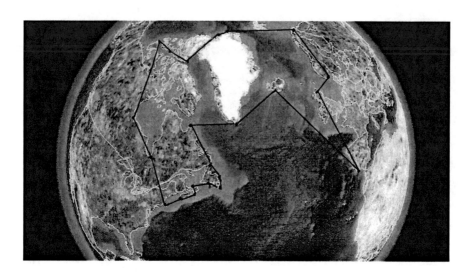

The boundaries of the new Celtic Territory as described in the Tiniteqilaq, Greenland geoglyph, c1100 AD.

The Tiniteqilaq geoglyph was intended to revise the Celtic Territory, depicted by the Stonehenge geoglyph. As previously stated, the Tiniteqilaq geoglyph extends the Stonehenge Territory from Nova Scotia down to Newport, Rhode Island USA. The fact that one of the bearings obtained from the Tiniteqilaq geoglyph points to an ancient glyph at the northern tip of Norway and from there to the city of Farum, Denmark shows a direct connection between the Tiniteqilaq geoglyph and the Danish Farums. You will encounter, later in the book, the many geoglyphic connections to the Faram family which are located in North America. This is a perfect example of how Geoglyphology can expand our range of historical knowledge.

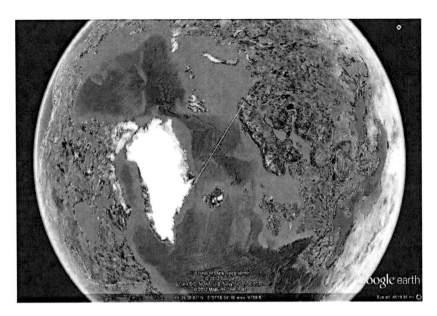

The 52 Degree radial from the Tiniteqilaq, Greenland geoglyph to the Norway geoglyph

The Norway to Farum City Geoglyph - 69 26 51.63N 30 03 38.95E

(The two submerged circle geoglyphs are at the extreme north end of Norway. When a line is drawn through the center of each one it points directly back to Faram City, Denmark)

After researching ancient European geoglyphs, the boundaries depicted in the Tiniteqilaq geoglyph correspond precisely with the territory to which the Celts would have initially migrated in order to escape the chaos in Europe and establish a new country. The territory defined by the Tiniteqilaq geoglyph has been extended past the Territory defined by Stonehenge to include Newport, Rhode Island. When the Tiniteqilaq geoglyph was built, the following eastern Celtic Countries were omitted from the territory described by the Stonehenge geoglyph. They were the Celtic countries of Wales, Cornwall, Brittany, the Netherlands, Denmark, Eastern England and Scotland. This says something as to who the early colonists of North America were. The missing countries are the same Celts who would have known about the Americas and who would have been part of the migration to the New World.

The weather conditions, called the "Little Ice Age", without a doubt, drove the Norse, previously called the Vikings, from their homes in Greenland and Iceland to the more temperate climates along the Eastern shores of North America. This is not to say that they did not venture further into North America later. Unfortunately, even in the face of overwhelming evidence to the contrary, mainstream science refuses to acknowledge that the Celts, Masons, Norse and Templars all colonized North America in pre-Columbian times.

After the Stonehenge and Tiniteqilaq geoglyphs outlined the first two, recorded, Celtic territorial ventures into North America, the next geoglyph expanding the Celtic Territory was the Searcy, Mississippi Geoglyph in 1332 AD. (See Chapter 10) Something that should be remembered is that, all the North American territorial expansions had to be granted by Portugal. Portugal had explored these lands centuries before and had the geoglyphic markers to substantiate their claim to both North and South America. At this point in time, Portugal had colonized the entire coast of Brazil and was gradually ceding

North America to the Celts, their previously Galician allies. This was done so that Portugal could open trade in South America, while knowing that North America would be colonized by their Celtic Allies. The Searcy geoglyph described the new Celtic territory in North America as being all the land east of the Mississippi River. It is no coincidence that this is exactly the same territory agreed to, by the British, as the boundary of the new United States, in the "Treaty of Paris", after the US War of Independence was signed in 1778 AD.

A larger territory extending from the Atlantic to the Pacific, as evidenced by the Kensington Runestone (described later in the chapter), was ceded to the Templars in 1362 AD by Portugal. Since Portugal was an ally of both Britain and the US, this fact was not revealed to the British during the negotiation for the Treaty of Paris after the US Revolutionary War with Britain.

The Newport Tower

The Newport Tower

The Mystery

The Newport Tower has been the subject of discussion and controversy since the Colonists first arrived in the new world and discovered the structure on Newport, Rhode Island, USA. Early explorers noted that the tower existed during their early explorations of North America. However, that did not deter skeptics from claiming that the tower was constructed in Colonial times. Adding to the controversy was the fact that no one knew the true purpose of the structure. Documented research by the Faram Foundation shows that the tower not only was made before the 16th Century AD, but was constructed on a site that is part of a geometric network that documents the history, and pre-Columbian colonization, of the USA.

The Newport Tower has been carbon dated as being over 500 years old. The island on which the tower was built is mentioned in geoglyphs as far back as the Gulfo de Cintra geoglyph, in Africa, constructed c5000BC. The mathematics associated with the Tower, as referred to below, were found to point to six important places in the evolving survey that would eventually be called the USA. The first point of reference is a survey marker in western Minnesota named Inspiration Peak; a second point was the location where the Nordic Runestone tablet named the Kensington Runestone was found. Another is the two survey markers (Islands) in the Saint Lawrence Seaway, a fifth is now named Cat Island in the Bahamas, and the sixth is the conjunction of the Newport 193 degree radial (the opposite of the important 013 degree radial) at the point where the equator meets the west coast of South America.

The central survey marker in the United States, Inspiration Peak, was identified not only by the Newport Tower but also by the 5100 year old monolith called Stonehenge in Britain. Carbon dating has suggested that the tower was first built c1473 AD, destroyed and then rebuilt c1673 AD on its

200th anniversary. (For information on the carbon dating of the Newport Tower please see (Appendix B.) The Newport Tower is one of the coded survey markers used to revise a North American land claim that was conceived thousands of years ago. This original claim was modified over time by the ancient Celts. Although the North and South American continents are the primary land masses that are addressed in this book, there are others that have been identified in other parts of the world.

Purpose

The Newport Tower was built by the early inhabitants of North America for two reasons. The first was to point the way to Inspiration Peak, a place of worldwide geographical importance. The second was to substantiate the builders land claim to North America by using the unique geographical location of Newport, RI and Inspiration Peak in the USA. The predecessors of the people that built the tower knew of the North American Territory, as well as the rest of the world, for over 7,000 years. This is substantiated by ruins in South America and Africa that also point to Inspiration Peak and the Newport Tower site. For some reason, Newport, Rhode Island held some special significance in antiquity. Geoglyphs found around the world show that people were mapping out what would later be known as the United States at least as far back as the building of the Stonehenge (c3100 BC) and the Mayan Pyramids (c200BC). Mayan Pyramids located in Central America outline the southern boundary of what would eventually become the United States. As you will ascertain later, the southern boundary of the USA was the northern boundary of the Mayan territory. This is confirmed by the bearings built into the Chichin Itza Pyramid complex in Mexico.

The 7000 year old Golfo de Cintra geoglyph, located in Western Africa, pointed out the location where the Newport Tower would eventually be built

6500 years later. Gavin Menzies book *"1421, The Year China Discovered America"* adds credence to the argument that Europeans or Egyptians, and their descendents, inhabited the Americas long before history is willing to admit. Menzies quotes from the 1524 AD logs of the Italian explorer Verrazano during his stay in what later became Newport, Rhode Island:

"The local people were the color of brass; some of them inclined more to whiteness.... The women are of like conformity and beauty; very handsome and well favored, of pleasant countenance and comely to behold; they are well-mannered and content as any woman, and of good education.... The women used other kinds of dressing themselves like unto the women of Egypt and Syria; ...."

Menzies goes on to say: ... *"Verrazano was not describing local women married to foreigners, but women resembling those from the East who had somehow ended up in North America. Clearly they were from a different civilization and were not natives of North America".*

Some people claim that these women were left there by the Chinese 100 years before; however, the women that the Chinese were carrying were concubines used to make money when the Chinese were in port. That would hardly fit the character, or the dress, of the Rhode Island women. It would however fit the character and dress of the Europeans and their Egyptian cousins.

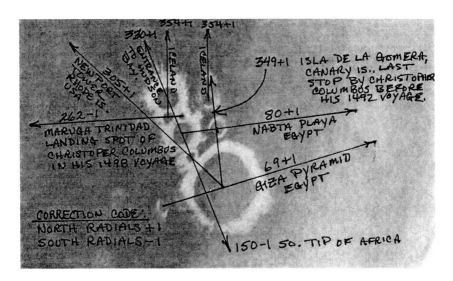

**The 7000 Year Old Gulfo de Cintra Glyphs, Western Sahara, Africa
Notice that the location of Newport, RI is shown.**

(Discovered by Arthur Faram, The Faram Foundation, 2008)

The Gulfo de Cintra Geoglyph's Radial End Points

The Gulfo de Cintra geoglyphs are some of the most spectacular encountered in all our investigations around the world. First of all, they are very clear. There is no doubt where the centers of the defining circles are. This is due to the fact that they consist of cement like circular slabs. These slabs now sit atop 40 foot tall sand castles that were formed from 7000 years of erosion caused by wind blowing away the surrounding sand. Secondly, all the resulting radials point to well established markers that leave no doubt as to where they were intended to point. The Gulfo de Cintra Glyph was discovered, by following the directions from the 7000 year old Egyptian geoglyph Nabta Playa, in Southern Egypt. Nabta Playa has been identified and accurately dated by accredited archeologists. The Golfo de Cintra geoglyph was discovered by Arthur Faram , of the Faram Research Foundation, in 2008.

As was mentioned, with Stonehenge, the most important glyphs require a uniform correction of a few degrees on all the bearings. This is apparently to preclude the uninitiated from accurately reading the glyph. In the Gulfo de Cintra Glyph the code is to add one degree to all bearings from 271 to 090, and subtract one degree from all bearings from 091 to 270. Did the Egyptians, Hebrews, Greeks, Celts, and their predecessors have some knowledge that others did not have; the knowledge to build the Pyramids, knowledge to build Stonehenge, knowledge of the geography of the entire world? The geoglyphs located around the world indicate that the answer is yes.

Other Ancient Geoglyphs That Point to Newport, RI.

The Geometry of the Newport Tower Mystery

The most important thing that must be remembered about the builders of geoglyphs is that they place little value on words. The builders, their predecessors and descendents, are men of numbers and symbols. You should also know that the builders, and their predecessors, never present a puzzle without setting up another solution to the same puzzle by some other method. This prevents the skepticism that has prevailed over the past centuries about the Newport Tower and other ancient geoglyphs which, unlike other geological finds, offer little or no verification from another source. It is a known fact that the Newport Tower is aligned along a 93/273 degree axis; in addition, there has always been a question as to why most European structures, of non-secular origin, have six legs while this one has eight legs.

Remembering a phrase I learned during my research about Europe, I decided to apply that information to the Newport Tower, to see what resulted. When asked where the Templar Treasure might be, a wise man said; *"The treasure lies under a giant triangle that is so large that only God can see it".* Newport seemed like a good place to start looking for a triangle. I personally have always thought that the treasure would be something more meaningful than a monetary treasure. That treasure may be the USA, which lies under, what I call, *"The Great Triangle"*. (Described later)

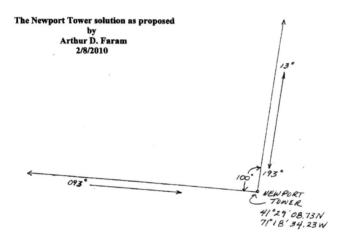

The Newport 013 Degree Radial

My experience told me that the eight legs on the tower were a symbol for 80 degrees. Navigators of this era oriented their maps and alignments to the East. As a result, the solution begins by subtracting 80 degrees from the East orientation of 93 degrees. This obviously left a bearing of 13 degrees. If this was correct, I now had one angle and two sides, of undefined length, to a triangle. In order for the 13 degree radial to be significant, a meaningful geographical location along the 13 degree bearing would have to be found to define the length of that side of the triangle.

The Island of La Haute-Cote-Nord
(48 23 53.32N 68 52 04.17W)

While tracing along the 13 degree bearing, I noticed that the line went directly over a small island in the Saint Lawrence Seaway which the locals call "La Haute-Cote-Nord". La Haute-Cote-Nord, loosely translated from the French language, means "The Highest Point on the North Dimension". This appeared to be a vital clue. If so, there were now two sides, one length and one angle of the triangle. But in order to make a triangle, one more angle or length was needed. From my previous research, I remembered several other triangles I had discovered, one had connections to Iceland.

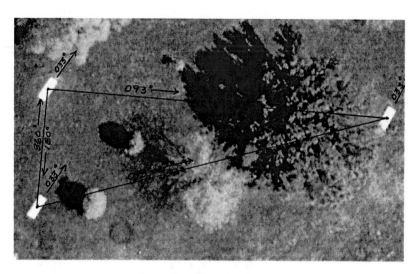

The Cemetery Triangle

**This triangle was found in an ancient graveyard
located in Druid Hill Park. Baltimore, MD USA.**

As I later discovered, the Druid Hill triangle contains all the interior angles needed to complete the Newport Triangle and solve the Newport Tower mystery. The name "Druid Hill", also peeked my interest. This triangle identifies itself as an important clue, by the fact that all three graves are oriented to 33 degrees and point to the ancient maritime port of Reykjavik, Iceland. Reykjavik was the prime port located midway between Europe and the Americas, and was the stopping place for most ancient ships in the North Atlantic, when transiting from Europe to the Americas. The importance of this triangle is that it provides the three interior angles that make up the Newport Triangle. This was just one more check provided to substantiate that the solution to the Newport Triangle is valid.

The Capiapo Chile Triangle

This triangle is located in Capiapo, Chili. These triangles are but two of the many glyphs scattered around the globe as clues to substantiate the Newport Triangle solution. These triangular geoglyphs were located by following the bearings emanating from other geoglyphs. This interconnection of geoglyphs, in itself, proves the validity of Geoglyphology.

These triangles consist of the three interior angles of 20, 60 and 100 degrees. In view of the fact that 100 degrees was the one angle that I had already decoded from the Newport Tower, it was decided to apply the remaining two angles of these triangles, to the partially completed Newport triangle, to see what developed. The sides of the triangle were extended to the west, because to the east there was nothing but water. If a significant landmark existed at the point of the western vertex, a solution to the mystery of the Newport Tower may have been found. As hoped, there was a significant landmark situated right

under the Western vertex of the triangle. The name of that landmark is
Inspiration Peak, MN. The resulting triangle was named the Newport Triangle.
The triangle is shown below.

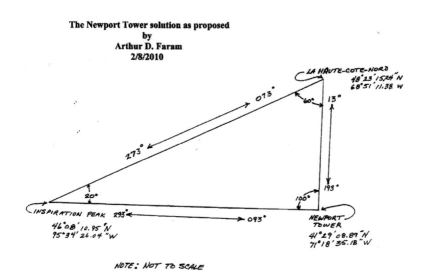

The Newport Triangle

I also learned, that directly across the Saint Lawrence Seaway, from the
Island of La Haute-Cote-Nord, was another island called Cote-Nord-Hauter,
which loosely translated means the higher dimension north. I then decided to
run a line from this island back to the Newport Tower location. To my surprise,
there was exactly one degree difference between the 13 degree line of the
Newport Triangle and this new 12 degree bearing. The next obvious move
would be to apply the same criteria to this new line as was applied to the 13
degree line. One degree was subtracted from each side of the original triangle
to see where the vortex would point. After checking, it was discovered that the
vertex of the triangle was directly above where the Kensington Runestone, of

which I was familiar, was discovered. I named this new triangle the Kensington Triangle. Could these two American mysteries be related? You will soon see that they are.

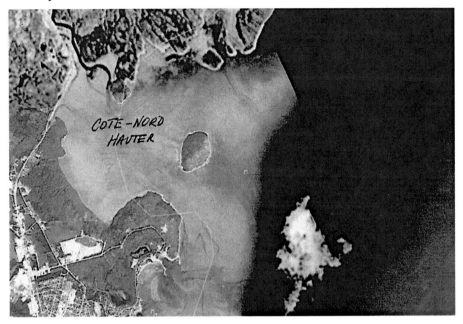

The Island of Cote-Nord Hauter
(48 45 06.12N 69 01 59.98W)

After applying the same criteria to the 12 degree radial, as had been applied to the 13 degree radial, another famous landmark showed up directly under the western vertex of the triangle. That landmark was Runestone Park, the location where the Kensington Runestone was found. Obviously, they were related since they were both found by using the calculations related to the Newport Tower.

Now I had a bigger puzzle. Why, and how, were the Newport Tower, the Kensington Runestone and Inspiration Peak related to one another? The answer would be found in the Runic writing chiseled on the Kensington Runestone, which is next.

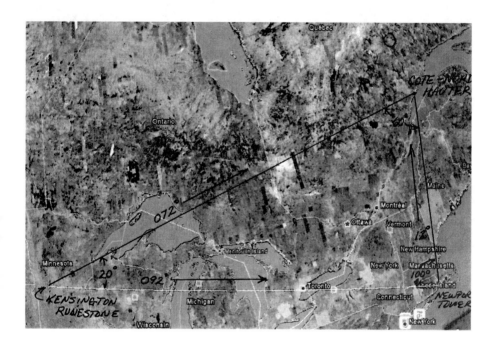

The Kensington Triangle

The Kensington Runestone

Mystery Solved

The Kensington Runestone
The key to the Inspiration Peak survey marker.

Just as the Newport Tower was used to establish the location of one of the most important survey markers of the early inhabitants of North America (Inspiration Peak), the Kensington Runestone is used to locate and validate that same location. As I have stated many times before, the builders of these markers never provide only one solution to a puzzle. There are always one or more other solutions to prove the first.

The Kensington Runestone Solution

The Runestone Front View

The Runestone Side View

Upon submitting the runestone to a handwriting analysis, it was determined that the writing had been done by two different persons. The first five rows were inscribed by one person and the last four rows, and side, were inscribed by a second person. The first tip off is the slant of the work. If you will check the slant in the pictures above, you will notice a distinct difference from one persons writing to the other. Another tip off is the way the letters are formed. For example, the first person brings the right leg of his "R" all the way down to the baseline. The second person stops short of the baseline.

As is common, when someone is attempting to copy another person's writing, the first half of the sixth line is similar to the first five lines. But, as is common, the copier gets tired of trying to copy the other person's style and towards the end of the first line, and thereafter, he reverts back to his own style. The second persons writing was added to redefine the boundaries of the North American territory. In 1362 Portugal ceded, what is now basically the USA, to the Templars for their service in ridding Iberia of the Muslims. This new territory had to be defined.

The fact that the writing was accomplished by two separate people should tell us that the stone is genuine. Not to mention the fact, as you will see later, the mathematical petroglyphs described on the stone are validated by geoglyphs found only in the Nordic area of Europe.

Text (Nielsen interpretation)
With one slight variation from the Larsson rune rows, using the letter þ (representing "th" as in "think" or "this") instead of d, the inscription on the face (from which a few words may be missing due to spalling, particularly at the lower left corner where the surface is calcite rather than greywacke) reads:

" 8:göter:ok:22:norrmen:po:
??o:opþagelsefarþ:fro
vinlanþ:of:vest:vi:
haþe:läger:veþ:2:skylar:en:
þags:rise:norr:fro:þeno:sten:
vi:var:ok:fiske:en:þagh:äptir:
vi:kom:hem:fan:10:man:röþe:
af:bloþ:og:þeþ:AVM:
fräelse:af:illu:
"

Translation: Unlike the version in the infobox above, this is based on Richard Nielsen's 2001 translation of the text, which attempts specifically to put it into a medieval context, giving variant readings of some words:

8 Geats and 22 Norwegians on ?? acquisition expedition from Vinland far west. We had traps by 2 shelters one day's travel to the north from this stone. We were fishing one day. After we came home, found 10 men red with blood and dead. AVM (Ave Maria) Deliver from evils.

The lateral (or side) text reads:

" har:10:mans:we:hawet:at:se:
äptir:wore:skip:14:þagh:rise:
from:þeno:öh:ahr:1362:
"

Translation:

(I) have 10 men at the inland sea to look after our ship 14 days travel from this wealth/property. Year [of our Lord] 1362

Dr. Nielsen's Translation

In order to discover how the runestone and the tower were connected it would be necessary to study a translation of the Kensington Runestone, done by Dr. Richard Neilsen. As previously stated, the builders of the Newport Tower and creators of the Kensington Runestone have little use for words and place most of their emphasis on numbers, geometry and symbols. Attention was directed to the numbers contained in the translation. The above translation is the original translation by Dr. Neilson. The decoded version follows below.

Text (Nielsen interpretation)
With one slight variation from the Larsson rune rows, using the letter þ (representing "th" as in "think" or "this") instead of d, the inscription on the face (from which a few words may be missing due to spalling, particularly at the lower left corner where the surface is calcite rather than greywacke) reads:

" 8:göter:ok:22:normen:po:
??o:opþagelsefarþ:fro
vinlanþ:of:vest:vi:
haþe:läger:veþ:2:skylar:en:
þags:rise:norr:fro:þeno:sten:
vi:var:ok:fiske:en:þagh:äptir:
vi:kom:hem:fan:10:man:röþe:
af:bloþ:og:þeþ:AVM:
fräelse:af:illu:
"

— SUBTRACT 80 DEGRSES FROM 093° ORIENTATION OF I.P. TO OBTAIN 13° STARTING POINT.
Translation: Unlike the version in the infobox above, this is based on Richard Nielsen's 2001 translation of the text, which attempts specifically to put it into a medieval context, giving variant readings of some words: FROM RUNESTONE SPACER TO I.P.
— 22° @ 2 MILES

8 Geats and 22 Norwegians on ?? acquisition expedition from Vinland far west. We had traps by 2 shelters one day's travel to the north from this stone. We were fishing one day. After we came home, found 10 men red with blood and dead. AVM (Ave Maria) Deliver from evils. — 10° @ 22 MILES FROM RUNESTONE TO SPACER

The lateral (or side) text reads:

" har:10:mans:we:hawet:at:se:
äptir:wore:skip:14:þagh:rise:
from:þeno:öh:ahr:1362:
"

Translation: — 110° RADIAL TO BERMUDA   — 140° RADIAL TO EAST COAST MARKER
(I) have 10 men at the inland sea to look after our ship 14 days travel from this wealth/property. Year [of our Lord] 1362 — DISTANCE FROM I.P. TO THREE CORNERS OF U.S.

Above: Dr. Nielson's translation decoded.

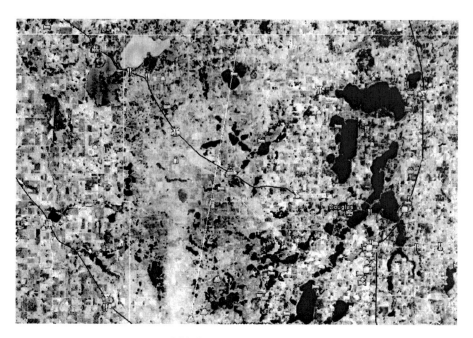

010 Degrees at 22 Miles

One solution derived from the numbers given on the Runestone, was a heading of 10 degrees at 22 miles. Although this interpretation seemed to be headed in the right direction, it still did not give any indication that it was a correct solution to the puzzle. Neither did any of the other combination of numbers. Further research was conducted to see if the method of measurement had changed between 1362 AD and now. Sure enough, Queen Elizabeth had changed the Universal Standard of measurement, the mile, from 5000 feet to 5280 feet, after becoming Queen in 1592 AD. That meant that 22 miles in new English miles would convert to 20.8 miles in old English miles.

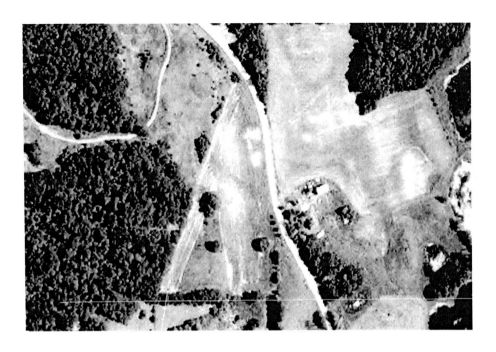

The Spacer

(46 06 33.05N - 95 35 05.68W)

After converting the English miles, the figures 10 degrees at 20.8 miles were used which placed the end point of the 10 degree radial on the south end of what became known as "The Spacer". It was called this because the measurements are so precise, that if you land on the south end of the spacer and begin your second leg from the south end, you will come up short of reaching the all important Inspiration Peak by the same length as the spacer. The second leg of the connection must start on the North end of the Spacer. The "Spacer" is the line on the left side of the following photos. It looks like a runway, but is in reality a stone wall that someone has mowed around.

Inspiration Peak - 22 Degrees at 2 Miles

(46 08 09.49N 95 34 14.61W)

Now that the Spacer has come into play, one must follow the new direction
which points 22 Degrees for two miles from the North end of the Spacer to
reach the main survey marker named Inspiration Peak. But remember, we are
dealing in old English miles so the real distance is 1.9 miles. The end of the last
line that is drawn lands precisely on Inspiration Peak, and at the location where
the west vertex of the Newport Triangle solution also landed.

The Campsite - One Day North

The figures displayed above are the figures used to transition from the place
where the Kensington Runestone was found, to "Inspiration Peak". However,
locating Inspiration Peak was meaningless unless you already knew the

geometry associated with it. It appears that the first writer on the runestone assumed that the reader would already know the geometry, and would only need to locate Inspiration Peak in order to apply the mathematics. There was enough information in the first five lines of the text to locate the "...*traps and two shelters one day north from this spot.*" (This is referring to a campsite containing the stone wall pointing to Inspiration Peak. This campsite is depicted in the next two photos.) However, the second writer had a different agenda and wanted to make the complete solution available to whoever might find the stone. This would be a prudent move, if the second writer knew the details had changed or would be lost to time. The change he was describing was the territory ceded to the Templars in 1362 by Portugal. At the time the Kensington Runestone was first carved, the Northern Territory extended all the way to the equator. The territory in its original concept included Meso (Central) America and Baja California.

The 110 degree radial and the 140 degree radial were added at the time of the second carving, and are critical in defining the revised boundaries of the Territory given to the Templars by Portugal. The new information was a crucial part of revising the ancient survey done in North America thousands of years before. The new North American Territory, given to the Templars, excluded Central America and retained Baja California. These boundaries were later confirmed by the Portuguese geoglyph built in the Canary Islands c1822 AD. The Canary Island geoglyph is explained later in this chapter. Unfortunately, Baja California was later traded in negotiations with Mexico after the Mexican American war.

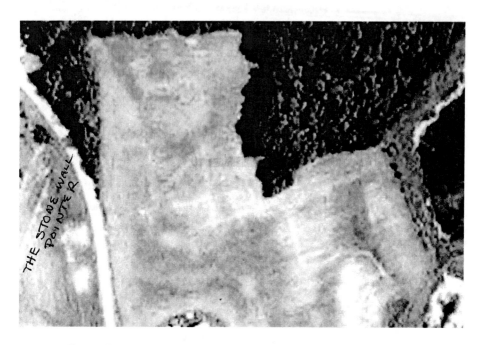

Campsite One Day North of Kensington Runestone Site

NOTE: This photo is presented so that you could see the geoglyphs on the ground before they were covered with the lines in the next photo. The geoglyphs were verified by a higher magnification than presented here. Unfortunately this field has since been plowed under since this photo.

186

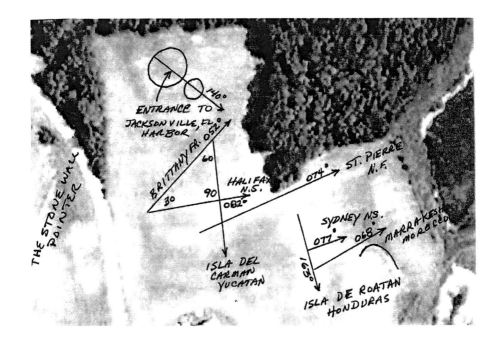

Campsite with Geoglyphs and Stone Wall Pointing to Inspiration Peak

Other research that has been conducted, which is not included here, confirms that this is the campsite that was mentioned in the first five lines on the Kensington Runestone. The stone wall here is oriented 22 degrees at 2 miles from Inspiration Peak. All that would be necessary from here is to follow the stone wall pointer, a common pointer in Geoglyphology at the time, to Inspiration Peak. The pre-Columbian geoglyphs at this campsite further confirm its authenticity, since placing geoglyphs at your campsite was a common practice. These geoglyphs possibly point to the birthplace of eight of the ten men mentioned on the Kensington Runestone. Nordic crews were comprised of men from many ports of call. The radial endpoints shown in the photo are all known, pre-Columbian, geoglyphic locations. The lines that exist in this geoglyph, unlike most, do not seem to form an organized territorial boundary.

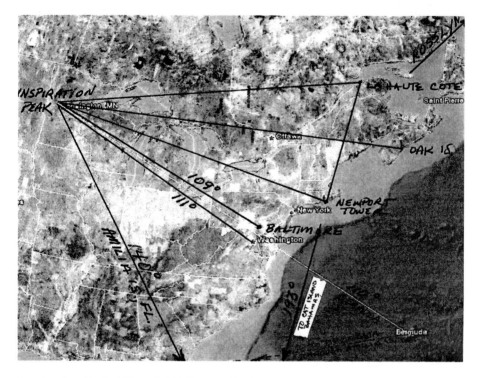

Inspiration Peak 110 and 140 Degree Radials as Defined by the Kensington Runestone.

(The other lines are added for relationship purposes. Notice that Oak Island, of Templar treasure fame, is identified by splitting the radials of the Newport Triangle. Also, notice that Washington DC lies on the 111 degree radial. The number three is sacred to the Freemasons.)

In the decoding of the Kensington Runestone, which verified the math in the Newport Tower solution, the bearings of 110 and 140 were mentioned and are shown in the previous photo. These are important radials and terminate at points used by other geoglyphs elsewhere in the USA.

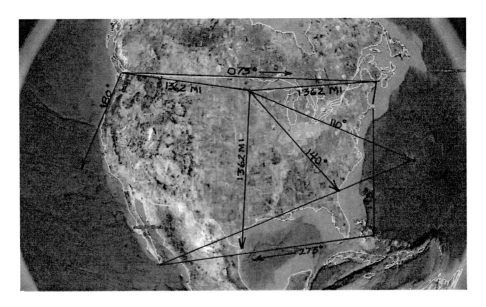

**Revised North American Territorial Boundaries, as Described by
the Newport Tower, Inspiration Peak and the Kensington Runestone.**

(This will also be referred to, in later chapters, as the Templar Territory.)

Notice that by running a line from Bermuda, the termination point of the 110 Degree radial, through Amelia Island, the termination point of the 140 degree radial, you have a line that terminates at the tip of Baja California. The 073 degree northern boundary was obtained from the Newport Triangle, as was the 273 degree boundary. The 193 degree radial is the opposite of the 013 degree radial of the Newport Tower. These are the new boundaries of the North American Territory which was ceded to the Templars, by Portugal, in 1362 AD. The fact that Portugal validated these boundaries, 460 years later, by building the Guimar geoglyphs on Tenerife, Canary Islands further proves the validity of Geoglyphology.

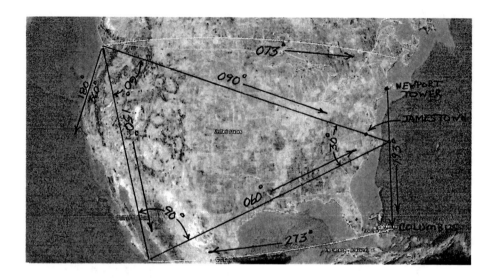

The Sacred Geometry Triangle, formed by the revised boundaries of the what would later become the United States, shows a well thought out process was used by Portugal before the allocation of this territory.

(In the solving of the Newport Tower Mystery, the magnetic bearings of 073 and 273 degrees revealed themselves in the Newport triangle and again in this solution. They are not reciprocal headings, because they originate from two different points on the earth's surface.)

The Runestone 1362 Controversy

The Kensington Runestone was first discovered, in 1898. Since then there has been controversy over the date of 1362 inscribed in the lower right hand corner of the stone. When it was discovered that the stone pointed to Inspiration Peak, MN, which was 1362 miles from the three corners of the current boundaries of the United States, the date became even more controversial as to whether it was a date or a measurement. Further research has revealed that it is both.

After the Templars were disenfranchised in Europe by the Vatican, they dispersed between Scotland, Portugal and North America. Portugal, who was their ally, solicited the Templars help in liberating the Iberian Peninsula from the Moors. They accepted, and for their efforts, c1362, were awarded the territory of North America, previously claimed by Portugal.

Knowledge of this land grant is why Columbus and the Spanish never approached the East coast of what would become the United States. It is also why President Polk said, just before the war with Mexico and Spain; A country from the Atlantic to the Pacific is our "*Manifest Destiny*". In Chapter 13, you will see where Columbus makes reference to the southeast corner of the Templar Territory.

Further Study has shown that, in typical Old Norse tradition, the number 1362 is also another cryptic clue to the validity of the Runestone puzzle. It is highly unlikely that the Swedish farmer that found the Kensington Runestone, in 1898, had the knowledge that Inspiration Peak even existed, or that it was exactly 1362 miles from the three corners of what would later become the United States.

After the Kensington Runestone was discovered, everyone naturally assumed that the 1362 AD date in the lower right hand corner of the Runestone was the date it was carved, but the date wasn't placed on the runestone until the second carver inscribed it. The date does, however, fit in nicely with the time the Portuguese would have given the North American Territory to the Templars for their help in liberating the Iberian Peninsula from the Muslims, and to prevent anyone but the Celts from colonizing and claiming the territory. This land grant was the embryo that eventually grew to be the United States. The land grant was confirmed by the Portuguese when they built the Pyramids on Tenerife Island in the Canary Islands c1822. The Tenerife Geoglyph radials terminate at the ends of the Inspiration Peak radials.

Further confirmation stems from the fact that Portugal, after hundreds if not thousands of years, would start a navigator's school in Segres Portugal in 1415 AD. By starting the navigator's school, Portugal was announcing that they were ready to begin commerce with Europe from the lands they had already colonized on the East coast of South America. Please take a look at the following map, and ask yourself if Portugal could have explored the entire country of what is now Brazil, colonized and named all the towns that are listed, in the few years since Columbus was supposed to have discovered the Americas. Also, please notice the Templar crosses on the sails of the ships. All this will be explained, in detail, later in the book.

1519 Map of Portuguese Brazil

Geoglyphs at the Ends of the Inspiration Peak 1362 Mile Long Radials

After assuming control of the North American Territory, ceded to the Templars by their Portuguese allies, the Celts were anxious to place survey markers, as civilizations had done for thousands of years before them, to mark their new territory. The following three geoglyphs were place at the termination points of the 1362 mile long radials that emanate from Inspiration Peak. Two of the three corner markers were destroyed by the land owners after the pictures were published. Only one marker, the southern 1362 mile long radial, still exists, at the time of this writing.

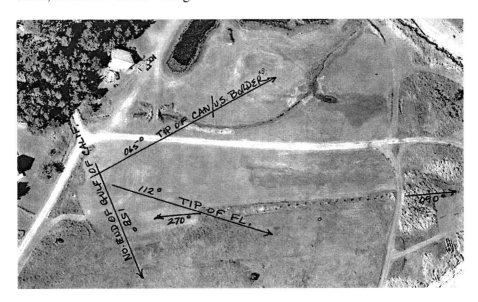

The 1362 Northwest Endpoint and Associated Square Geoglyph
48 40 26.90N 123 10 11.61W

Depicted above is the termination point of the Northwest 1362 mile long radial from Inspiration Peak. The associated square geoglyph is a survey marker validating the Northeast corner of the Northern Territory, later to become the United States. This geoglyph was on Stuart Island, the first island south of Vancouver Island, Canada, which is within the US borders. Based on protocols used in constructing the three geoglyphs depicted here, it is believed that the geoglyphs were made by the same group of people that revised the North American Land Claim. It is apparent that they wanted there to be no mistake as to the territory which they claimed, and as would be proven later, were willing to fight for. The land in this picture has since been plowed under by the owner to destroy the many geoglyphs on the property. The square shown here has been modified. There is another square geoglyph at the top of the photo under the "R" in the word border. This too was destroyed by the owner of the property.

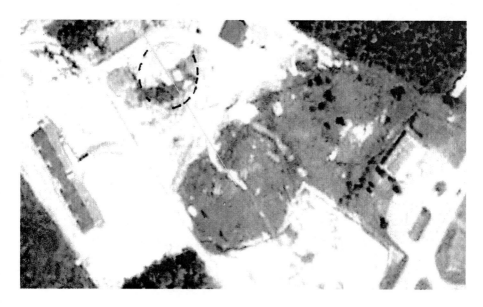

The 1362 Northeast Endpoint and Associated Geoglyph
45 07 57.09N 67 18 56.65W

194

Depicted above is the termination point of the Northeast 1362 mile long radial from Inspiration Peak. Unfortunately, at the time the photo was taken, the owners had not taken very good care of this geoglyph. Amazingly, a line run through the center of these two circles points directly to the island of La Haute-Cote Nord, the island in the Saint Lawrence Seaway that provides the first clue, the endpoint of the 13 degree radial, to solving the Newport Tower Puzzle. This geoglyph was located at the original northeastern boundary of the State of Maine. The land north of here was added to the state of Maine later. This geoglyph has also been destroyed by the owner.

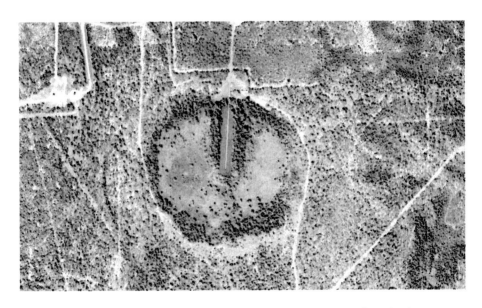

The 1362 Mile Southern Endpoint and Associated Geoglyph
26 26 33.42N 97 33 02.47W

When this Southern 1362 mile long radial was added, it extended to within 30 miles of the Rio Grand River, the current boundary between the US and Mexico. The end of this radial is closer to the Nueces River than the Rio Grand

River. Therefore, the US and Mexico were in dispute as to whether the Nueces river or the Rio Grand river was the boundary between the US and Mexico. This dispute was the excuse used to precipitate the Mexican American War and reclaim the western half of the US territory, which had, at the time, been claimed by Spain. This war was necessary for the USA to recover their land between Texas and the Pacific Ocean, which Spain had colonized during the intervening years since 1362 AD.

When the "Treaty of Hidalgo" was signed in 1828 AD, following the war with Mexico, the Rio Grand River became the Southern Boundary of the US, while the US recovered their western lands. During the negotiations the US agreed to give Baja California to Mexico. The treaty stated that the two countries agreed to never go to war against each other again. This agreement against ever going to war again serves to validate the homogeneous relationship which the two land masses had enjoyed prior to the intervention of Spain.

Cryptographic Translation of the Kensington Runestone

In January of 2012 the organization calling themselves "*Giants of the Earth Heritage Site*" produced a 30 minute interview with one of the worlds leading Runic Cryptographers, Howard Burtness. (You Tube Catalog # 4Uc6o00v3JE) Up to this time, the Kensington Runestone had only been translated by persons with recent educations in Runic Translation. Until Mr. Burtness was interviewed, only the context of the words had been translated. During the Runic education of Mr. Burtness, he had discovered that the Cistercian Monks that migrated to the Americas after 1100 AD had been taught cryptography, in addition to simple runeology. This fact was re-discovered by a man named Mr. Monge who was a cryptologist in WWII.

The interview of Mr. Burgness, by Kirsten Roble, revealed much more information about the writings on the Kensington Runestone than had ever before been learned. Mr. Burtness showed that there are several types of cryptography that were used in coding hidden messages into the Kensington Runestone. These protocols are the same type of cryptology taught to the Cistercian Monks/Templars of Europe c1000-1500AD.

You can view the video to obtain the full impact of this discovery; however, here are a few of the bits of information he found encrypted into the Kensington Runestone. The date on the Runestone is listed as Sunday, April 24, 1362. The writer of the text was listed as a Norse named Harrek and the carver of the stone was listed as a Norse named Tollik.

Inspiration Peak

Inspiration Peak - The North American Territorial Marker
(46 08 09.49N 95 34 14.61W)

The location of Inspiration Peak, along with its important geometrical properties, has been known and identified for over 5000 years. The existence of Inspiration Peak in ancient times is verified by the Stonehenge monolith in England. The dating of Stonehenge has already been established as circa 3100

BC by celebrated scientists and archeologists around the world and should not present fuel for controversy.

Inspiration Peak was also identified by the mathematics built into the Newport Tower, NJ USA. The island where the Newport Tower resides has been identified by many other geoglyphs around the world, including China. Some of these geoglyphs are as old as 7000 years.

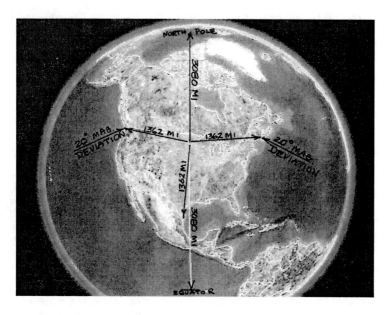

The original Inspiration Peak survey marker which spans from the equator to the North Pole. Although not yet verified, our current research indicates this survey could be as old as 25,000 years.

Incredibly, Inspiration Peak lies halfway between the Equator and the North Pole. In addition, the two Northern 1362 mile long radials mark the NW and NE corners of the territory, which not by coincidence, are now the "endpoints" of the boundary between Canada and the USA. The location is also 1362 miles from the southern tip of Texas.

As if this was not enough, the East/West line, that is now the border between Canada and the US, terminates on both ends at points that have exactly 20 degrees of magnetic deviation. For a culture to be able to locate and survey this location over 5000 years ago boggles the mind. Inspiration Peak, the Newport Tower and the Kensington Runestone are the most important of the survey markers which have been found in North America. They are important, because these three markers are able to combine together to delineate the original Northern Territory ceded to the Templars in 1362 AD, by Portugal.

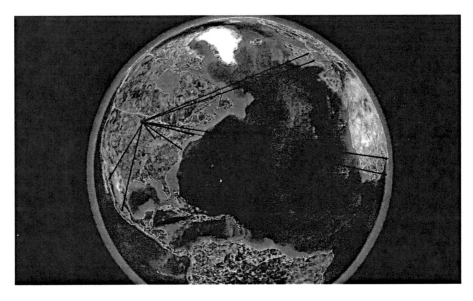

Photo showing known origination points of geoglyphs that point to the Inspiration Peak Location

199

Outlined below are the origination points for the pointers displayed in the previous photo. Included are the approximate dates the pointers were created.

Stonehenge Monolith, UK - c3100BC
Monte Alban Pyramid, Oaxaca Mexico - c500BC
Pigeon Point Geoglyph, Minnesota USA - c1200AD
Manchester, Ohio Geoglyph USA - c1300AD
Geoglyph near 23rd Street NW, Washington DC USA - c1400AD
Point du Raz Geoglyphs, Bretagne, France - c1400AD
Malabo Island Geoglyphs, Equatorial New Guinea, West Africa - c1400AD
Cape of Good Hope Geoglyphs, South Tip of Africa - c1400AD
Atanacio Geoglyphs, Mexico - c1400AD
Newport Tower, Newport, RI USA - c1473AD

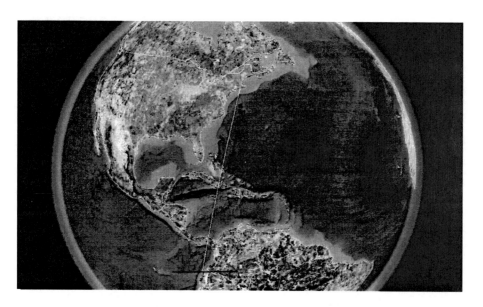

The 193 degree radial from the Newport Tower.

(The 013 degree bearing was the initial bearing that had to be discovered before the puzzles could be solved. The reciprocal of the 013 degree bearing is the 193 degree bearing which terminates at where the Equator and the West coast of South America meet. Just one more clue to let the person, solving the puzzle, know that they were on the right track.)

In 1492 AD, the early colonizers staked their final claim to the Americas. Christopher Columbus, working for Spain and the Vatican, was chosen, along with the Pizon brothers, to visit the Caribbean and claim Central America for Spain and the Church. Spain knew that North and South America were already colonized. During the first voyage of Columbus geoglyphs were placed claiming Mesoamerica and the Caribbean for Spain. One of these geoglyphs identifies the southeast corner of the Templar Territory. (See Chapter 13)

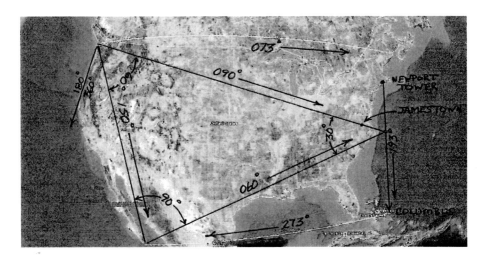

Map of the North America Land Claim, and the Sacred 30/60/90 Degree Triangle

(The combinations of mathematics, geometry, and survey skills necessary to accomplish such perfect geometrical puzzles are phenomenal. By including two of the same bearings used in the solution of the Newport Triangle, in the North American Territorial boundaries, the originators are not only showing their skill but, as usual, providing a crosscheck to verify to any investigator that they have the correct solution to the land claim.)

It is no coincidence that just south of the SE corner of the Templar land claim, at Cat Island, lays the original San Salvador Island. San Salvador was where Columbus landed to claim the Caribbean and South America for Spain. Can it be a coincidence that the British colony of Jamestown, the first "historically recorded" colony in the USA, was located under a leg of the 30/60/90 degree triangle? It is clear that 17th Century Britain was attempting to establish their claim to the land that belonged to the Templars, now the Masons. Land which would eventually became the United States.

The Portuguese Canary Island Geoglyphs (c1822 AD)

The geoglyphs on Tenerife, in the Canary Islands, are a 19th century Portuguese acknowledgement of the Territory which was given to the Templars in 1362 AD. This was done just prior to the US engaging Spain in a war to retrieve what is now the western United States.

The Guimar Pyramids

(Constructed by the Portuguese c1822. NOTE: Thor Heyerdahl, of Kon Tiki fame, spent the last half of his life on this site in an effort to determine why Mayan Pyramids were in the Canary Islands.)

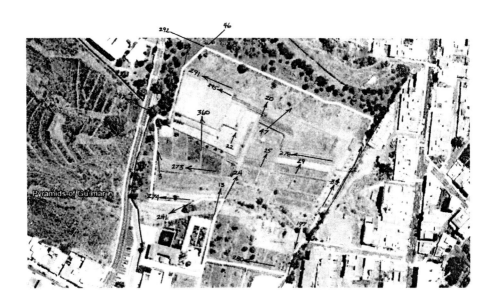

The Guimar Geoglyphic Complex

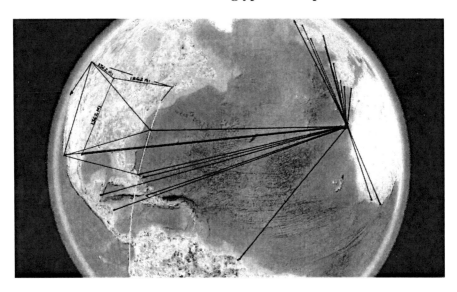

All the Guimar Geoglyph Radials

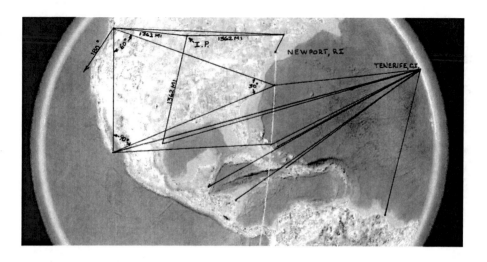

The Guimar Radials That Pertain to the American Territory

(These radials, originating from the Portuguese Island of Tenerife, validated the boundaries of the territory ceded to the Templars in 1362 AD, by the Portuguese. The Guimar Radials match the 1362 radials perfectly. The radials south of the Templar Territory indicate countries that achieved independence from Spain c1822.)

The Searcy Geoglyph

Up until now, some would say, there has been room for doubt about the validity and purpose of the Newport Tower. The following information leaves no doubt that the Newport Tower, the Kensington Runestone and Inspiration Peak were tied together and each played its part in the history of the formation of the Territory now known as the USA.

By being located 1253 miles from Inspiration Peak, and 1253 miles from the tip of Florida, the Newport Tower is trying to tell us to look for another, harder to find, geoglyphic point that is also 1253 miles from the Newport Tower. There is only one location in the US that is 1253 miles from Newport Tower and meets the protocols that were developed by the ancients. That point is

Vicksburg, Mississippi. At precisely 1253 miles from the Newport Tower is the Searcy Geoglyph. This geoglyph consists of geoglyphic bearings which outline the Templar territory that existed at the time the geoglyph was constructed c1332 AD.

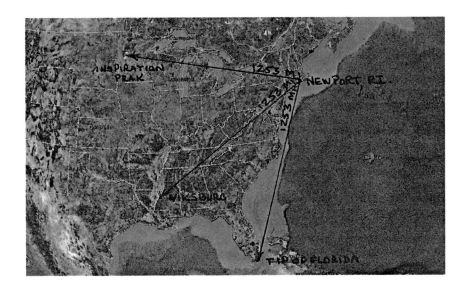

The Three Newport Tower 1253 Mile Long Radials

The Searcy Glyph - Vicksburg, Mississippi USA

Endpoints for the bearings displayed in the Searcy geoglyph.

037 Degree Radial - North Tip of Celtic Scotland
037 Degree Radial - Celtic Island of Zealand, Denmark
047 Degree Radial - Original NE Corner of the North American territory (North part of Maine added later.)
122 Degree Radial - Cat Island, South East corner of the original North American territory as described by the geometry of the Kensington Runestone, Inspiration Peak and the Newport Tower.
152 Degree Radial - Gulfport, Mississippi USA
163 Degree Radial - Mouth of the Mississippi River (Important trade route and western edge of the original western expansion.)
350 Degree Radial - Northwest Corner of the Celtic Territory. (Where the Rainey River meets the Lake of the Woods on the US/Canada border.)

Boundaries Established by the Searcy, MS Geoglyph

The Searcy geoglyph exists on property that has been in the Searcy Family since c1332 AD. 20,000 acres were given to the Searcy family for their service to the King of Portugal. This land was also designated as a place to construct the geoglyph which outlined the new North American Territory, which had just been given to the Templars. The Searcy Geoglyph verifies the information which had been handed down through his family for over 600 years, that being that their family was originally from Denmark. The property was deeded to Sir Bartholomew Searcy by the King of Portugal c1332. The Searcys only owned 20,000 acres of this Portuguese land grant. The Searcy geoglyph designated all the remaining land east of the Mississippi River to the Templars.

In 1362 AD, the rest of the North American territory, from the Atlantic to the Pacific, was ceded to the Templars. This is confirmed by the boundaries which were described by the Kensington Runestone dated 1362 AD. These boundaries, when combined with Inspiration Peak and the Newport Tower outlined the 1362 land grant. These 1362 boundaries were later confirmed by the Tenerife Pyramid geoglyphs, built by the Portuguese, in the Canary Islands c1822 AD. This was presumably done in preparation for the US reclaiming the western US territory, resulting in the Mexican American War.

THE NORTH AMERICAN TERRITORIAL TRANSITIONS

In order to make sense of the various territorial transitions which the North America Territory endured, and which this book illustrates, the following synopsis is presented.

The first Territory known to exist, in North America, was described by Inspiration Peak and served as a survey marker for a land claim that staked out the entire continent of North America, as well as Mesoamerica. This Territory, as were many of the Territories found around the world that are over 10000 years old, cover one or two continents. The geometry of their survey markers (geoglyphs), and the fact that they do not overlap, leaves no doubt that they are legitimate and surveyed by man.

The first division of the original Inspiration Peak (North American) Territory was the construction of Stonehenge c3100BC. Stonehenge established a southern boundary between what are now, basically, Canada and the United States. That line ran between the NW endpoint of the Inspiration Peak 1362 mile long radial, to Nova Scotia. This placed what is now Canada within the defined boundaries of the Celtic Empire of Europe.

The second amendment came with the construction of the Tiniteqilaq, Greenland Geoglyph. This geoglyph excluded some of the eastern Celtic territories outlined by Stonehenge and extended their North American territory down to Newport Rhode Island.

The third amendment came in the form of an emergency transfer of land to the Celts/Templars, which extended from the Mississippi River east to the Atlantic Coast. This allocation, by the Portuguese, was marked by the construction of the Searcy Geoglyph created c1332 AD, in Vicksburg, Mississippi. This transfer of land was apparently to exclude the Nordic Colonists, who were not Celts, from colonizing the Celts North American territory. After the catastrophic freeze in Greenland and Iceland in the early 14th century, the Norse began migrating south to North America. (See Chapter 6)

As a result of the necessity to move south from Greenland, the Norse began colonizing the territory just west of the Mississippi River from Minnesota to Louisiana. Had they been successful at colonizing and claiming this land, the Norse would have blocked any expansion of the Celtic Territory to the west. Presumably to counter this, there was a fourth grant by Portugal, c1362, which included all the territory from the Atlantic to the Pacific.

The short time span between the 1332 grant and the 1362 grant would seem to validate that the 1332 grant was an emergency measure to stop the Norse colonization of eastern North America. The later 1362 grant included what are now the entire United States, Baja California, and the northern part of Mexico. This territory was given to the Templars, by the legal claimant Portugal, to not only to thwart the colonization of the North American Territory, but as a reward for the Templars assistance, to Portugal and Spain, in ridding the Iberian Peninsula of the Muslims.

The next amendment occurred after the US war of Independence with Britain. The new boundaries were mapped out in the "Treaty of Paris", between Britain and the US in 1778. The boundaries established by the Treaty of Paris, except for the northern boundary, were essentially the same as the boundaries described by the Searcy geoglyph in c1332.

After the "Treaty of Paris" was signed, the US and Britain negotiated on the location of the Northern boundary of the US. The negotiations over the northern US boundary would end with the "Treaty of the Oregon Territory" in 1818 AD. For some reason, the US kept the fact that they also owned the land from the Mississippi River to the Pacific Coast a secret. This would come back to haunt them when the Spanish colonized the land west of the Mississippi River. This claim by the Spanish required that the Portuguese build the Guimar geoglyph on Tenerife Island in the Portuguese Canary Islands c1822 AD. This confirmation of the US land claim was necessary, if the US were to legally recover their land west of the Mississippi River from Spain.

In 1803 AD, the first step in stopping the colonization of the US land west of the Mississippi was accomplished by the Louisiana Purchase. This land was sold to the US by the King of France, Napoleon Bonaparte. Napoleon, himself a Mason, was a friend of the US and placed his brother in the position of King of Spain so that the transaction could be made. The negotiations to purchase the land, by France from Spain, took several years. One of the conditions of the sale was that France never sells the land; however, just three months after acquiring the land, France sold the land to the US. The urgency of this purchase would indicate that another reason existed for the US to acquire the land, other than just getting it back from Spain. After all, they were going to war with Mexico anyway, they could have acquired the land for free along with the rest of the western US.

Based on this, and other information, it is believed that the acquisition was another attempt to prevent non-Celtic Europeans from colonizing the territory west of the Mississippi River. Remember, it was never been made public that the 1362 AD grant to the US from Portugal had ever been made.

There is ample proof in the form of geoglyphs and runic artifacts, which have been found from Minnesota to Texas to validate that the Norse and their descendants were attempting a blockade west of the Mississippi River, through colonization. Another indication that this is the case is that the Masons have clamped a veil of secrecy on this period in US history; they own the land on which many major geoglyphs reside, and destroy them when they are discovered by the public. It is now believed that the need to prevent the colonization of America by foreign countries, especially the Norse, was the motivation for the Sinclairs and their military arm, led by the Farams, to move to the Americas c1398 AD.

The final territorial amendment resulted from the end of the Mexican American War and the "Treaty of Hidalgo" in 1848. The treaty returned the land north of the current US boundary to the US, and gave the land south of the current US boundary to Mexico.

There are many political, and economical, reasons for the US not divulging the fact that the Celts, as well as their predecessors, were in the Americas prior Spain's orchestrated voyage of Columbus. Most of those reasons are addressed in this book.

END CHAPTER

Chapter 6

The Vikings

THE VIKINGS

No saga about Europe and the Americas would be complete without the story of the Vikings. It was around 700 AD, when the Vikings simply appeared in the Baltic and North Sea. Until now, there did not seem to be a political or cultural evolution to the Viking story. Coincidently, that is the same time period that the Galicians moved to Denmark from their home in Iberia.

In the eighth and ninth century, previously unknown tribes begin to appear in the regions of Denmark, Norway and Sweden. Strange ships began appearing in the bays along the coasts of Europe. They were strongly built of oak and from 40 to 60 oarsmen sat on the rowers' benches. Each ship had a single mast with a square sail. The ships carried a shallow draft so that they could be maneuvered in shallow water, not unlike the roman ships. The ships were pointed at each end so that they could go forward or backward without turning around and had tall curved prows. These ships eventually evolved into what we now know as Viking ships. The Viking ships were usually carved in the shapes of dragons with shields along the side. These dragon ships, as they were often called, usually appeared in a bay at about dawn. As soon as the ships reached the beach, tall blond men jumped out, shouting battle cries. Armed with swords and battle-axes, they attacked the villagers and carried all the loot that their ships could carry. They then sailed away. Vik in Norse means "harbor" or "bay." The Norsemen who took part in these swift, cruel raids along the coast were therefore called Vikings.

Prior to relocating to Denmark, the Galicians were happy remaining in the background and letting the Roman government handle the politics and cost of defense, while they reaped the harvest of government contracts and a protected mercantile. Due to the crumbling of the Roman Empire, the Galicians had lost both their government contracts and their Roman protection. This, in itself, most likely would not have been enough to cause them to leave their home in Galicia; however, the advancement of the Muslims, in their conquest of Europe, tipped the balance and caused the Galicians move to Denmark. The Galicians, now the Danes, were faced with the prospect of the distrust of the Germans on one side and the hostility of the now Anglo-Saxon British on the other. Conditions and timing would indicate that the displaced Galicians made a pact with the Norsemen (Norway) to act as their military force. This would explain the Vikings sudden rise to power and their eventual conversion to Christianity. After all, the Galicians were now rich from their mining operations in Cornwall England and international trade. They were also expert ship builders. The Danes association with Norway would evolve, over time, to be called the "Denmark-Norway Alliance". The first indication that the Vikings were working for the Danes is the fact that, after their establishment, they went after the Catholic monasteries in England with a vengeance.

History states that 400 years after the Celtic Orthodox form of Christianity was formed in England, Catholic Monks went to Britain to establish the Catholic Church there. The Orthodox Christians (Celts), already living there, told them that they already worshiped Jesus, but that the Catholics could remain if they did not interfere with the Celts Orthodox Christian religion. The

Celts claimed that Jesus had established his church in Cornwall, England over 300 years before.

As might be expected, from an organization as large and powerful as the Roman Church, they did not listen. The Monks established monasteries all along the East coast of England, the place of least Celtic influence, collecting offerings, selling pardons for sins and levying taxes. As if these transgressions were not enough, they then sent the money back to the Vatican. After centuries of abuse by the Roman Christians, the Orthodox Christians were ready to recapture their land. It cannot be a coincidence that the primary objectives of the first Viking raids were the Monasteries on the East Coast of England. In the centuries to come, due to their actions against the Catholics, the Vikings were condemned as barbarians by most historians, who at the time were also Catholic. What most people were not told was that the Vikings were not indiscriminant barbarians but, were engaged in a holy war directed by the Danes. History indicates, that the Vikings slaughtered the Monks and took large sums of Gold and Silver as their prize from the monasteries. If this is true, the monks were not living their vow of poverty as they had promised. Being so, the Vikings were not barbarians but privateers in a Holy War.

The Vikings were the subject of the prayer, "*A furor normannorum libera nos domine*" ("*From the fury of the Northmen deliver us, O Lord!*"), no doubt attributed to monks of the English monasteries plundered by the Viking raids in the 8th and 9th centuries. This is also the period that the Danes, fighting alongside the Vikings, captured most of England. This period is known, to this day, as the period of "Danelaw".

More credible reports of the Viking age can be found in monastic chronicles, such as the Anglo-Saxon Chronicle and similar Frankish and Irish Annals, which broadly outline what happened, and at what date. There are also sources of a more directly religious nature, such as the much-quoted letters of Alcuin, and Wulfstan's famous *'Sermon of the Wolf'*, both of which chose to interpret the Viking raids as God's punishment on the Anglo-Saxon Catholics for their sins. Even the chronicles reflect the fact that the Vikings often attacked monasteries for their wealth, which created an obvious religious bias against them. This hostile tone of the contemporary accounts has done much to create the popular image of Viking atrocities. However, modern historians have noted that the same sources show Christian rulers behaving equally unpleasantly, but without being condemned on religious grounds.

The time of the earliest recorded raids occurred c790 AD and lasted until the Norman Conquest of England in 1066 AD. This time period correlates almost exactly with the arrival of the Galicians in Denmark (Circa 720 AD), and the beginning of the Baltic Hansiatic League (c1000 AD), which promoted trade rather than priveteering. Support for the theory that the Norsemen were doomed by the Hanse is strengthened by the fact that the names of Scandinavian kings are known only in the later part of the Viking Age. Only after the end of the Viking Age, did the separate Norwegian kingdoms acquire a distinct identity. Thus, the end of the Viking Age for the Scandinavians also marks the start of their relatively brief Middle Ages.

Viking Ships

There were two distinct classes of Viking ships: the longship (sometimes erroneously called "*Drakkar*", a corruption of "dragon" in Norse) and the "*Knarr*". The longship was intended for warfare and exploration, and was designed for speed and agility. It was equipped with oars to complement the sail as well as making it able to navigate independently of the wind. The longship had a long and narrow hull, as well as a shallow draft, in order to facilitate landings and troop deployments in shallow water. The Knarr was a dedicated merchant vessel designed to carry cargo. It was designed with a broader hull, deeper draft and a limited number of oars (used primarily to maneuver in harbors and similar situations). One Viking innovation was the beitass, a spar mounted to the sail that allowed their ships to sail effectively against the wind. This was a distinct advantage since their opponents had not yet learned this skill. All they had to do in order to escape another ship was to sail into the wind. While the Vikings maintained a relatively straight course their opponents would be required to zigzag, or tack, as it is called in nautical terms. Longships were used extensively by the Leidang, the Scandinavian defense fleets. The term "*Viking ships*" has entered common usage, possibly because of its romantic associations.

In Roskilde, Denmark are the well-preserved remains of five ships, excavated from nearby Roskilde Fjord in the late 1960s. The ships were scuttled there in the 11th century to block a navigation channel from a seaborne assault, thus protecting the city, which was then the Danish capital. (NOTE: Roskilde is on the island of Zealand, Denmark only 10 miles from Farum Sound, the home port of the Farum clan. The city is only 20 miles from the current capital of Copenhagen.) These five ships represent the two distinct classes of Viking ships, the Longship and the Knarr.

Much is known about the Viking Ships thanks, to archaeological discoveries of sunken ships and descriptions and drawings from the period. Only the very wealthy could afford the large ocean-going ships used in colonization and trade. Ships were either commissioned new from a master shipwright or purchased second-hand. There were no blueprints. Ship building was done by eye. Although the overall designs were similar, no ship was an exact replica of another. The smaller boats were, both then as now, built locally where many people possessed boat building skills.

Viking ships were built from the outside in and from the bottom up. The keel was laid out first and the hull was built up from it. To hold the boards in shape as they were attached one by one, to a "strongback" which was erected over the construction site. The strongback was an overhead frame, anchored in the ground to which the hull was temporarily attached in the configuration desired.

Trees were selected specially for each boat or ship. The favored species were oak, pine, and spruce. Pieces that were to be angled in the ship were made from natural bends in the tree, for instance a piece cut from branches. The wood was not seasoned because the newly cut, "green" wood was more flexible. Steaming the boards made it easier to bend them into shape. The best boat boards were planks that had been cut radially from the trunk, so that all planks included both the inner and outer portion of the trunk in the same proportions. This minimized the warping and shrinking as the wood dried, and it increased the tensile strength of the boards. Triangular in cross section, the boards were placed with their thinnest side placed downward, the thicker top overlapping the thin bottom part of the next plank. In big ships, planks had to be joined to produce the required length. This was done by scarfing; that is the ends of the planks to be joined were thinned so that the end of one plank could overlap the other. After the hull was built up, "ribs" were inserted into it and attached to the hull with strong lashes of leather or even baleen from whales. This made the construction flexible so that the hull moved slightly with the water pressure rather than breaking from it.

The boards were held together with iron nails. The iron nails extended through both boards and through a rove over which they were tightly bent, "clenched," with hammer blows. The upper boards could also be attached with treenails. Treenails were dowels carved out of wood with an expanded head like a nail. Such treenails were also used in house construction and furniture. Steering was done with a large oar attached to the right hand side, "starboard" ("steering board") side of the ship.

Most ships were stabilized with ballast of football-sized boulders which could be increased or discarded according to the weight of the cargo. The cargo ships also carried small open row boats which could be used for landing or loading and off-loading the ship.

Sails were large and rectangular, with a width of 10 meters or more and not quite as high as they were wide. They were made from lengths of wool, linen, or hemp sewn together as the widest piece of cloth one could produce on a loom of the era was 2 or 2.5 m. Most of us have seen the pictures of the Viking ships with the colorful striped sails.

Because the ships were relatively light, they rode the crest of the waves rather than cutting through them. Travelling in these ships cannot have been comfortable because they were largely open, like giant canoes. The cargo ships had a deck in the bow and could have one aft as well, but the rest of the ship was open. The crew and light goods were probably on the bow deck where they were covered by tarpaulins or tents. The heaviest cargo was stowed behind the mast. In addition to big ships, there was a variety of smaller vessels of all sizes, both for rowing and sailing. Roads were poor, and the easiest way to transport people and goods was via waterways. Viking ships were sometimes referred to as "*dragons.*" In Viking art, ships are often depicted with a dragon head atop the bow. One such carved head of wood has been found in the river Schelde in Belgium. It appears to have been removable.

Much of the inland areas traveled by the Norsemen cannot be accessed by ship today. By the end of the last ice age about 11,000 years ago, much of northern Europe and North America was covered by ice sheets up to 3 km thick. At the end of the ice age when the glaciers retreated, the removal of the weight from the depressed land led to a post-glacial rebound. Initially the rebound was rapid, proceeding at about 7.5 cm/year. This phase lasted for about 2,000 years, and took place as the ice was being unloaded. Once deglaciation was complete, uplift slowed to about 2.5 cm/year, and decreased exponentially after that. Today, typical uplift rates are of the order of 1 cm/year or less, and studies suggest that rebound will continue for about another 10,000 years. The total uplift from the end of deglaciation can be up to 400 m.

In the Viking Age, Malaren was still a bay of the Baltic Sea and seagoing vessels could sail up it far into the interior of Sweden. Birka was conveniently near the trade routes through Sodertalje canal. Due to the post-glacial rebound, the Sodertalje canal and the mouth of Riddarfjarden bay had become so shallow that, by about 1200 AD, ships had to unload their cargoes near the entrances. After a while the bay became a lake. The decline of Birka and the subsequent foundation of Stockholm at the choke point of Riddarfjarden were in part due to the post-glacial rebound changing the topography of the Malaren basin. The lake's surface currently averages 0.7 meters above sea level. Over time, this post-glacial uplift caused many rivers and harbors, such as Bremen, Germany and Farum, Denmark, to be unnavigatable to boat trade.

Maps

Mariners relied on charts called "portolans" to assist them on their voyages. The portolans contained maps of coastlines, locations of harbors, river mouths, and manmade features visible from the sea. As sailors' skills improved and the use of the compass was more widespread, portolans improved in accuracy.

The use of latitude and longitude has been understood, since before the time of Ptolemy in the second century A.D. He assigned coordinates to place names. However, the use of latitude and longitude posed difficulties while sailing on the high seas. Portuguese chart makers added the meridian line, a point useful for latitude sailing as well as for navigating solely by compass. A geographic feature could now be located through the use of its distance, in degree of latitude, from a ship's point of departure.

Navigation

When a sailor departs port and loses sight of land, he must have some method of determining his direction. Early captains relied on nature to provide the answers. We all know the sun rises in the east and sets in the west. A rising sun on the left-hand side of the ship, for example, meant it was sailing south. At night, the pilot could view the Pole or North Star. This star does not change its position by the hour and it remains constant in the north. The farther north the sailor traveled, the higher the Pole Star appeared in the sky. The farther south he sailed, the lower the star appeared in the sky. When mariners reached the equator, the star disappeared. Navigators in the Southern Hemisphere were accustomed to using different stars to determine direction. During and before this period, there was a worldwide obsession over astronomy and its various uses.

The quadrant, a quarter circle measuring 0 to 90 degrees marked around its curved edge, was a common instrument to assist in determining latitude. Its straight edges had tiny holes or sights on each end. A plumb line hung from the top. The navigator lined up the sights on the Pole Star and the plumb line would hang straight down over the curved area at a particular point. This would indicate the height of the star in degrees latitude.

Another way of determining latitude was with the use of the astrolabe. This was a simple wooden or brass disk with degrees marked around its edge. It had a rotating arm with small holes at either end. The disk would be hung vertically from a ring. The user could move the arm until the sunlight shone through the hole at one end and fell on the hole on the other end. The arm then would indicate the latitude by the degrees marked around the edge of the disk.

The drawback for both the quadrant and the astrolabe was the movement of the ship, which made it difficult to make an accurate measurement. The cross-staff, invented in the sixteenth century, solved this problem. (NOTE: Subsequent discoveries have hinted at the idea of sophisticated navigation devices available to a select few cultures well before the time of the Vikings.)

Determining longitude, the distance from east to west, was problematic. It is impossible to measure it without an accurate timepiece to compute the speed of the ship against the time at sea. (The chronometer was not invented until the eighteenth century.) For early sailors, the only way to measure it was to factor together variables of compass direction, speed, or dead reckoning. The compass was well known to Europeans by the fifteenth century. It had been used in China and Arabia centuries before. Compasses of the fifteenth century were made with an iron needle magnetized by a lodestone on a small piece of wood floating in a container of water. This was eventually replaced by a brass canister where a magnetic needle swung around an upright pin. The compass was not always accurate because magnetic north is affected by anomalies in the earth's magnetism and does not provide a straight line of travel.

Another method of navigating open sea was the complicated process of dead reckoning. The pilot had to estimate the ship's speed with a chip log, which had a weighted wooden float attached to a line with knots in it. This line would be thrown from the stern. The number of knots shown between the log and the ship denoted the ships speed. This information combined with the known direction of the compass would determine progress along longitudinal lines. Time, distance, and direction were measured each time the ship changed tack due to wind direction. This zigzag plotting was calculated with a traverse board. The trailing rope had knots at specified distances apart thereby leading to the current measuring of nautical speeds in knots.

Viking Decline

Following a period of thriving trade and Viking settlement, cultural impulses flowed from the rest of Europe to affect Viking dominance. Christianity had an early and growing presence in Scandinavia, and with the rise of a centralized authority and the creation of the Baltic trade organization known as the Hansiatic League, Viking raids became more risky and less profitable.

A new quasi-feudalistic system became entrenched in Scandinavian rule and, as a result, organized opposition sealed the Vikings' fate. Eleventh-century chronicles note Scandinavian attempts to combat the Vikings from the eastern shores of the Baltic Sea. This was a prelude to the development of the Hanse, a Baltic trade organization that did not want piracy to interfere with there trade in the Baltic Sea.

One of the primary profit centers of Viking trade was slavery. The Celtic Christian Church took a position that Christians should not own other humans as slaves, so chattel slavery diminished as a practice throughout Northern Europe. Eventually, outright slavery was outlawed, replaced with serfdom at the bottom rung of medieval society. This took much of the economic incentive out of raiding, though sporadic activity continued for a few decades beyond the Norman conquest of England. This anti-slavery belief was carried over to the newly established United States by its founding fathers.

The Vikings previous misadventures, and the initiation of the Hansiatic League, dictated that the Vikings find safe harbor in a place away from the countries which they had plundered. That even included Norway and Denmark, which the Vikings also attacked after the two countries adopted Catholicism. The fact that the Vikings were not considered Celts also precluded them from colonizing any Celtic countries. It now seemed that the actions of the Vikings had placed them in a group without a country. The only place suited to their climatic needs, and placement in a non-Celtic country, was Iceland. History confirms that the Vikings were not told about the rich Celtic lands west of Iceland in North America. This is one of the main reasons why Viking presence in North America is so difficult to substantiate. The true Vikings died off before the Nordic migration to America begin. The Celts went to great lengths to keep the Norse out of Celtic America. This included blocking all the routes to North America through the Saint Lawrence Seaway. Most of their attempts at discouraging the Norse were in vein.

ICELAND

According to Landnamabok (the Book of Settlements), possibly dating from the 11th century, Irish monks called Papars, had been living on Iceland before the Norse settlers arrived. These monks had left behind Irish books, bells and crosses, among other things. Hence, the Norse arriving at Iceland had no difficulty identifying the nationality of the Irish monks.

A source mentioning the existence of the Monks is the Islendingabok (Book of the Icelanders), dating from between 1122 and 1133. According to this account, the previous inhabitants, a few Irish monks, known as the Papar Monks, left the island because they did not want to live with the non-Celtic Norsemen. One theory suggests that those monks were members of a Hiberno-Scottish mission.

Recent archaeological excavations have revealed the ruins of a cabin in Hafnir on the Reykjanes peninsula (close to Keflavik Airport). Carbon dating reveals that the cabin was abandoned somewhere between 770 and 880, suggesting that Iceland was populated well before 874. This archaeological find may also indicate that the monks left Iceland before the Norse arrived. Could they have moved on to North America, as the Viking descendants did later on?

The first known permanent Norse settler in Iceland was Ingolfr Arnarson, who built his homestead in Reykjavik in the year 874 AD. Ingolfr was followed by many other emigrant settlers, largely Norsemen and their Irish slaves. By 930 AD, most arable land had been claimed and the Althing, a legislative and judiciary parliament, was initiated to regulate the Icelandic Commonwealth. Christianity was adopted c999–1000 AD with the arrival of the Vikings.

The Commonwealth lasted until 1262 AD, when the political system, devised by the original settlers, proved unable to cope with the increasing power of Icelandic chieftains.

GREENLAND

Greenland is an autonomous country within the Kingdom of Denmark, located between the Arctic and Atlantic Oceans, east of the Canadian Arctic Archipelago. Though physiographically a part of the continent of North America, Greenland has been politically and culturally associated with Europe,

(Specifically Norway and later Denmark) for more than a millennium. Greenland is, by area, the world's largest island that is not a continent. With a population of 56,615 (January 2011 estimate), it is the least densely populated dependency or country in the world.

Greenland has been inhabited, though not continuously, by Arctic peoples via Canada for at least 4500–5000 years. In the 10th century, during the Viking era, Norsemen settled on the uninhabited southern part of Greenland. In the 13th century, the Inuit natives arrived. In the early 14th century, the Norse colonies were abandoned due to a freak climatic freeze. In the early 18th, century contact between Scandinavia and Greenland was re-established and Denmark established rule over Greenland.

Greenland became a Danish colony in 1814 AD, after being under the rule of the Denmark-Norway Alliance for centuries. With the Constitution of Denmark of 1953 AD, Greenland became a part of the Danish realm in a relationship known in Danish as Rigsfællesskabet (Commonwealth of the Realm). In 1979 AD, Denmark granted home rule to Greenland, and in 2008 AD, Greenland voted to transfer more power from the Danish royal government to the local Greenlandic government. This became effective the following year, with the Danish royal government in charge of foreign affairs, security, and financial policy, and providing a subsidy of DKK 3.4 billion. This subsidy will be gradually diminishing over time as Greenland's own economy is expected to become stronger due to income from resource extraction.

History of Greenland

From 986 AD, Greenland's west coast was colonized by Icelanders and Norwegians in two settlements on fjords near the southwestern-most tip of the island. They shared the island with the late Dorset culture inhabitants who occupied the northern and western parts, and later with the Thule culture arriving from the north. Norse Greenlanders submitted to Norwegian rule in the 13th century, and the kingdom of Norway entered into a personal union with Denmark in 1380 AD, and from 1397 AD on was part of the Kalmar Union. Greenland became a part of the Kalamar Union at the time the Kalamar Union was initiated. As you may remember, both the Sinclairs and the Farams left for North America in 1398 AD.

Life was harsh in Greenland. The last written records of the Norse Greenlanders are of a marriage in 1408 AD, in the church of Hvalsey, which is today the best-preserved Nordic ruin in Greenland. The evidence may be an indication that the Norse made their final move to North America c1409 AD. This mass migration south to North America would influence the move of the Farams and Henry Sinclair to the North American Territory in 1397. The Norse settlements died off in Greenland and the area came under the de facto control of various Inuit groups. However, the Danish government never forgot or relinquished the claims to Greenland that it had inherited from the Norwegians, and when contact with Greenland was re-established in the early 18th century, Denmark asserted its sovereignty over the island.

In 1500 AD, King Manuel I of Portugal sent Gaspar Corte-Real to Greenland in search of a Northwest Passage to Asia; which, according to the Treaty of Tordesillas was part of the Portuguese area of influence. In 1501 AD, Corte-Real returned with his brother, Miguel Corte-Real. Finding the sea frozen, they headed south and, according to current history, traveled no further south than Newfoundland. Upon their return to Portugal the cartographic information supplied by Corte-Real was incorporated into a new map of the world which was presented to the Ercole I d'Este, Duke of Ferrara by Alberto Cantino, in 1502 AD. The following map of the Cantino Planisphere, made in Lisbon, accurately depicts the countries surrounding the Atlantic Ocean. Once again, we have hundreds of years of exploration depicted on a map just 10 years after the voyage of Columbus. This deception will be explained in Chapter 13.

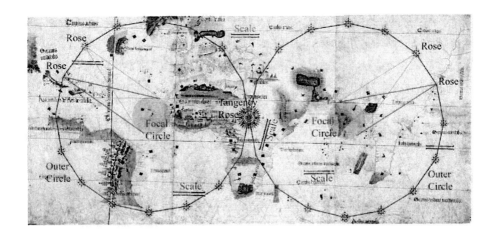

The Cantino Planisphere of 1502 AD

The 1502 AD, Map, the Cantino Planisphere, by Miguel Corte-Real, as with many maps printed shortly after the voyage of Columbus, clearly shows the exploration of the East coast of North and South America long before 1502. Between Florida and South America, the Islands of Cuba and Haiti can be plainly seen. Please take notice of the Portuguese flags planted in South America, but no flags planted in North America. This will become more important as you read on. By 1362 AD, the Portuguese had abandoned their interests in North America in accordance with the granting of North America to the Templars. Circa 1362 AD, the Templars took claim to North America in return for assisting the Portuguese and Spain to liberate the Iberian Peninsula from the Muslims. The Iberian liberation took until the year 1492 AD, the year

Columbus sailed for the Americas to re-establish Portugal's, and now Spain's, claim to the Caribbean and South America. (See Chapter 13) The Portuguese never returned to North America but continued development of the Eastern half of South America (Brazil), while Spain conquered and developed Central America and the Western half of South America

In 1721 AD, a joint mercantile and clerical expedition, led by Danish-Norwegian missionary Hans Egede, was sent to Greenland not knowing whether a Norse civilization remained there. After 15 years in Greenland, Hans Egede returned to Denmark where he established a Greenland Seminary. Gradually, Greenland was opened up to Danish merchants, and closed to those from other countries.

The Little Ice Age

Two great natural disasters struck Europe, in the 14th Century. One was climatic, the Little Ice Age. In 1303, 1306 and 1307 AD, the Baltic Sea froze over, something never before recorded. This meant that the Norse settlements in Greenland and Iceland were also cut off from trade. This would have required a move by the Vikings Nordic descendants to a milder climate. The last Icelandic ship sailed from Iceland in the early 1400's. Can there be any doubt, that the Vikings of Greenland and Iceland moved further south to the milder climate of North America? When contact with Iceland and Greenland was resumed in the 1700's, the settlements were long abandoned. Many reasons have been proposed to explain the demise of the Viking colonies. Clearly, this natural climatic disaster would be on the top of the list. During this same period, France experienced crop failure after heavy rains and in 1315; there was widespread famine, reports of cannibalism, and epidemics in Europe.

Scandinavian and Celtic Settlement c1200 AD

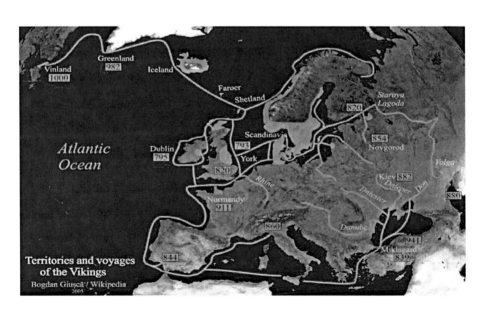

Recorded Viking Trading Routes, with Dates

THE NORSE MIGRATION TO AMERICA

Although the Celts had been traveling to the Americas for centuries, they did not let their Nordic military force, the Vikings, in on the secret. According to the Icelandic sagas ("*Eirik the Red's Saga*" and the "*Saga of the Greenlanders*", along with chapters of the *Hauksbók and the Flatey Book*), the Norse started to explore lands to the west of Greenland only a few years after the Greenland settlements were established in 985 AD.

While sailing from Iceland to Greenland with a migration fleet consisting of 400-700 settlers, and 25 ships (14 of which completed the journey), a merchant named Bjarni Herjolfsson was blown off course and after three days sailing he sighted land west of the fleet. Bjarni was only interested in finding his father's farm, but he did describe his discovery to Leif Ericson who explored the area in more detail and built a small settlement in North America fifteen years later. This confirms the Vikings lack of knowledge of the Americas.

The sagas describe three separate areas discovered during this exploration: **Helluland,** which means *"land of the flat stones"*; **Markland,** *"the land of forests"*, definitely of interest to settlers in Greenland where there were few trees; and **Vinland**, *"the land of wine",* found somewhere south of Markland. Many Early Nordic relics have been found north of the New England area. It was in Vinland that the settlement, described in the sagas, was built.

The fact that historical documentation shows that the Vikings did not originally know of the North American Territory, confirms that the Celts had not originally planned for the Vikings to be part of the colonization of North America, a land which the Celts had been visiting for centuries before this.

Although not originally planned to be part of the North America colonists, evidence of Norse voyages to the New England area continue to be discovered.

This includes the Maine Penny, a Norwegian coin from King Olaf Kyrre's reign (1066-80 AD) allegedly found in a Native American archaeological site in the U.S. state of Maine, suggesting an exchange between the Norse and the Native Americans late in, or after, the 11th century; and an entry in the Icelandic Annals from 1347 AD, which refers to a small Greenlandic vessel with a crew of eighteen that arrived in Iceland while attempting to return to Greenland from Markland, with a load of timber. In addition, Norse materials have been excavated in several Inuit communities. Then there are the scores of Nordic Runestones and geoglyphs that have been found, and are being found on a regular basis, in areas which include the New England and Central portions of the United States. As described in Chapter 8, it appears that the Farams and Templars took up strategic positions along the North American Territories northern border in order to prevent an influx of Norse into the Celtic North American Territory.

Nordic Mooring Stones in Newport, RI

The following Mooring Stones were found on the West coast of Newport Island, RI USA. These stones have traditionally been used by archeologists to validate locations where early Nordic mariners were known to have traveled. These stones were used to moor Nordic Ships in the 11th and 12th century.

Nordic Mooring Stones are unique in that they are large enough to secure a ship, and have a triangular hole in the top. Into the triangular hole hot lead is poured and then a metal rod, with a mooring ring attached, is driven into to hole. This makes for a secure attachment to the mooring stone. Although the mooring stones depicted here resemble Nordic Mooring Stones, that does not necessarily mean that they were placed there by the Norse. The Celtic Danes close association with Norway and the Vikings during this period would suggest that they could have adopted this same technology. (The Mooring Stones were photographed by Peter and Steve DiMarzo, Newport, RI USA)

The Typical Triangular Hole in a Mooring Stone

A Mooring Stone With a Hole in the Top, Newport RI

Mooring Stones in the Sunset, Newport RI

Nordic Landmarks in America

Many Nordic runestones and relics have been found in the United States, most dating around the 11th and 12th Century. Scholars have argued up to now that they were most likely fakes. However, there are so many of them being found now, that argument just doesn't hold water any longer. There is no doubt that there would be more evidence, if there were not people in the United States dedicated to hiding and destroying these artifacts. A runestone is typically a raised stone with a runic inscription, but the term can also be applied to inscriptions on boulders and on bedrock. Most runestones are located in Scandinavia, but there are also scattered runestones in locations that were visited by Nordic Cistercian Monks (Templars) during the colonization of North America. (Ref: Keywords Cistercians and runestones - http://www.wikipedia.com.)

CULTURAL LEGACY

More than any other single event, the attack on the monastery at Lindisfarne, England demonized the perception of the Vikings for the next twelve centuries. Not until the 1890s did scholars, outside Scandinavia, begin to seriously reassess the achievements of the Vikings, recognizing their artistry, technological skills and seamanship.

The first challenges to anti-Viking sentiments in Britain emerged in the 17th century. Pioneering scholarly editions of the Viking Age began to reach a small readership in Britain, archaeologists began to dig up Britain's Viking past, and linguistic enthusiasts started to identify the Viking-Age origins for rural idioms and proverbs. The new dictionaries of the Old Norse language enabled the Victorians to grapple with the primary Icelandic sagas.

In Scandinavia, the 17th century Danish scholars Thomas Bartholin, Ole Worm, and Olof Rudbeck of Sweden were the first to set the standard for using runic inscriptions and Icelandic Sagas as historical sources. During the Age of Enlightenment and the Nordic Renaissance, historical scholarship in Scandinavia became more rational and pragmatic, as witnessed by the works of a Danish historian Ludvig Holberg and Swedish historian Olof von Dalin. Until recently, the history of the Viking Age was largely based on Icelandic sagas, the history of the Danes written by Saxo Grammaticus, the Russian Primary Chronicle, and the War of the Irish with the Foreigners. Although few scholars still accept these texts as reliable sources, historians today rely more on the archeological and numismatic disciplines that have made valuable contributions toward understanding the period. As time progresses, other sciences are being developed which deserve close examination for the possibility of adding additional contributions to, not only the Viking era, but mankind's history in general.

The Celts, Portuguese and their predecessors had already enjoyed free and secret access to the Americas for millennia. Modern scholars already agree, that the Vikings colonized as far west and south as Newfoundland; however, they refuse to even consider evidence that would suggest that the Vikings entered what is now the United States.

After the year 1066 AD, the Viking Role in History came to a close. Historical evidence shows that, after leaving Europe, the Vikings moved on to colonize Iceland and Greenland. After their discovery of the North American continent, and the climactic freeze of the 14th century, the Viking descendants, not the Vikings, were forced to move south to a warmer climate.

For years I have wondered, why mainstream scholars would reject the idea that the Vikings colonized any further south than Newfoundland. There is undeniable proof that both Danish and Nordic artifacts have been found in North America. Then it hit me, the scholars were correct. The Vikings never did colonize any further south than Newfoundland; it was their descendants and Nordic cousins, not the Vikings, that traveled to North America. So the next time someone asks you did the Vikings travel any further south than Newfoundland; reply, no but their descendants did.

Can a rational person believe that the Norse would traverse the entire length of Europe and brave the seas of the North Atlantic to Newfoundland without proceeding the short distance across the Saint Lawrence Seaway to the other half of North America? As will be covered in a later chapter, access to the Templars North American Territory was eventually blocked by Templar military forces led by the Faram family.

Celtic Map Circa 1450AD

(English text added by author.)

If the Celtic map is studied closely, it soon becomes obvious that the map contains a diagram of the entire world, including North and South America. It is simply not in proportion to the rest of the map. The map clearly shows Canada, the Saint Lawrence Seaway leading into the Great Lakes, Florida, the Gulf of Mexico and South America. This map was originally attributed to the Vikings. Forensic studies have since confirmed it is genuine, but not Viking.

Recent North American discoveries reveal that the Norse settled outside the 1332 AD Searcy land grant, in the area just west of the Mississippi River, from Minnesota to Texas. After being blocked from access to the Templar Territory, through the Saint Lawrence Seaway, the Norse people were forced to find a new route to North America through Canada's Hudson Bay. On the west coast of Hudson Bay is the entrance to the Nelson River. Through this river, the Norse were able to find a route from Hudson Bay to both Lake Superior, and the Red River, in Minnesota. This answers the question of why the Norse culture, in the United States, is found predominantly west of Lake Superior. As you will discover in the Chapter titled "The Colonizing of America" the Farams and the Templars had the routes to the Great Lakes, through the Saint Lawrence Seaway, blocked.

There is the possibility, that the hasty ceding of the Searcy Territory to the Templars, by the Portuguese, in 1332 AD, was an attempt by the Celts to force the Norse outside of what would evolve into the United States. The timing would coincide with the Norse' migration south from Greenland and Iceland c1305 AD after the freeze in the North. The Norse colonization west of the Mississippi River was again thwarted by the award of the entire North American Territory to the Templars in 1362 AD; however, the 1362 transaction was not recorded until 1822 AD, by the construction of the Guimar Geoglyph in the Portuguese Canary Islands. The lack of the public knowledge, or recording, of the 1362 award of the western territories of North America required the acquisition of the Louisiana Purchase. This purchase was the government's only way of preventing the colonization of the land by the Norse, and early Celtic colonists (Native Americans) who were attempting to blockade government access to the west coast. It would appear from historical records that neither the Vikings, nor their descendants, were intended to be part of the colonization of North America.

It is possible that the Masons were not discriminating solely against the Norse. Research shows that the Masons may have been intent on preventing any colonists, except Masons, from colonizing America. A clue that the early Masonic colonists were attempting to establish a country of Masonic ideals, to the exclusion of the rest of the world, is demonstrated by the many land acquisitions which the government made as soon as they saw the threat of outside colonization of the North American Territory. Although this goal was never realized, many of the Masonic ideals were incorporated into the laws of the United States.

Chapter 7

The Knights Templar

THE BIRTH of the KNIGHTS TEMPLAR

The Poor Fellow-Soldiers of Christ of the Temple of Solomon, commonly known as the Knights Templar or the Order of the Temple, were among the most famous of the Western Christian military orders. The organization existed for approximately two centuries in the Middle Ages. The order was created earlier, but not officially endorsed by the Roman Catholic Church until 1129 AD. The Order became a favored charity throughout Christendom and grew rapidly in membership and power. Non-combatant members of the Order managed a large economic infrastructure throughout Christendom, innovating financial techniques that were an early form of banking. The Templars also built many fortifications across Europe and the Holy Land. Templar Knights, in their distinctive white mantles with a red cross, were among the most skilled fighting units of the Crusades against the Muslims in the Holy Land (c1129-c1313), in Scotland against the English in 1314 AD, and against the Muslims, in concert with Portugal, in the Iberian Peninsula c1319-1492 AD.

The Muslim presence in the Holy Land began with the initial Arab conquest of Palestine, in the 7th century. This invasion of the Holy Land eventually resulted in the conquest of the entire Mediterranean coastal states as well as a large part of Europe. The first crusade began in 1095 AD, when the Byzantine Emperor, Alexius I, asked for help from the Christians to fight against the Turks. Pope Urban II sent crusader troops to Jerusalem to fight with the

Byzantines. The Crusades were, in part, an outlet for an intense religious piety which rose up in the late 11th century among the lay public. A crusader would, after pronouncing a solemn vow as a Cistercian Monk, receive a cross from the hands of the Pope or his legates, and was thenceforth considered a "Soldier of the Church". The result was an awakening of intense Christian piety and public interest in religious affairs, and was further strengthened by religious propaganda, which advocated a "Just War" in order to retake the Holy Land from the Muslims.

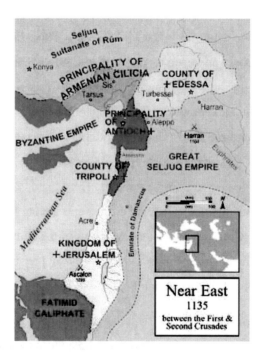

Holy Land States Captured by Crusaders c1135AD

Jerusalem, Tripoli, Antioch and Edessa.

The Crusader states were a number of mostly 12th and 13th century feudal states, created by Western European crusaders in Asia Minor, Greece, the Holy Land, and in the eastern Baltic area. The name also refers to other territorial gains (often small and short-lived) made by medieval Christendom against Muslim adversaries.

HUGO de PAYENS

Hugo de Payens (1070 - 1136 AD) was the first master of the Knights Templar. He was originally a vassal of Count Hugues de Champagne. Count Hugues de Champagne visited Jerusalem once with Hugo de Payens. Payens remained in Jerusalem while the Count returned home to France. Count Hugh of Champagne made pilgrimages to the Holy Land in 1104-07 AD and for a second time in 1114-16 AD. The fact that Hugo remained there is testified to by a charter, with *"Hugonis de Peans"* in the witness list, from Jerusalem in 1120 AD and again in 1123 AD. In 1125 AD his name appears again as a witness to a donation, this time accompanied by the title "Magister Militum Templi" ("Master of the Knights of the Temple").

Upon his return to Champagne, Hugo organized a group of nine knights ostensibly to protect pilgrims on their way to the holy land. It is more likely that the Knights were assembled to retrieve precious artifacts left behind by the Empire of King Solomon. This assumption is arrived at by the fact that the nine Knights lived on the Temple grounds for years after their arrival in Jerusalem, while digging under the temple itself. On the surface, it would appear that this search was self-serving; however, it is easier to understand if you realize that the Knights Templar, as they would be called later, were there to retrieve artifacts sacred to a secret organization, of which they were part. This organization had existed for millennia and still exists to this day. King Solomon was part of that political/religious lineage.

Hugo de Payens approached King Baldwin II with eight knights, two of whom were brothers and all of which were relatives of Hugo de Payens, some by blood and others through marriage, to form the first order of the Templars. The other riders were: Geoffrey of St. Omer, Payen de Montdidier, Archambaud Agnan St. Andre de Montbard, Geoffrey Bison, and two men recorded only the names Rossal and Gondamer. The ninth knight remains unknown, although some have speculated that he was Hugh Comte de Champagne.

De Payens was probably born in Chateau Payens, about 10 km from Troyes, in Champagne, France. He was also a veteran of the First Crusade (in 1099 AD) and spent 22 years of his life in Eastern Europe. It is likely that Hugues de Payens had served in the army of Godfroi Boullion during the First Crusade. As a teacher, he led the Knights Templar for almost twenty years until his death, helping to establish the foundation of the Order as an important and influential international military and financial institution. While visiting London in 1128 AD, one year prior to being acknowledged by the Catholic Church, he managed men and money for the Order. Hugh also founded the Orders first headquarters there, establishing the Templars in England.

Origin and early life

No early biography of Hugues de Payens exists, nor do later writers cite such a biography. None of the sources on his later career give details of his early life. Information is therefore scarce and uncertain; embellishments depend partly on documents that may not refer to the same individual, partly on histories written decades or even centuries after his death. The earliest source that pins down a geographical origin for the later Grand Master is the Old

French translation of William of Tyre's, "*History of Events Beyond the Sea*". The Latin text calls him simply Hugo de Paganis, but the French translation dated to c1200, describes him as Hues de Paiens delez Troies ("Hugh of Payens near Troyes"), a reference to the village of Payns, about 10 km from Troyes, in Champagne. (Eastern France).

In early documents of that region Hugo de Pedano, Montiniaci dominus is mentioned as a witness to a donation by Count Hugh of Champagne in a document of 1085-90 AD, indicating that the man was at least sixteen by this date. Being a legal adult and able to bear witness to legal documents, he would have been born no later than 1070 AD. The same name appears on a number of other charters up to 1113 AD, also relating to Count Hugh of Champagne, suggesting that Hugo de Pedano or Hugo dominus de Peanz was a member of the Count's court. By the year 1113 AD, he was married to Elizabeth de Chappes, who bore him at least one child, Thibaud, later abbot of la Colombe at Sens. The documents span Hugues' lifetime and the disposition of his property after his death.

The one belated statement, that the founder of the Knights Templars came from "Payns near Troyes", has some circumstantial confirmation. The now sainted Bernard of Clairvaux, who favored the Order and helped to compose its Latin Rule, also had the support of Hugh de Champagne. The Latin Rule of the Order was confirmed at the Council of Troyes in 1129 AD. A Templar command post was eventually built at Payns. It should be noted that in early European history the Champagne area was also the center of the La Tene Celtic culture. This is the same Celtic culture that spread to Galicia, Scotland, Ireland and North America.

There is also a claim that Hugues de Payens or Ugo de' Pagani came from Nocera de' Pagani in Campania, southern Italy. Reference to Nocera as his birthplace is found at least as early as Baedeker's Southern Italy (1869 AD) and is also found in the Old Catholic Encyclopedia. Two more recent writers say that, the theory is supported by a letter that Hugues wrote from Palestine in 1103 AD, in which he talked of writing to "*my father in Nocera*" to tell him of the death of his cousin Alessandro. If you will remember, half the Farum Clan remained in Italy after Galicia conquered Italy in 410 AD. This, along with other facts, might explain the Farum-Denmark connection with the Templars after the family's move from Italy to Denmark c1000 AD.

The Foundation of the Order

Champagne is a historic province in the northeast of France, now best known for the sparkling white wine that bears its name. Formerly ruled by the Counts of Champagne, its western edge is about 100 miles (160 km) east of Paris. The cities of Troyes, Reims, and Epernay are the commercial centers of the area. Most of Champagne is now part of the French administrative region of Champagne-Ardenne, which comprises four departments: Ardennes, Aube, Haute-Marne, and Marne. The name Champagne comes from the Latin campania and referred to the similarities between the rolling hills of the province and the Italian countryside of Campania located south of Rome. From this we can establish another possible connection with the Italian Farums.

One early chronicler, Simon de St. Bertin, implies that the Knights Templar originated earlier, before the death of Godfrey of Bouillon in 1100:

> "*While Godfrey was reigning, some had decided not to return to France after the first Crusade. On the advice of the leaders of "God's Army" they vowed themselves to God's Temple. They vowed that they would renounce the world, give up personal goods, free themselves to pursue purity, and lead a communal life wearing a poor habit, only using arms to defend the land against the attacks of the insurgent pagans when necessity demanded.*"

This would explain Hugh de Payens' stay in the Holy Land after his Master, Hugo de Champagne, returned to France after the first Crusade in 1099 AD. According to author Robert Lomas, the Sinclairs of Scotland and their French relatives the St. Clairs were instrumental in creating the Knights Templar. He claims that the founder of Templars, Hugh de Payns, was married to a relative of the Duke of Champaine (Henri de St. Clair), who was a powerful broker of the first Crusade and had the political power to nominate the Pope, and to suggest the idea of the Templars, and empower it, to the Pope. (During this period of history, the Pope was elected by the Royalty.)

Information on Hugh de Payns comes from the records from local church cartularies dealing chiefly with the disposition of the Grand Master's properties, the earliest alluding to his wife Elizabeth in 1113 AD. Others span Payen's lifetime, the period following his death and lastly her own death in 1170 AD.

In 911 AD, the village of Saint-Clair-sur-Epte, in France, saw the signing of a Treaty between the French and the Vikings which created the Duchy of Normandy. The Viking colonization of Normandy highlights the French Templar, Scotish Sinclair, and Danish Faram connection. The newly-created Norman Dukes then entrusted this region to Duke Richard II's nephew Walderne (1006-1047). This is the first recorded record of the Lord of Saint-Clair. Walderne's son William Saint-Clair (born 1028 AD) sought fortune in Saxon England, then in Scotland, where he was made Baron of Rosslyn by King Malcolm. Thusly, the Scottish Saint-Clair, later Sinclair Clan, was established in Scotland.

The Saint-Clairs were, from their early days, connected with the founders of the Order of the Templar Knights, either through Henry "the Holy", the son of William, who took part in the First Crusade and the taking of Jerusalem in 1099 AD, or through Henry's own son, Henry II, who greeted Hugues de Payens, one of the first Knights Templars, and his kinsman by alliance, when the latter visited Scotland in 1129. It also appears that the Saint-Clairs, both in Scotland as well as France, contributed several knights to the Order.

Count Hugh of Champagne himself joined the Knights Templar on his third visit to the Holy Land in 1125 AD. As Grand Master, Hugues de Payens led the Order for almost twenty years until his death, helping to establish the Order's foundations as an important and influential military and financial institution. On his visit to England and Scotland in 1128 AD, he raised men and money for the Order, and also founded their first House in London and another near Edinburgh at Balantrodoch, now known as Temple, Midlothian. The Latin Rule laying down the way of life of the Order, attributed to Hugues de Payens and Bernard of Clairvaux, was confirmed in 1129 AD at the Council of Troyes, over which Pope Honorius II presided.

Hugues de Payens supposedly died in 1136 AD. The circumstances and date of his death are not recorded in any chronicle, though the Templars commemorated him every year on the 24th of May. The 16th century historian Marco Antonio Guarini claimed that Hugues was buried in the Church of San Giacomo at Ferrara. He was succeeded as Grand Master by Robert de Craon.

THE CHURCH CONNECTION

Bernard de Clarvaux

ONE OF THE TWO FOUNDERS OF THE KNIGHTS TEMPLAR AND
THE FOUNDER OF THE ORDER OF CISTERCIAN MONKS TEACHING
THE VENERATION OF THE VIRGIN MARY.

In the year 1119 AD, Bernard was present at the first general chapter of the order convened by Stephen of Citeaux. Though not yet thirty years old, Bernard was listened to with the greatest attention and respect, especially when he developed his thoughts upon the revival of the primitive spirit of regularity and fervor in all the monastic orders. The zeal of Bernard did not stop here; it extended to the bishops, the clergy, and the faithful, and remarkable conversions of persons engaged in worldly pursuits were among the fruits of his labors. Bernard's letter to the Archbishop of Sens is a real treatise "De Officiis Episcoporum". About the same time he wrote his work on "Grace and Free Will".

In the year 1128 AD, Bernard assisted at the Council of Troyes, which had been convened by Pope Honorius II, and was presided over by Cardinal Matthew, Bishop of Albano. The purpose of this council was to settle certain disputes of the bishops of Paris, and regulate other matters of the Church of France. This is also the Council in which the Latin Order of the Knights Templar was adopted. It was here that Bernard originated the outlines of the "Rule of the Knights Templars", who soon became the ideal of the French nobility. The bishops made Bernard secretary of the council, and charged him with drawing up the synodal statutes. After the council, the Bishop of Verdun was deposed.

After this Council, there arose against Bernard unjust reproaches and he was denounced even in Rome, as a monk who meddled with matters that did not concern him. Cardinal Harmeric, on behalf of the pope, wrote Bernard a sharp letter of remonstrance. "*It is not fitting*" he said "*that noisy and troublesome frogs should come out of their marshes to trouble the Holy See and the Cardinals*". Bernard answered the letter by saying that, if he had assisted at the council, it was because he had been dragged to it, as it were, by force. "*Now* [*]

illustrious Harmeric", he added, "*if you so wished, who would have been more capable of freeing me from the necessity of assisting at the council than yourself? Forbid those noisy troublesome frogs to come out of their holes, and to leave their marshes. Then your friend will no longer be exposed to the accusations of pride and presumption*". This letter made a great impression upon the Cardinal, and justified its author both in his eyes and before the Holy See. (From the Catholic Encyclopedia.)

Templar Expansion and Domination

Though initially an order of poor monks, the official papal sanction made the Knights Templar a charity across Europe. Further resources came in when members joined the Order, as they had to take oaths of poverty, and therefore often donated large amounts of their original cash or property to the Order. Additional revenue came from business dealings. Since the monks themselves were sworn to poverty, but had the strength of a large and trusted international infrastructure behind them, nobles would occasionally use them as a kind of bank or power of attorney. If a noble wished to join the Crusades, this might entail an absence of years from their home. So some nobles would place all of their wealth and businesses under the control of Templars, to safeguard it for them until their return. The Order's financial power became substantial, and the majority of the Order was devoted not to combat, but to economic pursuits.

By 1150 AD, the Order's original mission of guarding pilgrims had changed into a mission of guarding their valuables through an innovative way of issuing letters of credit, an early precursor of modern banking. Pilgrims would visit a Templar house in their home country, depositing their deeds and valuables. The Templars would then give them a letter which would describe their holdings. Modern scholars have stated that the letters were encrypted with a cipher alphabet based on a Maltese Cross; however, there is some disagreement on this, and it is possible that the code system was introduced later, and not something used by the medieval Templars themselves. While traveling, the pilgrims could present the letter to other Templars along the way, to "withdraw" funds from their account. This kept the pilgrims safe since they were not carrying valuables, and further increased the power of the Templars.

The Knights' involvement in banking grew over time into a new basis for paper money. One indication of their powerful political connections is that the Templars' involvement in usury did not lead to more controversy within the Order and the church at large. Officially, the idea of lending money in return for interest was forbidden by the church, but the Order sidestepped this with clever loopholes, such as a stipulation that the Templars retained the rights to the production of mortgaged property. Or as one Templar researcher put it, *"Since they weren't allowed to charge interest, they charged rent instead."*

Their holdings were necessary to support their campaigns; in the year 1180 AD, a Burgundian noble required 3 square kilometers of estate to support himself as a knight, and by 1260 AD, this had risen to 15.6 km². The Order potentially supported up to 4,000 horses and pack animals at any given time, if provisions of the rule were followed; these horses had extremely high maintenance costs due to the heat in Outremer (Crusader states at the Eastern Mediterranean), and had high mortality rates due to both disease and the Turkish bowmen strategy of aiming at a knight's horse rather than the knight himself. In addition, the high mortality rates of the knights in the East (regularly ninety percent in battle, not including wounded) resulted in extremely high campaign costs due to the need to recruit and train more knights. In 1244 AD, at the battle of La Forbie, where only thirty-three of 300 knights survived, it is estimated the financial loss was equivalent to one-ninth of the entire Capetian yearly revenue.

The Templars' political connections and awareness of the essentially urban and commercial nature of the Outremer communities led the Order to a position of significant power, both in Europe and the Holy Land. They owned large tracts of land both in Europe and the Middle East, built churches and castles, bought farms and vineyards, were involved in manufacturing and import/export and for a time even "owned" the entire island of Cyprus.

THE TEMPLARS DEMISE

The Templar's existence was tied closely to the Crusades; when the Holy Land was lost, support for the Order faded. Rumors about the Templar's secret initiation ceremony created mistrust, and King Philip IV of France, deeply in debt to the Order, took advantage of the situation. King Philip coordinated with the Pope of the Catholic Church to eliminate the growing power of the Templar organization. In 1307 AD, many of the Order's members in France were arrested, tortured into giving false confessions, and then burned at the stake. Under pressure from King Philip, Pope Clement V disbanded the Order in 1312 AD. It was later learned, that King Phillip had borrowed tremendous amounts of money from the Templars. By creating a scandal and eliminating the Templars, he would also eliminate his debt. The abrupt disappearance of a major part of the European infrastructure gave rise to speculation and legends, which have kept the "Templar" name alive into the modern day.

In 1307 AD, the French King Philip le Bel decided to arrest the members of the order. Pope Clement V also joined the purge. Following a long period of interrogation and trial, many of the Templars admitted to heretical beliefs, that they had rejected the Christian faith and insulted Jesus in their masses. Finally, the leaders of the Templars, who were called "Grand Masters," beginning with the most important of them, Jacques de Molay, were executed in 1314 AD by order of the Church and the King. The majority of them were put into prison, and the order dispersed and officially disappeared.

With the Templar Order in disarray the remaining members, allegedly, collected the immense wealth that the Templers had amassed and boarded ships in France for a trip to Scotland and Portugal. Since the Farums had been training and transporting Templars for years, the ships most likely were from the Farum fleet in Farum Denmark.

A Typical Templar Ship
(Notice the square sail, similar to the Viking ships.)

Jaques de Moley
The Last Templar Master

Jacques de Molay's goal as Grand Master was to reform the Order, and adjust it to the situation in the Holy Land during the waning days of the Crusades. King Philip IV of France convinced the Pope to have Molay, and many other French Templars, arrested and tortured into making false confessions. When Molay later retracted his confession, Philip had him burned at the stake on an island in the Seine River in Paris, on Friday, March 13, 1314. The sudden end of both the centuries-old order of Templars, and the dramatic execution of its last leader, turned Jacques de Molay into a legendary figure.

The "**Fraternal Order of Freemasonry**" was established in Scotland in the 15th Century, to continue and safeguard the secrets of the Templars. The Freemasons and others drew upon the Templar mystique for its own rituals. Today, there are many modern organizations which draw their inspiration from the memory of Jacques de Molay, the Templers, and the ancient principles for which they stood.

In 2001, a document known as the *"Chinon Parchment"* was found in the Vatican's Secret Archives, apparently after having been filed in the wrong place in 1628. It is a record of the trial of the Templars and shows that Pope Clement absolved the Templars of all heresies in 1308 AD, before formally disbanding the Order in 1312 AD. It is currently the Roman Catholic Church's position that the medieval persecution of the Knights Templar was unjust; that there was nothing inherently wrong with the Order or its rule; and that Pope Clement was pressured into his actions by the magnitude of the public scandal and the dominating influence of King Philip IV of France.

The Farums were deeply committed to the Templers, and supported them both financially and militarily. The Galicians, who were close allies with Portugal when they left Iberia, remained close throughout history. History states that Portugal was the Templars new headquarters after their banishment from France. The history of the new order that was founded to replace the Templars, *"The Military Order of Christ"*, was established c1319. History makes it clear that the Order was formed to provide a safe harbor for the Templars in their reclaiming of Iberia and the retention of the Knight's treasures. In Scotland, the Scottish independence movement provided an excellent cover for the disbanded Templars. The Templars would repay their Scottish hosts, by defeating the English at the Battle of Bannockburn in 1314. During the late 13th and early 14th century, England, under King Edward I, was at war with Scotland. In 1314 AD his son, Edward II, engaged the Scotts at the Battle of Bannockburn. The Scotts won the battle largely due to the intervention of the Knights Templar on the side of their King Robert the Bruce. There are no records of the Knights Templar engaging in the battle of Bannockburn. The excommunicated King Robert the Bruce had very good reason to hide the Templars part in the battle. King Bruce was desperate to keep on the right side of the Pope and of the King of France. It is also worth noting that two members of the Knights Templar had fought for Edward I, at the battle of Falkirk in 1297. This legend is the basis for degrees in the Masonic Order, known as the Royal Order of Scotland, since the Templars became the Masons in the 15th century, I would say this is a good indication that the story is true.

Templar accomplishments after 1312 AD:

1. The Templars fought for Robert of Bruce, King of Scotland, and helped secure Scottish independence from England at the battle of Bannockburn in 1314.

2. The Templars joined, and converted, the Scottish "Wall Builders" Lodges into Masonic Lodges (c1450)

3. The Templars fought for Portugal, and later Spain, to rid the Iberian Peninsula of the Muslims c1320 - 1492 AD.

4. The Templars colonized and assisted in settling North America, and the establishment of what would become the USA, c1314 until c1450 when the order became the Masons.

TEMPLAR BELIEFS

Before we can explore the depths of Templar accomplishments, it is important to understand a few of their beliefs, and appreciate the knowledge they possessed. Based on their beliefs, much of their wisdom was no doubt handed down through the Egyptians from Ancient Tibet. Great knowledge was required of their predecessors as the builders of the pyramids and Temples. In order to protect themselves, and their valuable knowledge, they resorted to secret societies that have existed down through time to this very day. The Templars were one of those societies. The reason that their secrets have never been discovered is that they seldom record them. Secrets are memorized, and are known by only the highest of the secret society members.

The Celts, Etruscans and their predecessors, from which the Templars evolved, were experts at Geometry and Astronomy. They enjoyed, and excelled at, putting together numeric and geological puzzles that we are just today deciphering. The Celts were also very spiritual; however, when the Roman Emperor Constantine instituted the Roman version of Christianity, 300 years after the death of Jesus, the Celts now had two reasons to keep their religion hidden. The Celts, who believed that Mary was also to be revered, had to go underground or be persecuted by Rome for their beliefs. The Nazarenes were the Celtic followers of the teachings of Jesus, before the Catholic Church was established. The Nazarenes believed that Mary, having had an Immaculate Conception, was the earthly embodiment of the feminine side of God, just as Jesus was the earthly embodiment of the Son of God.

Historically, one of the accusations that caused the downfall of the Templers was that they were worshiping a woman. During its formation, the Catholic Church adopted many ancient symbols in order to entice Nazarenes to convert to Catholicism. Giving a woman any status above motherhood was not one of them.

TEMPLARS AND THE MILITARY ORDER of CHRIST (Portugal)

Tomar , also known in English as Thomar, is a city of some 20,000. It was founded as headquarters of the Knights Templar in Portugal, prior to the Vatican's condemnation of the Order in the 12th century. Tomar contains some of the most significant Templar monuments in Europe. Tomar was especially important in the 15th century, when it was a center of Portuguese overseas expansion under Henry the Navigator, the Grand Master of the Order of Christ, and the successor organization to the Templars.

Under the modern city lays the Roman cities of Nabantia and Sellium. After the conquest of the region from the Moors, the land was granted in 1159 AD as a fief to the Order of the Knights Templar. In 1160 AD, its Grand Master in Portugal, Gualdim Pais, laid the first stone of the Castle and Monastery which would become the Headquarters of the Templar Order in Portugal. The feudal contract was granted in 1162 AD by the Grand Master to the people. The Templars ruled a vast region of central Portugal from Tomar, which they pledged to defend from Moorish attacks and raids. Like many lords of the unpopulated former frontier region of central Portugal, the villagers were given relatively liberal conditions in comparison with those of the northern regions of Portugal, in order to attract new immigrants. Those inhabitants who could sustain a horse were obliged to pay military service in return for privileges. They were not allowed the title of Knight, which was reserved for the monks. Women were also admitted to the Order, although they didn't go to battle. In 1190 AD, the town was besieged by the Muslim Almohad King Yakub of Morocco, but the Knights successfully defended it.

During the banishment of the Knights Templar from Europe (c1312 AD), the Pope decreed that all the property of the Templars be placed under the control of organizations subservient to the Church. King Denis of Portugal, himself associated with the Templars, argued that the Order's assets should stay in any given State, instead of being taken by the Church. King Denis re-instituted the Templars of Tomar as the "Order of Christ', largely to enlist their aid during the Reconquista (Removal of the Muslims from Iberia) and in the reconstruction of Portugal after the wars. King Denis was successful in negotiating with Pope Clement's successor, John XXII, for the new order's recognition and right to inherit the Templar assets and property.

There are only two Templar churches remaining which represent the classic style of the Templar church. The following two photographs are presented to show the similarities of the Rosslyn Chapel in Edinburgh Scotland, and the

Tomar Convent. The similarities are undeniable. It is evident that they were constructed by the same group of people.

Knights Templar's Convent of Christ - Tomar, Portugal (c1250 AD)

Knights Templar's Rosslyn Chapel - Edinburg, Scotland (c1450 AD)

The Military Order of Christ (*Ordem Militar de Cristo*), previously the Royal Order of the Knights of Our Lord Jesus Christ (*Real Ordem dos Cavaleiros de Nosso Senhor Jesus Cristo*), was the heritage of the Knights Templar in Portugal. After the suppression of the Templars in 1312 AD, the "Order of Christ" was founded in 1319 AD. The first, and successive, Grand Masters have been the King or President of Portugal. In 1319 AD, this new Order moved south to Castro Marim, but in 1356 AD, it returned to Tomar. In the 15th century, the position of Grand Master of the Order was henceforth nominated by the Pope, and the Grand Master was bestowed upon the King of Portugal, instead of being elected by the monks.

Henry the Navigator was made the Governor of the Order, and it is believed that he used the resources, and knowledge of the Order, to succeed in his enterprises in Africa and in the Atlantic. The cross of the Order of Christ was painted in the sails of the caravels that crossed the seas to the new lands. These ships were under the authority of the Tomar clerics until 1514 AD. Henry, enriched by his overseas enterprises, was the first ruler to upgrade the buildings of the Convento de Cristo since its construction by Gualdim Pais. He also ordered dams to be built to control the river Nabo, and swamps to be drained. This allowed the burgeoning town to attract more settlers. Henry ordered the new streets to be designed in a rational, geometrical fashion, as they can still be seen today.

Important people associated with the Order of Christ.

Vasco da Gama	Gaspar Corte-Real
Pedro Alvares Cabral	Martim Afonso de Sousa
Henry the Navigator	Joao de Castro
Gonçalo Velho Cabral	Ferdinand Magellan
Francisco de Almeida	Cristavao da Gama
Miguel Corte-Real	All the Kings of Portugal and Emperors of Brazil

History

Portugal saw great riches and importance within the Age of Discoveries. The Portuguese Order became the focal point for the descendants of the original Knights Templar Order. The Knights Templar, and their descendants, assisted the Portuguese to rid the Iberian Peninsula of the Moors. The Templars assistance originated from their new locations around the western hemisphere. It was the Templars service to Portugal which prompted the ceding of the North American Territory, previously explored and claimed by the Portuguese, to the Templars. That land grant would later evolve into the USA.

In 1789 AD, Queen Maria I of Portugal secularized the Portuguese Order. In 1910 AD, with the end of the Portuguese monarchy, the order was eliminated. However, in 1917 AD, the order was revived and the Grand-Master of the Order was again the President of Portugal. The Military Order of Christ, together with the Military Orders of Aviz and of St. James of the Sword, formed the group of the "Ancient Military Orders", governed by a Chancellor and a Council of eight members, appointed by the President of the Republic. The Order, despite its name, can be conferred on civilians and on military personnel, whether Portuguese or foreign.

Emblem of the "Order of Christ"

THE RECONQUISTA

Historians date the Reconquista as beginning at the Battle of Covadonga in 722 AD. This is right after the Celtic Farums left Galicia for Denmark, ahead of the Moor's invasion of the Iberian Peninsula. The campaign was completed when the last remaining Islamic state in Iberia, the Emirate of Granada, was defeated in 1492 AD. With the fall of the Granadian emirate, the entire Iberian Peninsula had been returned to Christian rule. Because of its great duration, the Reconquista has a complex history. Christian and Muslim rulers commonly became divided among themselves and fought. Alliances across faith lines were not unusual. The fighting along the Christian and Muslim frontier was punctuated by periods of prolonged peace and truces. Blurring matters even further were the mercenaries from both sides who simply fought for whoever paid the most.

In the Celtic hierarchy there are three classes; The Royal Class, the Elite Warrior class, and the Freemen. During the period of the Templars, the Sinclairs of Scotland were the head of the Royal class and the Farums of Denmark were heads of the Warrior class. Since they were both responsible for the inception and training of the Templars, it is logical to assume that the Templars, soon to call themselves the Masons, came with them to Scotland and then "La Merica", as the Templars called the North American Territory.

Shortly thereafter, we find the Templars supporting Portugal in their battle against the Moors. It would make sense that a group of Celts (The Galicians, now the Templars), which were run out of Iberia c700 AD by the Muslims, and then run out of Europe in 1312 AD by the Catholic Church, would return to liberate their allies, the Portuguese, and their countrymen the Galicians, from the Muslims.

Expansion into the Crusades and military orders

In the High Middle Ages, the fight against the Moors in the Iberian Peninsula became linked to the fight of the whole of Christendom. The Reconquista was originally a war of conquest. It only later underwent a significant shift in meaning toward a religiously justified war of liberation (see the Augustinian concept of a "Just War"). The papacy and the influential Abbey of Cluny in Burgundy not only justified the acts of war, but actively encouraged Christian knights to seek armed confrontation with Moorish "infidels" instead of with each other. From the 11th century onwards, indulgences were granted: In 1064 AD, Pope Alexander II allegedly promised the participants of an expedition against Barbastro (Tagr al-Andalus, Aragon) a collective indulgence, 30 years before Pope Urban II called the First Crusade. (An indulgence is the forgiveness of sin in return for some spiritual action.) The legitimacy of such a letter, establishing a grant of indulgence, has been disputed at length by historians, notably by Ferreiro.

Papal interests in Christian-Muslim relations in the Iberian Peninsula were not without precedent - Popes Leo IV (847-855 AD), John VIII (872-882 AD) and John XIX (1024–33 AD) are all known to have displayed substantial interest in the region. The papacy left no doubt about the heavenly reward for knights fighting for Christ (Militia Christi). In a letter, Pope Urban II tried to persuade the Reconquistadores fighting at Tarragona to stay in the Iberian Peninsula, and not to join the armed pilgrimage to conquer Jerusalem, saying their contribution for Christianity was equally important. The pope promised them the same rewarding indulgence that awaited the first crusaders.

Later military orders like the Order of Santiago, Montesa, and Order of Calatrava were founded or called to fight in Iberia. The Pope called the various orders of knighthood, in Europe, to the Crusades in the peninsula. After the so called Disaster of Alarcos, French, Navarrese, Castilian, Portuguese and Aragonese armies united against the Muslim forces in the massive battle of Las Navas de Tolosa (1212). The big territories awarded to military orders and nobles were the origin of the Latifundia in today's Andalusia and Extremadura in Spain, and Alentejo, in Portugal.

Many are not familiar with the Templars participation in the Iberian war against the Muslims. Most people believe, that the Templar Order ceased to exist upon the death of its last acknowledged Master in 1313 AD. The assistance provided to Portugal and Spain by the remaining Templars, during their battles to rid Iberia of Muslims, is the basis for the Portuguese land grant in 1362 AD that would later become the United States of America.

FROM TEMPLARS to MASONS

The trial of the Templars ended with the termination of the Order, however, although the order "officially" ceased to exist, it did not actually disappear. During their sudden arrest in 1307 AD, some Templars escaped. According to a thesis based on various historical documents, a significant number of them took refuge in the only kingdom in Europe that did not recognize the authority of the Catholic Church in the fourteenth century, Scotland. There, they reorganized under the protection of the Scottish King, Robert the Bruce. Sometime later, they found a convenient method of disguise by which to continue their clandestine existence. They infiltrated the most important guild in the medieval British Isles; **"The Wall Builders' Lodge"**, and eventually, fully seized control of those lodges.

Later the "Wall-Builders' Lodge" changed its name, calling itself the "Masonic Lodge." This name satisfied both the Wall-Builders and the Church builders. The "Scottish Rite Lodge" is the oldest branch of Masonry, and dates back to the 15th century. The names given today to the highest degrees in the

263

Scottish Rites are titles attributed centuries earlier to the Order of the Knights Templar. These are still employed to this day. In short, the Templars did not disappear, but their philosophy, beliefs and rituals still persist in the form of Freemasonry. These facts are supported in a thesis by Haran Yahya which is supported by much historical evidence, and is accepted today by a large number of western historians. (*"The New Masonic Order"* - by Harun Yahya)

The thesis that traces the roots of Masonry to the Templars is often referred to in magazines published by Masons for its own members. Freemasons are very accepting of the idea. One such magazine is called Mimar Sinan (A publication by Turkish Freemasons.), which describes the relationship between the Order of the Templars and Freemasonry in these words:

"In 1312, when the French king, under pressure from the Church, closed the Order of Templars and gave their possessions to the Knights of St. John in Jerusalem, the activities of the Templars did not cease. The great majority of the Templars took refuge in lodges that were operating in Europe at that time. The leader of the Templars, Mabeignac, with a few other members, found refuge in Scotland under the guise of a wall builder under the name of Mac Benach. The Scottish King, Robert the Bruce, welcomed them and allowed them to exercise great influence over the Wall Builder's lodges in Scotland. As a result, Scottish lodges gained great importance from the point of view of their craft and their ideas.

Today, Freemasons use the name Mac Benach with respect. Scottish Masons, who inherited the Templars' rituals, returned to France many years later and established there the basis of the rite known as the "Scottish Rite." It is clear that the roots of Freemasonry stretch back to the Order of Templars and before. Masons themselves do not deny this." ("Global Freemasonry" - Harun Yahya)

Ancient Crosses

Crosses have been used by civilizations for millennia, to represent different icons at different times, by a diverse number of people. Sometimes these crosses tell a history, and can be an important part of any research on a civilization or group of people. No other cross has been more misunderstood and misrepresented than the cross used by the Knights Templar, their predecessors and descendants. The first appearance of a cross signifying the "Soldiers of God" appeared on the walls of secret religious meeting places of Roman Soldiers, prior to the advent of the Roman Catholic Church. The infiltration of the armies of Constantine, by people of the Celtic persuasion, not only provided for valuable intelligence gathering, but also begin to have a religious effect on the non-Christian soldiers. It was inevitable, that some Roman Soldiers would convert to the teachings of Jesus. The following is a depiction of an early military cross, which was found inscribed on the wall of an underground church, used by Roman Soldiers for worship. The meeting place was dated to c200 AD, and was located near a Roman encampment near the city of Jericho, in what is now Palestine.

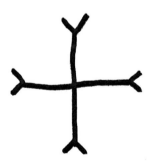

Cross found carved on the wall of an underground church used by Roman soldiers c200 AD, near Jerico.

Look at the cross closely. Notice the forks at the ends of the cross. These were evidently placed there to differentiate the Soldiers cross from a typical round Celtic cross. By placing the forks on the cross, the soldiers are claiming their own secret Greek Orthodox cross, by simulating a square surrounding the cross, rather than a circle, as in the Celtic Cross.

The cross inside a square can be seen decorating the floors in the Clairvaux Monastery. The Clairvaux Monastery was built by Bernard de Clairvaux, a monk and one of the founders of the Knights Templar. The symbol of a cross within a square later became the spiritual sign of the Orthodox Christians of the Byzantine Empire, in whose religious and political affairs the Farams were deeply involved.

The cross which the Templars wore on their robes was a stylized cross with the ends flared and squared. This was a secret symbol of their allegiance to Christian Orthodoxy, whose Byzantine symbol was the cross within a square.

The red color of the cross that the Templars wore on their robes was a symbol of martyrdom. To die in combat was considered a great honor that assured a place in heaven. There was a cardinal rule that the warriors of the Order should never surrender unless the Templar flag had fallen, and even then they were first to try to regroup with another of the Christian orders, such as that of the Hospitallers. Only after all flags had fallen were they allowed to leave the battlefield. This uncompromising principle, along with their reputation for courage, excellent training, and heavy armament, made the Templars one of the most feared combat forces in medieval times.

You may have already guessed, that the Templars were but a small part of the history of a dynamic and resilient group, called the Celts. As you discovered, in the previous text of this chapter, the Templars did not simply disappear after their ouster from mainland Europe. The Templars were simply one link in a chain of organizations which have carried the secrets of the ancient past, down through time, to the present day.

It is a well-known fact that George Washington, the first president of the USA was a Mason. What is not widely known, is that down through time preceding organizations have known about the Americas and have profited from their solitary knowledge of this information. The Celts did not suddenly appear in North America after 1492, they were here long before that, in the form of all the secret organizations that had preceded them. Although these facts have been widely known by major world governments, the majority of people have been kept in the dark about our past history and the pre-Columbian colonization of the Americas. With the advent of computers and satellites, which can detect these ancient survey markers, this is no longer a secret. Ancient mariners left us evidence of their conquests and travels during the past millennia. Until now, those ancient signposts were known only to the people who placed them. They are just now being discovered through the use of modern technology.

THE FARAM CREST IN ROSSLYN CHAPEL

As mentioned earlier, the crest of the Farum Family originated in the town of Farum, Denmark. The crest is a combination of the Celtic cross and the Byzantine Cross, both spiritual symbols of the same belief system. The marriage of these two symbols stems from; the Celtic cross being the symbol of the Galician Farums, and the Byzantine Cross being the symbol of the Italian Farums. There are only three places that this ancient crest is known to exist. One is in the Town of Farum, Denmark, another adorns the main window of Rosslyn Chapel in Edinburg, Scotland, and a third, whose location will not be divulged, is in the United States. Rosslyn Chapel was built as a monument to the Knights Templar, after the original Templars were replaced by the Masons.

The Faram Topiary Crest in the City of Farum, Denmark

The Main Window of Rosslyn Chapel, Edinburgh, Scotland.
(Notice the Faram Crest at the top of the window)

It is documented, in Edinburgh, Scotland, that a Robert Faram was serving on the City Council in Edinburgh Scotland, while Rosslyn Chapel was being constructed. This the first known recording of the family name of Faram. The changing of the Danish spelling of Farum to Faram, upon the Farums move to Scotland, will be explained in a later chapter. Rosslyn Chapel is only one of at least five churches that, over the centuries, the Faram family are known to have built.

As you see, the Templars did not simply fade away after their disappearance from Europe. Their followers changed the name to the "Freemasons" and were instrumental in the founding of the United States of America. In addition to all the other information available in historical records, all that is necessary to confirm that the Masons played a substantial role in the forming of the United States, is to view the life size painting of our first president, George Washington, proudly adorned in his Masonic regalia.

President George Washington in his Masonic Regalia

END CHAPTER

Chapter 8

The Sinclairs of Scotland

THE FARAM/SINCLAIR RELATIONSHIP

The Farams' initial move to Scotland was only temporary. Their true intention was to assist the Templars and the Sinclairs in settling the newly acquired territory of North America. For over two hundred years, the Sinclair and Faram families had worked together in supporting the Templar organization. The fact that they mysteriously disappeared from Europe at the same time, and have left us evidence of their time in North America, infers that it is likely that the Faram ships were part of the transportation used to get the Sinclair party to Baltimore, Maryland USA.

After depositing Sir Henry Sinclair in Baltimore, there is evidence that the Farams traveled to the Saint Lawrence Seaway. From their actions it appears that the timing of the movement of the Sinclairs, the Farams and the Templars to North America was not by chance but was the result of the Norse beginning to colonize parts of the Templars North American Territory. In previous chapters you read that in 1332 AD, the Templars had been ceded the land east of the Mississippi River; and in 1362 AD, they were deeded the land from the Atlantic to the Pacific. As the result of a freeze in Iceland and Greenland, the Norse began moving south during the apocalyptic climatic conditions of the 14th century. In order to counter the colonization of the North American

Territory, the Sinclairs, Farams and their Danish military force moved their organization to North America in 1398 AD.

SINCLAIRS PREPARATION FOR HIS TRIP TO AMERICA

There exists a map, called the Zeno Map, which is a map of the North Atlantic, dating from the 15th century. The map was first made known in Venice in 1558 AD by Nicolo Zeno, a descendant of the Zeno brothers. The younger Zeno published the map, along with a series of letters, claiming he had discovered them in a storeroom in his family's home in Venice. According to Zeno, the map and letters date from around the year 1400 AD, and purportedly describe a long voyage made by the Zeno brothers in the 1390s under the direction of a prince named Zichmni (Sinclair). The voyage supposedly traversed the North Atlantic, and reached North America.

The Zeno documents reveal that in 1393 AD, five years before Sinclair's departure, *"the Prince of the Orkney Islands"* sent a Venetian admiral, Nicolo Zeno, to carry out a survey of Greenland.

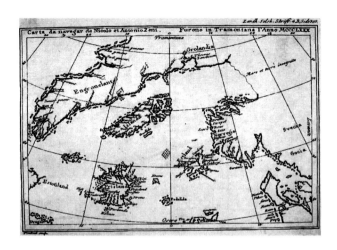

The Zeno Map (c1394 AD)

Many historians regard the map and accompanying narrative as a hoax. They claim that the younger Zeno made a retroactive claim for Venice to have discovered the New World before Christopher Columbus.

The argument against the authenticity of the map is based largely on the appearance of many supposedly "non-existent" islands in the North Atlantic, and off the coast of Iceland. One of these non-existent islands was *Frisland*, where the Zeno brothers allegedly spent some time.

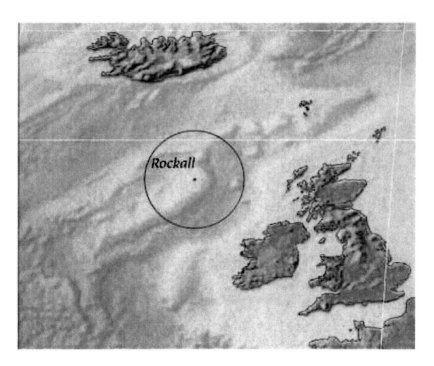

Frisland, the Uninhabitable Outcropping Now Called Rockall

Rockall Island can barely be called an Island since it is so small; however, on a 1579 AD Scandinavian map, the island appears and is named *Frisland*. Although uninhabitable, this reef would have been the perfect spot for Zeno to drop anchor and delay his return to Scotland. If Zeno's private mission were to see if the Norse had left Greenland, but his public mission were to map Greenland, he would have had to delay his return to Scotland or his true mission would have fallen under suspicion. Although the island is uninhabitable it would be a good place to fish and collect birds for food.

The Zeno map is a hoax in the sense that it maps the entire Atlantic, and does not come close to mapping Greenland. It does, however, show the extent of exploration prior to 1400 AD by the fact that Antarctica is displayed at the bottom of the map.

Based on the surrounding events, it is clear that Zeno was not sent on his voyage to map Greenland. This was not necessary, because the Celts already had maps of the entire world. One of the reasons that the Zeno map is so contentious is that it has nothing to do with mapping Greenland, but was presented simply to validate his voyage.

The real reason Zeno was sent to Greenland, by Henry Sinclair, was to assess the number of Greenlanders (Norse) that were still on the Island. The number of persons remaining on the island must have been small, or non-existent. This is what prompted Henry to gather all his troops and plan his voyage to North America. European colonization along the Mississippi River would have blocked Sinclair's, and the Celts, plans to establish a country from the Atlantic to the Pacific.

Zeno's mission was to see if Sinclair's journey to the New World was necessary. Before embarking on this endeavor, Sinclair made provisions for transferring some of his lands to his brothers and eldest daughter. He then took to the sea with 12 vessels, with Zeno navigating, and 200-300 fellow voyagers, made up of monks and Templars. According to the Zeno Narratives, Sinclair set foot on American soil on June 2, 1398.

Eminent historians have corroborated Sinclair's 1398 voyage from Zeno's ship's log, called "Zeno's Narrative", which documented the exploration of Nova Scotia during the next year. There is evidence that they erected a small castle in New Ross, near Oak Island. There currently exists a 14th century cannon in Louisburg Harbor that dates back to Henry's time. In addition, a stone wall near Halifax also dates back to the 14th century and has a distinctly

Scottish design to it; however, it is Henrys home and geoglyphs in Baltimore, Maryland USA that put the icing on the cake. (See Chapter 12)

A Celtic Petroglyph

Later, Zeno returned to Orkney while Sinclair continued along the North American coastline. According to the narrative, one evening, upon seeing smoke, the explorers traveled inland for a better view. Along the way, Sir James Gunn, lifelong friend to Sinclair, died. In honor of his memory, they carved his effigy on a horizontal stone ledge in Westford, MA which depicts the helmet of a medieval knight, a shield bearing the coat of arms of the Gunn family, a sword with a break in the blade (indicating the death of a knight), a falcon, and a rosette, which served as a lance rest. The carving is comprised of various sized holes punched into the stone by a sharp tool, driven by a mallet. Archaeologists have confirmed that the holes were punched into the rock 600 years ago and the effigy contains elements known only by northern Europeans. Located in the basement of the library in Westford, MA is a flat oval-shaped stone, measuring about 2 feet in diameter. Carved into its surface is the image of a 14th century ship, an arrow, and the numbers 184, possibly indicating the calendar number of the day of Gunn's death. A construction crew discovered the boat stone when a road was being built; the stone was subsequently moved to someone's garage, until it was donated to the library. Archaeological evidence indicates these images were probably carved at the same time as the Westford Knight carving, most probably by the same voyagers.

Certainly, the number of Norse and Gaelic words in the languages of the Algonquin tribes indicates that trade had been taking place between Europe and the Americas, before the time of Columbus. Micmac Indians of the 14th century (The same period as the Nordic migration from Greenland.) tell legends of a blond haired, blue eyed god who they called "Glooscap," whose friendly manner won the hearts of the natives. He treated them fairly and taught them to fish with nets. Indeed, fishing was a natural pastime for the Greenlanders.

According to a Micmac Legend, "Glooscap" claimed himself an island, planted trees on it, and sailed away in his stone canoe. They also spoke of the men who built the Newport Tower as "fire-haired men with green eyes." (Scotts ?) Prince Henry Sinclair's historic voyage of 1398 AD is indelibly hewn in stone at the Rosslyn Chapel in Scotland. Included in the interior decorations are stone carvings of Indian maize and American aloe cacti. These were carved c1460, before the voyage of Columbus, and were plants native only to the Americas.

THE BUILDING of ROSSLYN CHAPEL

Rosslyn Chapel, properly named the Collegiate Chapel of St Matthew, was founded on a small hill above Roslyn Glen, as an (Orthodox) Catholic collegiate church. The chapel was founded by William Sinclair, 1st Earl of Caithness (also spelled "Sainteclaire/Saintclair/Sinclair/St. Clair"), who was the grandson of Henry Sinclair. The Sinclair family was a noble family descended from Norman Knights of France. The purpose of the college was to celebrate the Divine Office, and also to celebrate Holy Mass for all the faithful departed, including the deceased members of the Sinclair family.

Knights Templar's Rosslyn Chapel - Edinburg, Scotland (c1480 AD)

Built to honor the Knights Templar, you will notice that the structure required a large amount of concrete. At the time of the chapel's construction, the Farums were operating two Gypsum mines, one in Sweden and one in Denmark. Gypsum is a key ingredient in concrete. In 1488 it is recorded, in the official archives of Edinburgh, that Robert Faram was an official in the city government. Who better to build a lasting monument to the Templars than the Family which had led them for hundreds of years? Notice the new spelling of the name Faram. This is the first record of this spelling in any document found to date. This most likely was done to differentiate this branch of Orthodox Christians Farams from their Latin Catholic relatives, the Farums, still in Denmark and Germany. (A more in depth explanation of the name change will be covered later.)

Around this same time, Scotland was able to obtain preferential treatment for passage of their ships, from the Hansiatic League in the Baltic Sea. This treatment was sought after by other nations, but was not extended to any other country but Scotland. This suggests that Scotland received preferential treatment from the "Hanse". The only possibility of an accord occurring with Scotland would be if someone known to the Hanse, a Faram, were in Scotland negotiating the agreement.

The fact that the Robert Faram had already been to North America would explain why the plants native to America were incorporated into the designs of Rosslyn Chapel. The original plans for Rosslyn have never been found or recorded. This is an indication that the architect may have come to Edinburgh, Scotland to build the Chapel and departed with the plans. Its architecture is considered to be some of the finest in Scotland.

Author Henning Klovekorn has stated that one of the interior pillars of Rosslyn Chapel is representative of one of the roots of the Nordic Yggdrasil tree, prominent in Germanic and Viking Mythology. He is of the opinion that the dragons at the base of the pillar are feeding at the base of the tree on the Yggdrasil root. The top of the pillar is carved tree foliage. Klovekorn argues that a Nordic association is plausible, considering the many auxiliary references in the chapel to Celtic and Nordic mythology. This mix of Celtic and Nordic icons may have stemmed from the Faram's intimate past with the Norsemen. In addition, there are carvings of what authors Robert Lomas and Christopher Knight believe are ears of New World corn, or maize, depicted in the chapel. This crop was unknown in Europe at the time of the Chapel's construction, and was not cultivated there until several hundred years later. Knight and Lomas view these carvings as evidence supporting the idea that Henry Sinclair I, Earl of Orkney, travelled to the Americas well before Columbus. This would tend to indicate that a relative of someone, that accompanied Sinclair to America, returned to construct the Chapel.

The pinnacles on the rooftop have been a subject of interest during renovation work in 2010 AD. Nesting birds had made the pinnacles unstable and as such had to be dismantled brick by brick revealing the existence of a chamber specifically made by the stone masons to harbor bees. The beehive is a Celtic symbol of working together in harmony.

END CHAPTER

Chapter 9

The Portuguese Explorers

PORTUGUESE DISCOVERYS

While researching Portuguese history, I learned that mainstream scholars, for the most part, avoid the subject of world nautical history for any period prior to 1419 AD. This is the year that Henry the Navigator began his Portuguese school of navigation at Sagres Portugal. Henry the Navigator was from royal Portuguese blood and had great influence on the affairs of State in Portugal. It is no accident that his name should be associated with such an important institution of learning. Portugal had been the leading producer of Navigators for ships of exploration for centuries, prior to Henry the Navigator.

In order to fully understand the contributions of the Portuguese navigators, down through time, it will be necessary to clear your mind of all preconceived notions, and all ill-conceived text, that has presented the idea that man did not have the intelligence to sail the seven seas prior to the "miraculous" voyage of Christopher Columbus in 1492. Even casual investigation will expose evidence of man's domination of the oceans of the world since ancient times. Anyone that would say otherwise has not done their homework.

The land within the borders of today's Portuguese Republic has been continuously settled since prehistoric times. The history of the City of Lisbon, Portugal can be traced back thousands of years. However, the Celtic cultures began there after their long migration across Europe to the Iberian Peninsula. After occupying almost the entire continent of Europe, during their initial migrations, Northern Portugal and Galicia became Celtic strongholds after being pushed to Western Europe by warring cultures. Northern Portugal and Galicia were where the largest Celtic cultures were located. These Celts, which came to be known as "Lusitanians," had a culture similar to the groups already in Iberia (Spain). This allowed them to settle in Western Iberia in peace and cooperation. The Celts created groups that were named "Celtiberians".

While retaining their Celtic identities, Portugal and Galicia were integrated into the Roman Republic (Later called the Roman Empire). The two countries cultivated a close association with Germanic peoples such as the Suebi and the Visigoths. This was demonstrated in the 5th Century when the four cultures banded together to conquer Italy.

The Portuguese were not the first world navigators. They were, however, in possession of much of the knowledge handed down from their predecessors, and were therefore the most knowledgeable mariners of their time. The fact that they had experience in sailing the world's oceans, and had a vested interest in keeping it secret, was appealing to others who knew of the existence of the New World. This secret was a large asset for groups, including the Celts, who were accessing the new world for lumber, minerals and other resources.

The Egyptians were visiting the Americas long before the Portuguese. As the Eastern plains of South America are now being cleared for farming, it is becoming clear that the area was once inhabited by hundreds of thousands of citizens who created geoglyphs similar to the Egyptian and Mayan geoglyphs. A close examination of the Pyramids of Egypt, Mexico, and China, shows that they all exhibit identical geoglyphic characteristics tying them all together. It is not inconceivable that the area, that is now Brazil, was an inexhaustible source of manpower for the building of the Egyptian and Mayan pyramids.

During the Reconquista, of the 15th Century, Portugal established itself as an independent kingdom from León, claiming to be the oldest European nation-state. The oldest international boundary in Europe is the boundary between Portugal and the ancient country of Galicia. Galicia lies to the North of Portugal, and is the earliest known origin of my familial ancestors. Galicia is now part of Spain, but retains its ancient borders in the form of a Spanish province. Portugal, who had up to this time repulsed Spain's attempts to conquer them, suddenly created an alliance with Spain in the 15th Century and together, with the help of the Templars, expelled the Moors, their mutual 8th century conquerors.

The last battle that the combined army of Portuguese, Spanish and Templars fought, against the Muslims, was in 1492. It is no coincidence that this is the same year that Columbus made his famous voyage to the Americas. This was simply the first opportunity for Spain and the Vatican to use the information that Portugal had provided to them about the New World. After Portugal's ceding of the North American Territory to the Templars, it was imperative to establish Spain's claim to the Caribbean and Mesoamerica, and re-establish Portugal's claim to Eastern South America. The fact that Henry the Navigator was now training navigators, along with the pending revelation of the existence of North America, required quick action by Spain to secure their position in the Americas.

The Age of Discovery

Prior to Portugal's alliance with Spain, the Spaniards had tried many times to take over Portugal. There were several invasion attempts, ending with a Portuguese victory in the Battle of Aljubarrota in 1385 AD. This victory saw

Portugal's colonial expansion in Africa and the voyages of discovery responsible for Portugal's rise as the leading maritime and colonial power in Western Europe. During this time period, Lisbon developed into a major commercial city. In 1415 AD the trading post of Ceuta in Morocco was captured by Portugal. In 1419 AD, King Joao's son, Prince Henry the Navigator began promoting voyages of discovery by opening his "School of Navigation" in Sagres, Portugal. As a result, the Portuguese were the first Europeans to publicly open the way into the Atlantic by training future explorers in navigation. And why not, they had already colonized the East Coast of South America.

On 25 May 1420, Henry the Navigator gained appointment as the governor of the very rich Order of Christ, the Portuguese successor to the Knights Templar, which had its headquarters at Tomar, Portugal. The organization of the Knights Templar was a wealthy, Celtic, European organization that was disbanded by authority of the Vatican c1319 AD. Much of the wealth from the Templers was transported to Portugal to establish the Order of Christ. Many of the Templers that survived the 1307 massacre made their way to Scotland, Denmark, and Portugal.

Henry the Navigator would hold his position as Governor of the "Order of Christ" for the remainder of his life. The Order was an important source of funds for Henry's ambitious plans, especially his persistent attempts to conquer the Canary Islands. Henry also had other resources. When the 10th King of Portugal John I died, Henry's eldest brother, Edward became head of the castles council, and granted Henry all profits from trading within the areas he discovered. He also held various valuable monopolies on resources in the Algarve. When Edward died eight years later, Henry supported his brother Peter for the regency during Alfonso V's minority, and in return received a confirmation of this levy. Henry also promoted the colonization of the Azores during Peter's regency (1439–1448 AD). The Portuguese Navigator's school spelled the end of the secret colonization, and lack of competition, in the plundering of the New World resources by the Celts and others.

The Faram Foundation has discovered clear evidence (See Chapter 13) that Columbus was on a mission to claim the Caribbean and Mesoamerica for Spain and the Vatican, not to discover the Americas. Within a year after the return of Columbus to Spain, based on some self appointed political right, the Vatican ceded all the Islands West of the Canary Islands to Spain. The fact that the term Islands was used, referring to the Islands of the Caribbean and the Gulf of Mexico, reveals the fact that the Vatican knew of the previous occupation of North America by the Templars and South America by Portugal. One of the many interesting facts confirming the true mission of Columbus is that on his first voyage Columbus landed on San Salvador Island, which is just a few miles from Cat Island, the SE corner of the previously established Templar North American land claim. In addition, during the voyages of Columbus, Spain's attention was directed to the Caribbean, another indication that North and South America was already known to be colonized. Thanks to worldwide trade, and their head start on the colonization of Brazil, Portugal enjoyed an upsurge of prosperity, making it the wealthiest country in Europe.

The following is a Portuguese map depicting the voyage of Portuguese explorer Cabral, showing his purported discovery of South America in 1500. This looks more like a visitation than an exploration. What do you think?

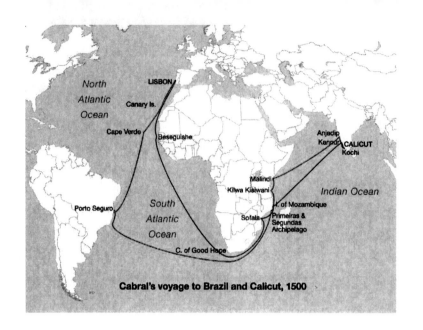

Cabral's voyage to Brazil and Calicut, 1500

A 1519 AD Portuguese Map of Brazil

The preceding map is a 1519 map of South America. According to mainstream historians, the intelligent person of today is expected to believe that; in just the 18 years from the time Cabral was supposed to have been the first person to step foot on South American soil, the entire coast of South America was explored, colonized, cities named and the entire continent mapped. It is clear that South America was colonized long before this. Notice the Templar Cross on the sails of the ships.

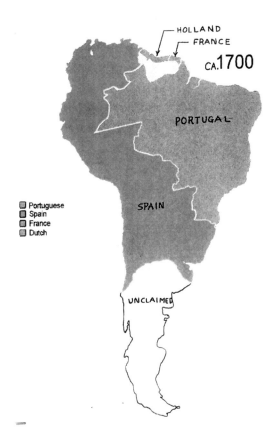

Spanish/Portuguese Split of South America

In the 16th and 17th centuries, Portugal ascended to the status of a world power during Europe's "Age of Discovery". Portugal built up a vast empire, including possessions in South America, Africa, Asia and the near East. And why not, Portugal already had settlements in all those places from centuries of earlier exploration. In the next two centuries, Portugal gradually lost much of its wealth and status as the Dutch, English and French took an increasing share of the spice and slave trades (the economic basis of its empire), by surrounding or conquering the widely-scattered Portuguese trading posts and territories. This left Portugal with ever fewer resources to defend its overseas interests.

THE FIRST PORTUGUESE NAVIGATORS MONUMENT

The following three photos are an example of the lengths to which Masons went to destroy any signs that the Celts and Portuguese were in any way associated with North America. Whether the following Newport land formation was natural or man made is not known. It was most likely a combination of both. The monument was configured into the typical two circle geoglyphic configuration which, when a line was drawn through the center of the two circles it pointed to the Portuguese capital of Lisbon. What gave the cover-up away was the fact that, the explorer, John Cabot's navigator made a map of Newport during his visit in 1497AD. That map, dated 1508, is depicted below.

(**Author's note**: You may find it interesting that there are few, if any, important nautical maps dated before 1500. After many years of deception, it would have been difficult to explain maps that existed before that date. However, it is not difficult to find information on post 1500 AD maps that would have taken hundreds of years to discover.)

Map of Newport, RI USA, from John Cabot's 1497 Expedition,
Published by Cabot's Navigator in 1508.

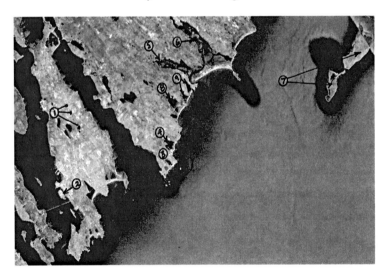

Current Day Landmarks in Newport, RI USA, Matching the Cabot Map
The land missing from Cabot's map, over the bay, is added in ink. The numbers
indicate points matching Cabot's map.

The Newport, RI Geoglyph Pointing to Lisbon, the Capitol of Portugal.

The Original Purpose of this Newport geoglyph, depicted on the map, was to mark the Portuguese claim in the Americas. The early Masons took extreme measures to destroy this Portuguese monument, after they obtained control of the North American Territory. This practice of destruction continues to this day, as more geoglyphs are published. Is this to cover up the true history of the Celts and Templars role in America?

THE SECOND PORTUGUESE NAVAGATORS MONUMENT IN NEWPORT, RHODE ISLAND USA

In order to understand the importance of Newport, RI USA, to the ancients, the following photo is presented. Newport, RI USA has been a special place from before the time of the Egyptians. Below is a photo showing all the many places that depict Newport in their geoglyphs. Included are the locations and the date the geoglyphs were constructed. There are many more that are not listed.

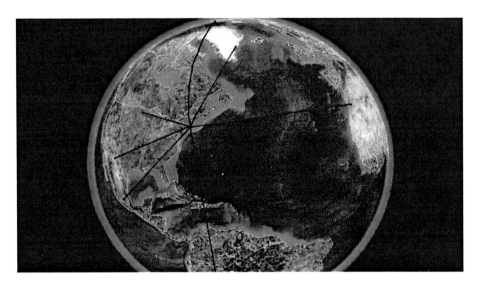

Locations of the pointers to Newport, RI, displayed in the above photo, are listed below. Included are the approximate dates the geoglyphs were created.

Gulfo de Cintra Geoglyphs, Sahara West Africa - c7000BC
Inspiration Peak, Minnesota USA - c7000BC - 3100BC
Cahuachi, Nazca Peru - c5AD
Pyramids of China - c100BC - 400AD
The Tiniteqilaq Viking Geoglyph, Greenland - c1100AD
River Geoglyph El Paso, Texas USA - c1300AD
Mexico City Geoglyph - c1325AD
"Michoacan", Mexico, Mural Glyph by Diego Rivera - c1925AD

After studying the city of Newport, RI USA, reviewing its history, and becoming familiar with its people, it became obvious that the people of Newport, if not Rhode Island, have a clear understanding of their ancient history but have been reluctant to speak about it, or share it with the outside world. This became evident when our team discovered that in 1988 AD, the City of Newport, RI USA, in cooperation with the Portuguese Government, installed an elaborate memorial to the Portuguese Navigators who had rediscovered and mapped most of the new world.

The Portuguese Monument in Newport, Rhode Island USA is the realization of the efforts of Arthur Raposo. This Portuguese-American was born in Fall River, but lived for many years in Middletown, Rhode Island. In his great desire to pay homage to the Portuguese Navigators, who once called Newport their home away from home, he organized the Miguel Corte Real Committee. Composed of ten Portuguese-American leaders, this committee was created for the purpose of erecting a monument to the Portuguese Navigators somewhere in Newport, RI "The City by the Sea" USA.

With enthusiasm and persistence, he negotiated with Rhode Island officials until he secured the best spot in the State of Rhode Island for the monument, Brenton Point State Park. Mr. Raposo first presented his plan to Attorney Robert M. Silva, president of the Portuguese Cultural Foundation. Together with Portuguese Cultural Foundation Executive Secretary, Peter Calvet de Magalhaes, they obtained the cooperation of the National Committee of the Commemorations of the Discoveries of Portugal. From this agreement, they developed mutual cooperation between Portuguese and American officials, which eventually led to Portugal offering the Portuguese Discovery Monument as a gift to the American people.

Meanwhile, through the joint cooperation of Governor Edward DiPrete, Portuguese-American Legislators, and the Environmental Department of Rhode Island, over $110,000 was allocated to landscape Brenton Point State Park to ready it to receive all the pieces of the Monument. This amount of money was matched by the Portuguese Government, which expended over $110,000 to build and transport the monument to Rhode Island. Adding the cost of the Interpretive Plaque, the total expense for this Monument reached a quarter of a million dollars.

The Portuguese Navigator's Monument – Newport, RI USA

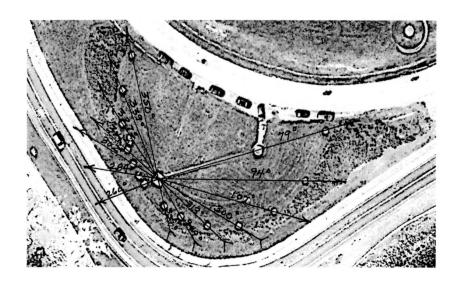

The Radials Generated by the Monument

Information contained on the Interpretive Plaque:

"The monument before you honors the Portuguese navigators of the Golden Age of Maritime Exploration, which spanned from the early 1400's to the late 1500's. era. (No doubt dates of political correctness.) *Portugal was the forerunner in maritime exploration -- both coasts of the United States were discovered and colonized by the Portuguese. "*(Notice they said both coasts.)

Brenton Point was chosen as the site for this monument because it is very reminiscent of Sagres, the point in southern Portugal where Prince Henry founded his School of Navigation in 1419 AD. It was in Segres Portugal that the maritime data, collected over hundreds of years, by the foremost scholars in mathematics, astronomy, cartography and those that were experts in the compass, the astrolabe, water currents and the winds, were taught. Newport is also the closest point in the USA to Segres, Portugal.

There are eighteen elements in the Portuguese Navigators Monument: the sixteen elements placed in a semicircle are an abstraction of the circular compass rose at Sagres, which is all that remains of Prince Henry's School of Navigation today. The elements are placed in a three-quarter sphere, which symbolizes the three-quarters of the world discovered by the Portuguese navigators. As it turns out the Rhode Islanders, unknowingly, got more than they expected from the Portuguese Monument. The monument was not a random display of elements. Unknown to the residents of Newport, each element points to a specific spot in America where Portuguese navigators placed a survey marker (Geoglyph), in the early days of Portuguese exploration of the Americas. Many of these survey markers still exist.

The World Sphere of the Monument

The large multifaceted stone marker was designed to evoke the tradition of explorers leaving behind a marker of their presence. The final element represents an armillary sphere, a navigational instrument which is one of Portugal's most significant and enduring symbols. The sphere was added to the Portuguese flag, in 1522 AD, to commemorate Magellan's circumnavigation of the globe, and is still included on the country's present flag.

The Interpretive Plaque was inaugurated on Sunday, June 8th, 1997, at 2PM, sponsored by The Portuguese American Federation, Inc. and the Division of Parks and Recreation of Rhode Island. The main speakers at this event were: President of the U. N. Committee on the Oceans: Dr. Mário Soares, Former President of Portugal, and the Vice-President of United Nations World Committee on the Oceans: Honorable Congressman Patrick J. Kennedy In attendance at the inauguration of the Interpretative Plaque: Aida Sousa, Executive Secretary of the Federation, Dr. Luciano da Silva and Dr. Mário Soares, President of Portugal.

The words engraved on the tall pillar of the Portuguese Discovery Monument:

"TO THE MEMORY OF THE NAVIGATORS, MAPMAKERS, EXPLORERS, FLEET COMMANDERS AND THOSE OTHERS WHO ENABLED THE DISCOVERY BY THE PORTUGUESE OF TWO-THIRDS OF THE WORLD."

So you see, even though the Portuguese geoglyphs at Newport RI, and other locations, were destroyed in the 16th Century, the Portuguese finally received the recognition they so richly deserved.

TWO IMPORTANT PORTUGUESE GEOGLYPHS IN THE USA

As declared on the Portuguese Navigators Monument in Newport, RI, the Portuguese "...*discovered and colonized both coasts of the United States.*" Anyone who doubts that the Portuguese sailed the globe, long before any other Europeans, only has to experience the following two geoglyphs in order to change their mind. The Portuguese, and their predecessors, marked the entire globe with their survey markers (Geoglyphs) long before most Europeans knew the New World existed. In spherical geometry, there are no parallel lines that can be drawn on a sphere. All lines will cross on the sphere at two points. That being so, calculating where two bearings of the same value, inscribed in geoglyphs located in two different places on the earth will cross, can make quite a statement. This situation can be found in two West Coast geoglyphs, one which can be found at the Northwest corner of the US, in Washington State, and another one located 988 miles South, on the coast of Santa Barbara, California. The Santa Barbara Geoglyph, was pointed out, and discovered, from one of the radials emanating from the geoglyph in the state of Washington.

The Washington geoglyph, in addition to designating the Northwest corner of the US, also pointed to at least seven other places on the globe. One of the places it pointed out is the Point Conception geoglyph in Santa Barbara, California. (See Below) Another place it pointed out is the Southern tip of Portugal. In itself, this is nothing unusual. What is unusual is that the makers of these two geoglyphs have tied them together in a way that shows who made them, and the skill which they possessed. The Washington State geoglyph (Shown below), and others on the same property, have since been plowed under by the land owners.

Both geoglyphs use a 48.5 degree radial, and both intersect and terminate at the Southern tip of Portugal. This ties the explorers, their country, and the two glyphs together for as long as the glyphs exist. This connection may not last much longer because the Santa Barbara geoglyph is already under several feet of water.

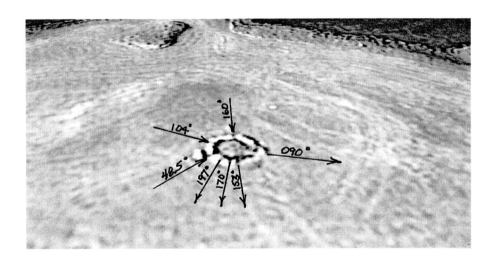

The Portuguese Geoglyph located in Washington State USA

Endpoints for the bearings displayed in the previous photo.

48.5 Degree Radial - So. Tip of Portugal
090 Degree Radial - Point Lookout, Scotland, MD USA - Entrance to the Potomac River, USA
104 Degree Radial - Amelia Island, FL – Also the termination Point of the all important Kensington Runestone and Inspiration Peak 140 Degree Radial
153 Degree Radial - So. Tip of Baja Mexico
160 Degree Radial - Punta Euginia, Baja Mexico
170 Degree Radial - Point Conception, Santa Barbara, California USA.
197 Degree Radial - Leadbetter Point Glyphs, WA USA - Entrance to Willapa Bay

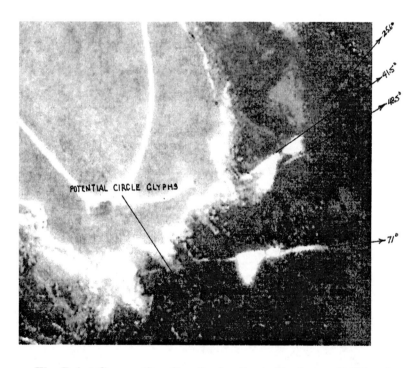

The Point Conception Geoglyph - Santa Barbara, California

Endpoints for the bearings displayed in the previous photo.

25.6 Degree Radial - Southern Tip of Norway.
41.5 Degree Radial - North Shore of Galicia at the Southeast corner of the Celtic Empire, as also pointed out by the 45 degree radials from the Southern tip of Baja, Mexico and the Southern tip of South America.
48.5 Degree Radial - Southern Tip of Portugal. Met by the 48.5 degree radial of the geoglyph in Washington State, USA.
071 Degree Radial - Point Lookout, Scotland, MD USA - Entrance to the Potomac River.

By combining the major Celtic countries of Norway, Galicia and Portugal in one geoglyph, located 14,200 miles by sea from Portugal, and then bringing together the radials of two separate geoglyphs at Lisbon Portugal, the creator of this geoglyph is making a statement to 21st Century man that should echo around the world. The tangible evidence that Columbus was the first European to visit the Americas is minimal, in comparison to the physical proof that others preceded him to the Americas. Thankfully there are free thinking individuals, not bound by historical inaccuracies, who are not afraid to strike out on their own and make important discoveries. One such individual was Frank Calvert, the true discoverer of the *mythical* City of Troy.

PORTUGUESE INFLUENCE IN AMERICA

As will be disclosed in later chapters, there is ample evidence to substantiate that early European explorers had a significant influence on the ancient tribes of North America in Pre-Columbian times. In fact, five tribes of the Mississippian Indian Culture, called the "**Five Civilized Tribes**" by the US Government, were most likely Portuguese or other European immigrants that stayed in North America. The following illustrations are early European and Near East icons that show up in most of the Eastern Indian decorations in America.

Cross used by the Sumerians to signify the planet of their origin c4000BC

Cross used by the Native Americans at Chaco Canyon, NM USA c1000 AD. Notice the similarity to the Sumerian cross.

Eris/Nibiru

Posted: 15:00 October 15, 2007 by Dr. Cristian Negureanu

"Eris/Nibiru was also known under the name of "The Planet of the Cross" because, in its passage between Mars and Jupiter, it crosses most of the orbits of the planets in our solar system."

Zecharia Sitchin, in his book The Twelfth Planet, writes about the way the Sumerians graphically represented Nibiru:

> *"The pictographic sign for this planet was ... a cross. This cuneiform sign also meant Anu. The Leader of the Planet of the Kingdom revealed himself to the Jews under the name of "Yahweh" and "The Divine". This evolved in the Semitic languages to the letter "tav", which meant "the sign". A cylindrical seal discovered in Nippur shows a group of ploughmen astonishingly looking up to the sky at the Twelfth Planet, represented by its symbol the cross, which was visible. Not only were the ancients waiting for the arrival of this planet but they were also observing its orbit. In fact, all the ancients considered the approach of this planet as a sign for great changes and the beginning of a new era".*

> *"Then will appear in heaven the sign "Tav" the Planet of the Cross of the Son of Man, and then all the tribes of the earth will mourn, because of the extreme phenomena caused by the Planet of the Gods and they will see the Son of Man coming on the clouds of heaven. He will send out his angels with a loud trumpet call and they will gather his elect from the four winds"* (Mathew 24: 30 - 31).

Starting with the Sumerians, the cross, the symbol of the Planet of the Gods, was adopted by many of the religions around the world. Therefore, according to the dictionary "*An Expository Dictionary of the New Testament Words*", the cross was also a symbol for the Babylonians from ancient Chaldea.

Details: *The Cross in Tradition, History and Art; Encyclopedia of Religions, Eris - The Planet of the Cross and the Natural Extreme Phenomena* by Dr. Cristian Negureanu. Throughout history, the spiritual cross has consisted of a cross with four legs of equal length. It was not until the Romans killed Jesus, on the Crucifix, that the Crucifix was adopted by the Catholic Church as its spiritual symbol.

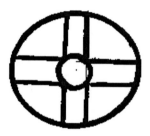

Symbol used by the Caddo Indians of Caddo, Texas. C1000 AD

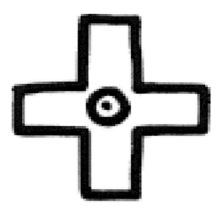

Cross used by Incas in Mesoamerica c1400 AD. Once again we have the cross and the Egyptian symbol for Ra the Sun God.

Crosses and quartered circle used by the Spiro Mounds Indians in Oklahoma c1200AD. In addition, there appear circles with dots, the Egyptian symbol for Ra the sun god.

The Spiritual Spiral. Found in most American Indian, and Celtic Petroglyphs, as well as Petroglyphs around the World.

The spiral is probably the oldest known symbol of human spirituality. The spiral has been in rock carvings thousands of years old, on every continent in the world. The religious significance can only be guessed at, but it has been found on tombs, and almost certainly has a connection with the sun, which traces a spiral shape every three months in its travels. The double spiral found in Neolithic Celtic stone art also follows the path of the sun, describing the movements of the heavenly body over the course of a solar year.

The Celtic Triple Spiral.

Also found in many American Indian petroglyphs.

A triple spiral motif found on Celtic tombs is drawn in one continuous line, suggesting a cycle of rebirth or resurrection. This hypothesis is bolstered by the fact that many of these appear to be deliberately placed where they catch the first rays of the sun on the winter solstice. The sun, dying and rising every day, is a natural symbol of rebirth. These spirals can be found in many North American Indian cultures as well as many locations previously occupied by ancient Celtic Cultures. In modern times, the spiral is still spiritually significant.

END CHAPTER

Chapter 10

The Celts in America

In order to understand the Celt's role in the Americas, it is necessary to remember that the Celtic influence in North America essentially ended with the transition of the Templar Order to the Freemasons.

Until the initiation of the Freemasons, in Scotland c1450 AD, most of the culture, traditions, spirituality and geoglyphs that were in place in North America were brought here by the Celts and their allies. When the Sinclairs and the Farams landed in North America, in 1398, this kinship was still in tact. This is validated by historical and physical evidence that the Sinclairs traveled to Baltimore, Maryland and lived peacefully with the American natives.

This peaceful relationship began to crumble when the Freemasons, in which later members of the Sinclair family were elected as Grand Master, began to change the peaceful existence of a spiritually based society into a regulated, Protestant, materially based society.

One might argue that the history of the Celts was not spiritual, but that their history contains as much violence as any other culture. There is some merit in that argument; however, if you will remember, from Chapter 2, the Celts were spiritual first, but were well equipped to defend their land or beliefs, if necessary. The Celts moved from the Near East to Europe, from Europe to Western Europe, to the British Isles, and then to North America seeking asylum from physical and religious persecution. Upon the inauguration of the Freemasons, and by the Sinclairs, migration to North America, the Celtic American culture was once again subjugated by a group of international Europeans which considered profit more important than spiritual peace and living off the land.

In all fairness to the Freemasons, by challenging the philosophy of the previous inhabitants of North America, most likely saved the Celts from themselves. Obviously, based on the Celts spiritual concept of living off the land, without a central government or economic base for supporting a military force, North America would have surely fallen prey to some militaristic culture from outside their borders. As it turns out, the world is not yet ready for world peace and, in their wisdom; the Masons must have known this. Consequently, we are now privileged to live as free men and women in a less than perfect democracy.

The geoglyphs that are presented throughout this book are presented as a road map of that story.

NORTH AMERICAN CELTIC GEOGLYPHS

The Searcy Geoglyph (c1332 AD)

This is the only geoglyph located, thus far, that has an unbroken line of descendants that have owned the land from the time it was settled until the present. According to the Searcy family, this geoglyph was on land granted to Benjamin Searcy c1332 AD. During the time period that this land was granted to the Searcy family, the Templars were assisting Portugal and Spain in ridding the Iberian Peninsula of the Muslim Moors. The Searcy Geoglyph outlines the entire eastern US. The Searcy land grant only covered 20,000 acres, and at one time had a runic marker at each corner of the 20,000 acres. The land was most likely granted to Mr. Searcy, a Templar, for his service to the King of Portugal. It was also a good location to construct the geoglyph designating the land east of the Mississippi River as belonging to the Templars. The location would have also been ideal for preventing travel up the Mississippi river. It was later, c1362 AD, that the Portuguese presented the Templars with the entire North American Territory, now known as the United States. This 1362 grant is recorded on the Kensington Runestone. The Searcy land is currently designated as a nature preserve, while it is involved in a court action over back taxes.

The Three 1253 Mile long Radials from the Newport Tower

The Searcy Geoglyph is positioned exactly 1253 miles from the Newport Tower. That is exactly the same distance from Newport Tower as to two other important geoglyphic locations. They are; the distance from Newport Tower to

Inspiration Peak, and the distance from Newport Tower to the southern tip of Florida. This was no doubt done to validate the authenticity of this important geoglyph.

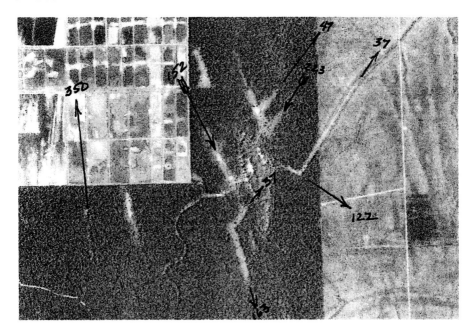

The Searcy Geoglyph Located 1253 Miles from the Newport Tower

Endpoints for the bearings displayed in the previous photo.

037 Degree Radial - North Tip of Celtic Scotland
037 Degree Radial - Zealand Denmark (The Searcy Family Came from Zealand Denmark)
047 Degree Radial - Original NE Corner of the USA. More land was added to the State of Maine Later.
122 Degree Radial - Cat Island. SE Corner of the North American Territory ceded to the Templars by Portugal.
152 Degree Radial - Gulfport, Mississippi 163 Degree Radial - Mouth of the Mississippi River
350 Degree Radial - NW corner of the expanded Viking Vinland. Where the Rainy River meets the Lake of the Woods on the current US/Canada border

The Territory Outlined by the Searcy/Vicksburg Geoglyph

The Searcy geoglyph seems to describe all the land east of the Mississippi River. Interestingly, this is the same territory which was agreed upon as the US boundary, in the Treaty of Paris, after the war between Britain and the United States. Little did Britain know, that in 1362 AD Portugal had already ceded the land, from the Atlantic to the Pacific, to the United States. This land transfer was recorded on the Kensington Runestone. The following excerpt from an article in Stanford University explains why the United States could not tell Britain that Portugal had ceded all the United States to the Templars.

> *"In 1762 Portugal, which stuck to the alliance with Britain during the Seven Years War with France, was invaded by Spanish and French forces, but with British help repulsed them."* (Source: Google Keywords - *Jameson World History*, Stanford University – Portugal)

310

Clearly, Portugal and Britain were allies during the Seven Years War in 1762 against the French. The end of the Revolutionary War in 1778, which Britain lost, would not be a good time for the US to tell Britain that Portugal, an ally of both countries, had previously ceded the entire North American Territory to the US.

THE BANAMICHI GEOGLYPH

Just as the Searcy Geoglyph is 1253 miles from the all important Newport Tower, and was located between two other important points 1253 miles from Newport, the Banamichi Geoglyph is located 1362 miles from Inspiration Peak, and between two other important points, also 1362 miles from Inspiration Peak.

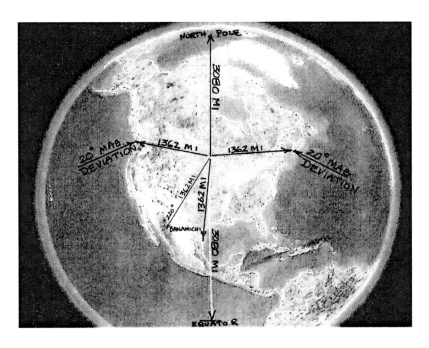

Location of the Banamichi, Mexico Geoglyph

Bearings of the Banamichi Geoglyph

Before the Mexican American war, this geoglyph was located within the North American Territory, which was granted to the Templars by Portugal. After the Mexican American war, this land fell within the boundaries of Mexico. When Mexico became aware of this geoglyph, they built a military outpost around it to protect it. This geoglyph was just one more example of the survey markers that the pre-Columbian colonists left behind to establish their claim to the North American Territory which, before several revisions, existed from the Equator to the North Pole. Other countries protect their geoglyphs. Sadly, the United States is the only country that has people that, for some reason, intentionally hide and destroy our heritage.

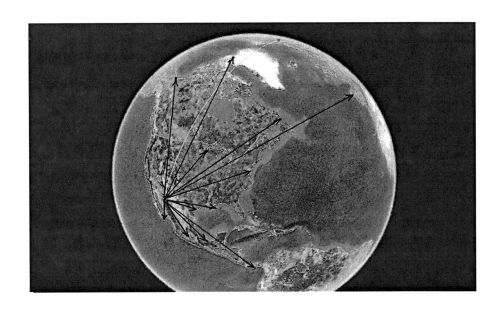

Radials Associated with the Banamichi Geoglyph

The Banamichi Geoglyph was, most likely, constructed circa the 14th century. This was a period when North American colonists were attempting to include Mesoamerica, and their allies the Aztecs, as part of the North American territory. (Google – Keyword, Medicine Hat Geoglyph)

I possess photos of many geoglyphs that existed on the lawns of the Capital and the White House, before the geoglyphs were covered by construction. This substantiates that geoglyphs were an important ritual connected to all Celtic and Masonic Monuments. Many have speculated about why the streets of Washington, DC bear Masonic Icons. It is because they were commissioned by the most famous Freemason of all time, President George Washington. George Washington hired a Mason from France, who knew all the ancient protocols of the science of Geoglyphology, to layout the streets of Washington, DC.

THE AMERICAN MOUND BUILDERS

Most accounts of Native American life and culture were written by European Americans, while being threatened by the Native Americans which they were displacing.

Even observers who were more thoughtful and sympathetic had difficulty comprehending the character of Native American peoples or interpreting their cultures as anything but primitive, and doomed to fall before the advance of civilization. Surviving European American texts and documents present only discontinuous glimpses of indigenous cultures that were diminished and dispersed before they could be fully understood. These misunderstandings served to discount and destroy important relics of the Early North American culture which would have explained their complete history.

When European Americans first entered the western country, they were intrigued and puzzled by numerous mounds and earthworks found in abundance along rivers and highlands. As early as 1750, Dr. Thomas Walker noted earthworks at the head of the Cumberland River in Kentucky.

Clusters of earthen mounds were discovered throughout the Ohio River Valley and Kentucky, at locations such as Grave Creek in what is now West Virginia and at the site of Marietta on the Ohio.

Larger and more elaborate mound complexes were discovered further west and south, some of the most notable on the Ohio near the Wabash and on the Mississippi near its confluence with the Missouri. In some places, mummified human remains and other artifacts of ancient life were uncovered.

The Native American peoples living near these formations had not built them, and European Americans with dismissive racist assumptions found it impossible to believe that any immediate forbearers of the indigenous tribes could have constructed such impressive complexes.

A variety of imaginative theories were advanced to identify the mysterious "mound builders" who had created the earth forms. Some observers claimed that they had been constructed by the lost tribes of Israel or by Tartars or Greeks. Some saw clear ties to the culture of the Welsh, Norse, Hindus, or Phoenicians.

*Whatever was made of their origin, most of the mounds were not considered sufficiently valuable to be preserved for more careful study. Farmers routinely leveled mounds while plowing their fields, and rectilinear patterns of urban streets were surveyed directly through rather than around the larger earthworks. (*Source*: University of Chicago Library and Filson Historical Society, **Library of Congress**.)*

The mound builders of North America seem to have been grouped into one large Indian tribe, called the "**Mississippians**". Although the ethnic association is correct, the name is not. The groups that constructed the North American mounds were the early Celts which colonized North America from 800 AD to 1500AD. All "Mississippian" sites pre-date 1500. This date coincides with the Masons' coming into being, c1450 AD, and the subjugation of the North American Territory from the control of the previous inhabitants.

The Poverty Point, Louisiana Mounds

"Now a nearly forgotten culture, Poverty Point at its peak, 3000 years ago, was part of an enormous trading network that stretched for hundreds of miles across the continent. It was - and is - also an engineering marvel, the product of five million hours of labor." - **U.S. National Park Service**

"Poverty Point comprises several earthworks and mounds built between 1650 BC and 700 BC, during the Archaic period in the Americas, by a group of Americans of the Poverty Point culture. The culture extended 100 miles (160 km) across the Mississippi Delta. The original purpose of Poverty Point has not been determined by archaeologists, although they have proposed various possibilities including that it was: a settlement, a trading center, and/or a ceremonial religious complex." The Ancient Mounds of Poverty Point: Place of Rings. Gibson, Jon L., Gainesville, Florida: **University Press of Florida. (2000)**

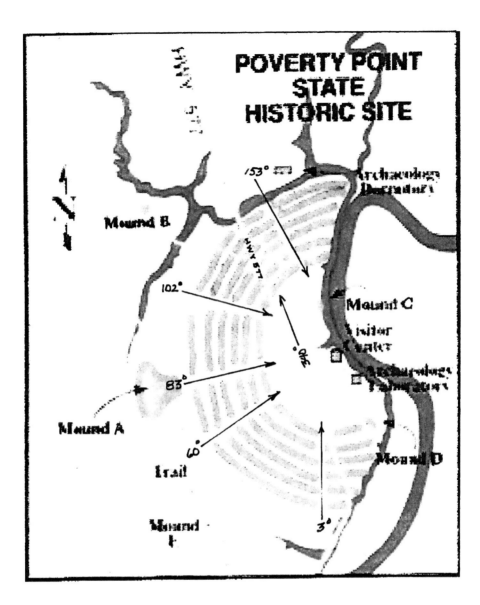

The Poverty Point, Louisiana Geoglyph bearings. (c1650-700 BC)

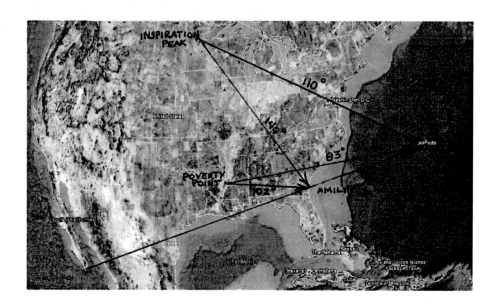

The Connection of the Poverty Point Geoglyph 085 and 102 degree radials with the 110 and 140 Degree Radials of the Kensington, Runestone and Inspiration Peak.

Notice that two of the radials of the Poverty Point geoglyph (c1000 BC) point to the same places that the Kensington Runestone/Inspiration Peak 110 and 140 degree radials (c1362 AD) point. This is indisputable proof, that the Celts were in the United States prior to 700 BC, the latest date attributed to the builders of the Poverty Point Geoglyph. This also confirms that the people, whom the US labeled as the Mississippians, were in reality ancient Europeans.

Both the Poverty Point 083 and 102 degree radials, and the Kensington Runestone Radials 110 and 140 degree radials, are key radials in defining the same territory that was given to the Templars in 1362 AD. Some might say that the Celts learned about this territory from the Mississippians. This premise would bring up even more questions. Namely, where did the Native Americans learn spherical geometry?

The Spiro Mound, Oklahoma Geoglyphs

In addition to having been dated by accredited archaeologists, the points to which this mound glyph refers are consistent with other points common in geoglyphs constructed by the Celts during this time period. Two good examples are the NW corner of the current United States and the Newport Tower.

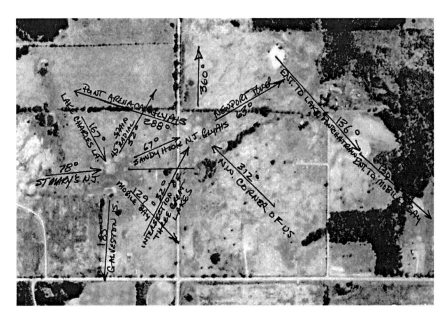

**Spiro Mounds, Native American, Geoglyphs. Pointing
to places important to the Celts. (c800-1500 AD)**

**Celtic Crosses on Spiro Mounds Pottery dated 1200 AD,
in Oklahoma USA**

The Monks Mound Illinois Geoglyph

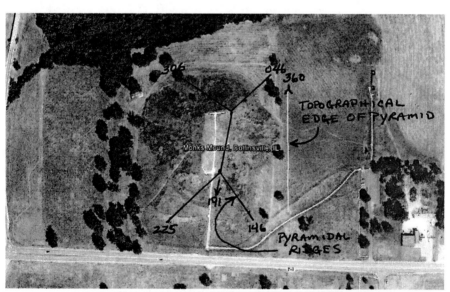

Monks Mound with Bearings Marked (c900-1200 AD)
(The mound looks lopsided but topographically the edges are as described.)

Endpoints for the bearings displayed in the above photo.

046 Degree Radial - Stonehenge, UK (Refers to the northern boundary of the Monks Mound Territory as outlined by the Stonehenge geoglyph, in particular the southern boundary of what is now Canada as defined by Stonehenge.)
146 Degree Radial - Southern Tip of Florida, USA (Southeast corner of the Monks Mound Territory.)
191 Degree Radial -New Iberia, Louisiana and Vermillion Bay (Southwest corner of the Monks Mound Territory)
225 Degree Radial - Runestone Park - Heavner, Oklahoma USA (Site of numerous Celtic petroglyphs.)
306 Degree Radial - Niobrara, Nebraska - Junction of the Niobrara River and the Missouri, River, near the city of Vermillion, Iowa. (Western edge of the Monks Mound Territory.)
360 Degree Radial - Radial leading back to the West tip of the boundary created by the Stonehenge geoglyph.

The construction of Monks Mound by the Early Celtic colonists began about 1000 AD. Deep excavations in 2007 confirmed findings, from earlier test borings, that several types of earth and clay from different sources had been used successively. The most recent section of the mound, added some time before 1200 AD, is the lower terrace at the south end.

Monk's Mound is one of the oldest and largest of the ancient mounds in North America. Based on the territory that it describes, it appears to be the first attempt by the Celts to define the initial area of what would become the United States. Notice that the area west of the Mississippi is claimed. Further validation is denoted by the names of some of the endpoints of the Monk's Mound geoglyph. This refers to the name Vermillion, which appears twice in this geoglyph, and is a major territory on the boundary between France and Spain. The northern boundary shown in the photo is incorrect. Until the Treaty of Paris after the Revolutionary War, the end points of the Inspiration Peak NW and NE 1362 mile long radials were used as the northern boundary of the US.

The northern boundary that is depicted is the boundary as described in the Treaty of Paris after the Revolutionary War.

Boundaries Established by the Monk Mound Geoglyph

It can be easily deduced from the boundaries generated by the Monk's Mound Geoglyph, that the territory extends further west than any territory described prior to this time. Was this the Celts first attempt at preventing anyone from colonizing the land just west of the Mississippi River? According to the Monks Mound map, anyone that would attempt to settle within the area several hundred miles west of the Mississippi would be colonizing territory claimed by the Celts. The Monks Mound territorial outline includes the area known to have been colonized by the Norse after their move to the North American Territory from Greenland. That territory extends from Minnesota to

Texas. The later Norse settlement of the territory west of the Mississippi would explain the North American Celts request for Portugal, the legal owners of the Americas up to that time, to cede the land east of the Mississippi to them in 1332 AD. This would, at least, prevent any Norse from settling east of the Mississippi River. It would also explain why, only 30 years later in 1362 AD, the Celts were successful in obtaining the entire North American Territory, as outlined by the Kensington Runestone, Newport Tower and Inspiration Peak. This second grant would prevent any group from blocking the route from the Atlantic to the Pacific. Unfortunately, the 1362 AD land grant would not become public knowledge until the construction, by the Portuguese, of the Guimar geoglyphs, in the Canary Islands, c1822 AD. This was necessary to confirm the US land claim in preparation for the Mexican American War. This meant that Monks Mound was the only proof of the Celtic claim to the land just west of the Mississippi River until the Portuguese geoglyph at Guimar c1822. Since the evidence indicates that the Celts did not wish the any other country to colonize the North American Territory, it would stand to reason that they would have tried to protect, and claim, the territory by the construction of Monks Mound during the Templar phase of their colonization.

The Territory, west of the Mississippi River, was not included in the Searcy geoglyph of 1332 or the Treaty of Paris in 1778. The first publicly recorded US addition of the territory, which was being colonized by the Norse, was the Louisiana Purchase in 1805 AD. This was just one more move to prevent Europeans from colonizing the territory west of the Mississippi River, which would have blocked the US from their rightful claim of the land between the Atlantic and the Pacific. Organized opposition to exposing this information continues to this day. An example is contained in the following article.

"The team's samples of Native American genomes were drawn mostly from South America, with a handful from Canada. Samples from tribes in the United States could not be used because the existing ones had been collected for medical reasons and the donors had not given consent for population genetics studies, Dr. Ruiz-Linares said. Native Americans in the United States have been reluctant to participate in inquiries into their origins. The Genographic Project of the National Geographic Society wrote recently to all federally recognized tribes in the United States asking for samples, but only two agreed to give them, said Spencer Wells, the project director." (Earliest Americans Arrived in Waves, DNA Study Finds. Nicholas Wade, July 11, 2012, **New York Times-science section.**)

What is it that intimidates so many people into covering up the history of this country?

As is the case with many of the older geoglyphs, the Monk's Mound geoglyph has one pointer that points to the main survey marker for the territory that exists next to it. In the case of the Monk's Mound survey marker, that adjoining territory is the Stonehenge territory. The names associated with the other endpoints also tell a story. There is New Iberia, Louisiana at the end of one of the radials, which says that the builders of Monk's Mound were from Old Iberia. There is also the correlation of Vermillion Bay at the end of one radial, and Vermillion City at the end of one of the other pointers. It is no coincidence that the Pyrenees Mountain range, which forms the southern border of France, terminates at what is called the Vermillion Coast. The connection between the builders of Monks Mound naming the two locations Vermillion, and one location New Iberia (Old Iberia being the location of Galicia), and then pointing to them in their geoglyph is another crosscheck to show the mound

324

was built by Europeans. As I have said before, the ancients always provided two ways to prove that a solution to a geoglyphic puzzle was correct.

Two More North American Mounds

Newark, Ohio Mound (c250-500 AD)

Etowah, Ohio Mounds (c1000-1500 AD)

There are hundreds of these mounds spread around North America, and they all lend themselves to the use of the ancient geoglyphic protocols. An entire chapter on the Mound Culture can be found in the book titled "Ancient Signposts" at Amazon.com.

CELTIC ARTIFACTS FOUND in NORTH AMERICA

Several runestones have been found in the United States, most notably the Kensington Runestone in Minnesota, and the Heavener Stones in Heavner Park, Oklahoma. It is no coincidence, that these locations are identified by other Celtic geoglyphs around the world. A runestone is typically a stone with a runic inscription, but the term can also be applied to inscriptions on boulders and on bedrock. The tradition began in the 4th century, and it lasted into the 12th century. Most runestones are located in Scandinavia, but there are also runestones scattered in locations that were visited by Norsemen during their colonization of North America. (Keyword "runestone" - http://www.wikipedia.com)

There has been considerable debate over the age and validity of the runestones which have been found up until this time. However, as the years pass, evidence is accumulating, in quantities too large to ignore. As more evidence is found it validates and supports the fact that there was pre-Columbian colonization in North America. There is evidence, that many of the runestones found in past few centuries were being destroyed. This is confirmation, that some organization does not want the true history of the United States known.

The Heavner Oklahoma Runestones

Inscription on Heavener Runestone #1

Stones similar to the Kensington Runestone have been found the East Coast, in the Ohio Valley and on the Great Plains of North America. The "Heavener Runestone" of Oklahoma is a slab about 12 feet high, 10 feet wide and 16 inches thick with runic letters spelling out the word "Gaomedat". By reversing two runes which appear to be different from the others, the inscription becomes "Glomedal", or "Glome's Valley". It could also be rendered "G. Nomedal". Nomedal is a Norwegian family name. Thanks to the efforts of Gloria Farley, the author of "*In Plain Sight*" the area surrounding the stone is now the Heavner Runestone State Park. The stone is now protected inside a building erected around it. The official theory is that the stone was erected as a boundary marker, between 600 A.D. and 900 A.D.

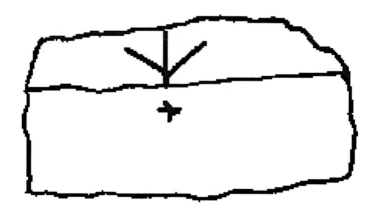

Inscription on Heavener Stone #2

The second stone, which measures 30 by 14 inches and which is 20 inches thick, shows 12-inch, three-pronged symbol on a stem. Below it on the side surface is a small mark, which proved to be a "bindrune," or combination of two runes. These markings are similar to other markings in the western world which serve as geoglyphic markers. The three pronged symbol would typically point to three predetermined and well known points, which would validate this location as having been visited by a person that was aware of the geometric protocols used by runeologists of the period. The stone could provide a claim to this spot, and possibly a certain amount of land around it. Since the stone was moved, and no orientation has been provided, it would be difficult to determine which landmarks the originator was using to validate his claim.

Inscription on Heavener Stone #3

On Heavener Stone number three, a cross, a direction symbol similar to the mark on Stone #2, and an arrow appear on the stone. The symbols are 6 to 9 inches tall and appear in a triangular pattern on a stone 5 1/2 feet long. Similar survey markers have shown that each line on the marker may point to a predetermined point to further validate the stone marker. Most survey markers include an orientation line that points North, South, or East. That marker is most likely the arrow. However, since the stone was moved, it would be difficult to determine its' orientation.

The Poteau Oklahoma Runestone

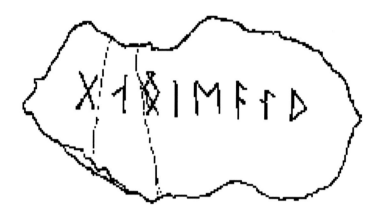

The Poteau Stone

The Poteau stone, found by schoolboys in 1967, is 15 inches long. There are seven characters in a straight line, 1 1/2 to 2 inches high. The runes show very plainly, because the bottoms of the grooves are in a lighter colored layer of the stone, while the surface was dark. Tool marks in the grooves showed that the letters had been made with a punch, like the Heavener and Kensington Runestones. Four of the runes are duplicates of those on the Heavener Runestone, and three seemed to be variants of others on it. The Heavener Runestone lies approximately 10 miles southeast of the Poteau Runestone. The original sites of Heavener Runestones, numbers two and three, fall in a line between the two others.

The Shawnee Oklahoma Runestone

Shawnee Runestone

Shawnee Runestone was found in 1969 near

The Shawnee Runestone

Yet another stone was found in Shawnee, Oklahoma. Its five runes, all from the 24-rune Elder Futhark alphabet, spell out "MEDOK." Medok is similar to Madoc, the name of a Welsh prince. Welch records state that he came to America in the year 1170 AD, then returned to Wales for ten shiploads of colonists which he led up the Mississippi River. (Just more people that would be called Indians later in history.) However, the Welsh did not use third century AD Norse runes, and the name Medok is not Madoc. Alf Monge, a noted rune cryptologist, studied the inscription on the Shawnee Runestone and said it was another Norse cryptopuzzle, giving the date November 24, 1024 A.D.

It is this writer's opinion, that the persons who discovered these stones should return to the place where they found them to find a mate. If people are finding stones, some with names on them and others with survey markings on them; it would stand to reason that there would be one of each type of stone at each location. Interestingly enough, all the stones found in Oklahoma are in close proximity to the Sulpher City Geoglyphs, which also confirm the existence of pre-Columbian exploration in North America.

The Maine, "Spirit Pond", Runestones

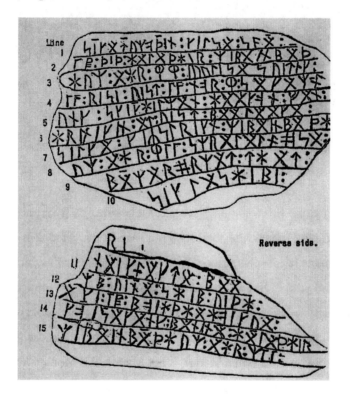

Stone Number One of the Spirit Pond Stones

The Spirit Pond Runestones were found in Maine in 1971. One bears a rough map of the area; the second has runic writing on one side. On the third, there are ten lines of runes on one side and six on the other. One stone appears to be poem, one appears to be a ship roster, and another is a map. The inscription tells of a sudden storm and fearful men trying to save their ship from "*The foamy arms of Aegir, angry god of the sea*". These stones have also been called a hoax, although no scientific evidence has been presented to prove those assumptions. The cryptologist Alf Monge believes that the stone is genuine. After reading the following dialog, you will most likely come to the conclusion that the stones are authentic.

Line1: **S 10 Na 4 umf 6 in** : **Nilsa** - Spain : **Sela** - Hebrew for rock :　　　　　　～Ｌ～

Line2: **Lo** : **Did** : **Haladhir** - Hungarian : **Miraisasuitln** - Nederlands :

Line3: **Hum** : **Ahr** - German : **PP** : **Mul** - Spain : **Sasuiten** :

Line4: **Lf** : **Risi** - Italian : **Uist** - Scotish : **Lf** : **Nor** - Norway : **O** : **Sanamn** - Iran :

Line5: **Uxn** : **Sninhilman** - Jewish : **Haanon** - Norway : **Fan** :

Line6: **Hrixinin** - Egypt : **At** : **Uist** - Scotish : **Baalaana** - Buddist for Good Luck :

Line7: **Silna** - Polish : **Kirslrikn** - Morocco : **Mibainbadhum** - Egyptian :

Line8: **Ahr** - Germany : **Oll** - Sweden : **Smralalneisa** :

Line9: **Bamareermat** : **That** :

Line10: **Sinlashibi** - Turkish :

Line11: **Naineanta** - Newfoundland : **Baatb** :

Line12: **Uina** - Germany : **Shib** - Afgan : **Uidh** - England :

Line13: **Ani** - Turkish : **Tq** - Iraq : **Boihdhaheinda** - Arab :

Line14: **Noisanann** - Nederlands : **Banina** - Spain : **Haiadhir** - Pakistani :

Line15: **Mibainbadhum** - Egyptian : **Ahr** - Germany : **MII** - Year 1002 :

The preceding runestone translated as possibly being the names of a ships crew.

The preceding runestone has confounded scholars for years in that some of the writing was said to be undecipherable. Could that be because the writing is composed of 18 different ethnic origins? Study has shown that the writing on the stone could be the names of the seamen that were shipwrecked. This is validated by the fact that the names are of various ethnic origins from the ports which the Norse ships were known to frequent. It is further validated by the fact that there appear to be approximately 40 names on the list. This is approximately the number of men known to have manned one Nordic Ship. It is documented that their ships were not manned solely by Norsemen. The Roman numeral date 1002 AD, in the lower right-hand corner, coincides with many other dates around North America, which indicate pre-Columbian exploration of North America and the possibility of a Celtic exploration

.

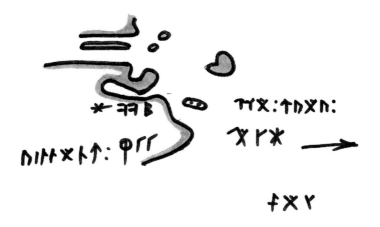

The Map Depicted on Stone Number Two of the Three Spirit Pond Stones

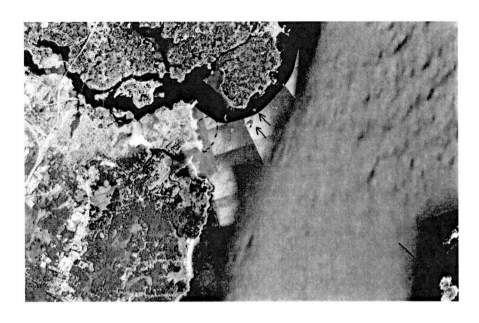

Portsmouth New Hampshire

Portsmouth New Hampshire is located just south of the S10 Na 4 UMF 6 Nordic coordinates spelled out by the runes on the map. The topography appears to match the map on the stone. The tip of the peninsula could have eroded away from river and tide currents. The extension that would most likely have eroded away is drawn on the photo in ink. After adding back the part that most likely would have eroded, the map on the rock matches the entrance to the river and surrounding islands. If the stone was a fake it would have matched the current shoreline.

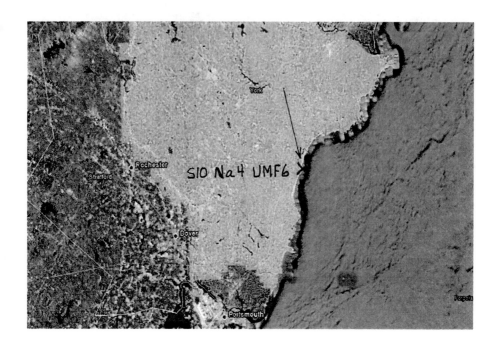

Position Calculated from Coordinates on Stone #2.

The translated runic numbers on the stone, S10 Na 4 UMF 6, appear, by their very nature, to be coordinates of some kind. Research shows that a position on the Maine Coast can be calculated using these numbers. It was discovered that by using the early mariner's archaic form of plotting a position, any position on the earth can be plotted with an accuracy of within several feet to several hundred feet. The position illustrated above was calculated prior to discovering that it lies precisely on the 090 degree bearing from Inspiration Peak. The 090 degree radial is the most important radial on a geoglyph. Also, the area just north of this position is named Salisbury, which shows many geoglyphs on the ground. Curiously, Stonehenge is located at Salisbury England. The ancient Celts always provided a way to validate the correct solution to their puzzles. The Inspiration Peak 090 Degree Bearing is that double check.

The Spirit Pond Stone Location When Discovered.

Displayed in the previous Plate is the position that is recorded as having been the location of the Spirit Pond Stones when they were discovered. The stones were most likely carried North to this location by the originators.

The Geoglyph Associated with Spirit Pond

THE FORT BRAZOS TEXAS GEOGLYPHS

Location of Fort Brazos, Southern Tip of Texas

Fort Brazos Geoglyphs

Fort Brazos Bearings

Notice the portion labeled as the Mexican Barricade. That is the only portion built by the Mexicans. The remainders of the geoglyphic pointers were constructed by General Zachery Taylor as a remembrance of our heritage, the Portuguese explorations, and a claim to the North American Territory described in this, and the Kensington Runestone, geoglyph.

Endpoints for the bearings displayed in the above photo.

031 Degree Radial - South Tip of Lake Erie
035 Degree Radial - South Tip of Lake Huron
036 Degree Radial - Edinburgh, Scotland
039 Degree Radial - Northeast Tip of the Current USA
042 Degree Radial - Southern Tip of the New Jersey Peninsula
051 Degree Radial - Galicia (Where the Farams Originated)
054 Degree Radial - Portugal (World Explorers)
059 Degree Radial - Tip of Cape Hatterus, Eastern Most Point in the USA
070 Degree Radial - Bermuda (Termination Point of the 110 Degree Radial
Inscribed on the Kensington Runestone and Emanating From Inspiration Peak.

090 Degree Radial - A geoglyph Orientation Radial Usually Reserved for an Important Point. This Radial Points to Cat Island the SE Corner of the North American Territory, prior to the Mexican American War.
152 Degree Radial - Western Most Edge of South America
172 Degree Radial - Vera Cruz, Mexico
236 Degree Radial - Western Tip of Mexico
237 Degree Radial - Punta de Mita, Mexico
244 Degree Radial - Southern Tip of Australia
252 Degree Radial - Fiji, Island in the West Pacific. Strangely, Fiji Island is mentioned in many Celtic geoglyphs.
316 Degree Radial - Lake Amistad, on the Rio Grande River between Texas and Mexico.

A Brief History of Brazos-Santiago Island

Brazos Island is a barrier island on the Gulf Coast of Texas in the United States, south of the town of South Padre Island. The island is also known as Brazos Santiago Island, a reference to the town of Brazos Santiago, the first Spanish settlement on the island. The area was granted by the State of Tamaulipas to Ygnacio Trevino on January 24, 1829, as part of the Potrero de San Martin Grant. (Brazos Island was granted separately and earlier by the King of Spain.) The island is the southernmost barrier island in Texas, separated from the delta landmass of the Rio Grande by unnamed channels. The island's northern end is separated from South Padre Island by the Brazos Santiago Passage. The island is oriented generally north-south, with the Gulf of Mexico on the east, and South Bay on the west. In the course of the natural processes of erosion and sedimentation, the island is not always surrounded by water, and is currently connected to the mainland. A portion of Brazos Island is now designated as a Texas State Scenic Park, also known as Brazos Island State Recreation Area. The beach at this state park is known as "Boca Chica Beach."

Brazos Santiago, Texas

The original recorded inhabitants of Brazos Island were the Mexicans. The island was inhabited intermittently from 1830 to 1867. The Mexicans established the original Fort Brazos Santiago, a Mexican customs house and military outpost at the entrance to Brazos Santiago Pass. Before 1848, the port had wharves on the lagoon side of Brazos Island. Goods destined for ports up the Rio Grande had to be offloaded at Brazos Santiago, because the bars at the mouth of the Rio Grande were too shallow for ships capable of sailing the Gulf. Trade for Matamoros and interior Mexico was landed at the harbor on Brazos Island and then transported to Matamoros by oxcart. In 1840 AD, the government of the Republic of Texas debated the construction of a fort on the north end of Brazos Island, exactly where the Mexicans established Brazos Santiago, six miles north of the Rio Grande at Brazos Santiago Pass. This installation would not only have controlled navigation through the vital pass between Padre and Brazos islands, but would also have established a Texas military presence in the disputed territory, between the Rio Grande and the Nueces Rivers. However, since the site lay 120 miles to the south of the nearest Texan settlement, only nominally in disputed Texas territory and on the site already occupied by the Mexican army, the planned fort never materialized.

Sometime prior to 1846 AD, a Mexican garrison was established on the site where the current remains of the US Union Supply Depot exists. In March 1846 AD, the Mexican fort was abandoned when the Mexican Commander received word that General Zachary Taylor, Later to be President Taylor, and two brigades of 2400 men, with cannon, were headed his way. In 1849 AD, the Fort became Brazos Island Depot, a U.S. Army arsenal and encampment protecting the inlet to Port Isabel and Fort Polk. The marine transfer station, required to transfer cargo from deep draft ships to shallow draft ships, for Forts Polk and Brown was also located on Brazos Santiago Island.

During the Mexican War, Gen. Zachary Taylor established a supply depot on Brazos Island, which handled all logistics concerning northern Mexico supplies and men, and where several thousand American troops debarked and waited for assignments to other locations. After 1848 AD, Richard King developed shallow-draft steamboats that could negotiate the shallow bars at the mouth of the Rio Grande. His boats could then offload in the lee of Brazos Island, go around to the Gulf side, and cross the bars and travel up the Rio Grande to their destination. A road was built down Brazos Island, across Boca Chica Bay to the Rio Grande in 1846. To cross Boca Chica Bay, General Zachary Taylor built a floating bridge to transport military supplies. Some of the Cypress pilings can still be seen there. In 1846, General Ulysses S. Grant crossed here returning from the fighting in Mexico. In 1847, Robert E. Lee crossed the tract similarly several times.

The Mexican American War

In May 1845, General Taylor was ordered to correspond with the government of the Republic of Texas, then negotiating annexation to the United States, and to repel any invasion of Mexicans. In July he moved his army of 4,000 men to the site of Corpus Christi, Tex. In January 1846 AD, he was ordered to the mouth of the Rio Grande to support the American claim to that river as the boundary of Texas.

When Mexican forces attacked his troops, General Taylor did not wait for Congress to declare war. On May 8, 1846, at Palo Alto he defeated a Mexican army three times the size of his own force, largely through the accuracy of his artillery. The next day, he won the Battle of Resaca de la Palma and then occupied Matamoros. President James K. Polk thereupon named him commander of the Army of the Rio Grande and promoted him to Brevet Major General. A grateful Congress voted him thanks and awarded him two gold medals.

United States President James K. Polk, who envisioned a nation stretching to the Pacific Ocean, had been elected the year before. Much of the territory he sought was claimed by Spain, which then encompassed New Mexico, Arizona, and California. This is the same land ceded to the Templars by Portugal in 1362 AD. Senate records show that Polk, and others in the Senate, all Masons, knew this. Polk hinted that if Mexico wouldn't sell these territories, the United States would seize them.

"*Manifest Destiny*" was a popular slogan of the day, reflecting a view that the United States was destined to control vast territories. Bolstered by such sentiments, Polk sent an emissary to Mexico to buy western lands. When Mexican officials rejected the offer, Polk ordered U.S. troops, led by General Zachary Taylor, to occupy the disputed region between the Nueces and Rio Grande Rivers in Texas. The president was knowingly courting war. If bloodshed erupted, however, he wanted Mexico to be perceived as the aggressor. Having United States forces in the disputed region, between the Nueces River and the Rio Grande Rivers, would have increased the likelihood that Mexican troops would cross the Rio Grande and strike the first blows. Powerful voices in the United States spoke against Polk's provocations, including John Quincy Adams, a former president; John C. Calhoun, a former vice president; and philosopher Henry David Thoreau.

END CHAPTER

Chapter 11

Sir Henry Sinclair I
(Baron of Baltimore)

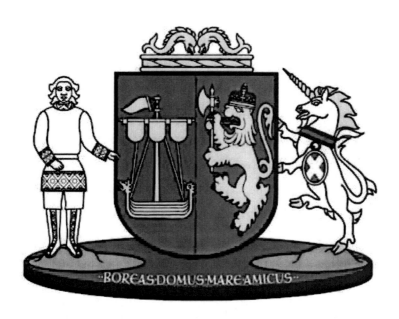

Orkney Islands Coat of Arms

Norway Coat of Arms

Scottish Flag

The preceding emblems are presented to illustrate the close association of Scotland, Norway and Denmark. Nothing could be more descriptive of this association than the Coat of Arms of the Earl of Orkney, shown on the previous page. The COA shows a Dane, in a Jelling winter costume, and a Unicorn with a Scotish emblem, supporting Norway and the Vikings.

Henry Sinclair, Earl of Orkney.

Henry I Sinclair, Earl of Orkney, Baron of Roslin (c. 1345 – c. 1400) was a Scottish nobleman. Henry Sinclair inherited the titles of Baron of Roslin, Lord Chief Justice of Scotland and Admiral of the Seas from his father. Due to Henrys success in resolving issues in the Orkney Islands, located just north of Scotland, on 2 August 1379 he was bestowed the title of the 1st Earl of Orkney by King Haakon of Norway. Sinclair held the title Earl of Orkney under the King of Norway, who laid claim to the Islands at the time. The presentation of this title from the King of Norway highlights the close association between Scotland, Denmark and Norway. Earl Henry was succeeded by a son named Henry, who was followed by his son Earl William, to whom the Earldom of Caithness was granted by the King of Scotts in 1455. Henry was the grandfather of William Sinclair, 1st Earl of Caithness, who commissioned the building of Rosslyn Chapel in Edinburgh, Scotland.

The Sinclair family originated in Normandy, France in the 9th century AD. Not surprisingly, France is also the birthplace of the Templars. The family moved, at the time of William the Conqueror, to England and Scotland, in the 11th century. With very close ties to the French Kings, this family played a key role in medieval history. Roslyn has been their most revered home for nearly 1000 years. Gordon Sinclair Flaws combines much of the research of Niven Sinclair with his own natural talent to bring family history alive to the audience. (*Sinclair History*, by Gordon Sinclair Flaws)

Orkney Islands, Just North of Scotland

The Sinclair family first came to England with William the Conqueror during his invasion of England. The family name was originally "Saint-Clair" the name of a city in France. The Sinclair lineage can be traced back to the Normandy area of France, and earlier to the Scandinavian Viking days. The family's history is closely intertwined with the crowns of France, England, Scotland, and Norway. Their ancestors, as were the Farams, have been involved in many of the pivotal events in Western Civilization. The Sinclairs have left an indelible mark in the history books. The Farams, who worked with, and alongside, the Templars and Sinclairs, never received the recognition that the Sinclairs enjoy today. That is because the Farams were leaders of the Warrior Class, which not only did not share the spotlight with Royalty, but avoided publicity due to their clandestine duties.

The name Sinclair is of Norman origin from "Saint-Clair-sur-Elle" and was established in Scotland in 1162 AD when Henry de St Clair of Roslin was granted lands in Lothian. His descendant Sir William became guardian to the heir of Alexander III, and gained the Barony of Rosslyn in 1280 AD . I find it very interesting that the sponsor of the Templars, Sir Henry, should choose to move to the remote country of Scotland right after the Viking era ended. Does this mean that the Celts in France replaced the Vikings with the Templars? The close associations of Scotland, Norway and Denmark, and the fact that the Templar training facilities were in Denmark would seem to confirm this. Sir Henry fought with King Bruce at Bannockburn, and was one of the Scottish barons who signed the letter to the Pope asserting Scottish independence. His son, Henry married Isobel, co-heiress of the Earldom of Orkney and Caithness and thus transported the Sinclairs to the far north of Scotland. Their son, Henry Sinclair of Roslin became Earl of Orkney in 1379.

In 1455 AD, William , Son of Henry Sinclair I, was granted the Earldom of Caithness. In 1446 AD, William Sinclair commissioned the celebrated Rosslyn Chapel, in homage to the Templers. The Chapel is filled with hundreds of stone carvings having great significance to the Templars and Freemasonry. It was during this same time period, in Scotland that the Templars became the Freemasons.

The Sinclair Leadership of the Masons

"It is interesting to note that a later descendant, named William Sinclair of Roslin, became the first Grand Master of the Masonic Lodge in Scotland, and subsequently, several other members of the Sinclair family have held the position of Grand Master." (Brother Alexander Steuart MacNabb, *http://www.grandlodgeofvirginia.org,* Henry Lodge No. 57)

"The Saint Clairs of Roslin, or, as it is often spelled, of Rosslyn, held for more than three hundred years an intimate connection with the history of

Freemasonry in Scotland. *William Saint Clair, Earl of Orkney and Caithness, was, in 1441, appointed by King James II the Patron and Protector of the Freemasons of Scotland, and the office was made hereditary in his family. Charles Mackie says of him.*" (*Preernasen*, May, 1851, page 166) that "*he was considered one of the best and greatest Masons of the age.*"

"*He planned the construction of a most magnificent collegiate church at his palace of Roslin, of which, however, only the chancel and part of the transept were completed. To take part in this design, he invited the most skillful Freemasons from foreign countries; (Including the Farams from America) and in order that they might be conveniently lodged and carry on the work with ease and dispatch, he ordered them to erect the neighboring town of Roslin, and gave to each of the most worthy a house and lands. After his death, which occurred about 1480, the office of hereditary Patron was transmitted to his descendants,*" (Lawrie-*History of Freemasonry*, page 100)

"*The prerogative of nominating the office-bearers of the Craft, which had always been exercised by the kings of Scotland, appears to have been neglected by James VI after his accession to the throne of England.*

Hence the Freemasons, finding themselves embarrassed for want of a Protector, about the year 1600, if that be the real date of the first of the Saint Clair Manuscripts, appointed William Saint Clair of Roslin, for himself and his heirs, their "Patrons and Judges." After presiding over the Order for many years, says Lawrie, William Saint Clair went to Ireland, and in 1630 a second Charter was issued, granting to his son, Sir William Saint Clair, the same power with which his father had been invested. This Charter having been signed by the Masters and Wardens of the principal

Lodges of Scotland, Sir William Saint Clair assumed the active administration of the affairs of the Craft, and appointed his Deputies and Wardens, as had been customary with his ancestors. For more than a century after this renewal of the compact between the Laird of Roslin and the Freemasons of Scotland, the Craft continued to flourish under the successive heads of the family.

But in the year 1736, William Saint Clair, to whom the Hereditary Protector ship had descended in due course of succession, having no children of his own, became anxious that the office of Grand Master would become vacant at his death. Accordingly, he assembled the members of the Lodges of Edinburgh and its vicinity, and represented to them the good effects that would accrue to them if they should in future have at their head a Grand Master of their own choice, and declared his intention to resign into the hands of the Craft his hereditary right to the office. It was agreed by the assembly that all the Lodges of Scotland should be summoned to appear by themselves, or proxies, on the approaching Saint Andrew's Day, at Edinburgh, to take the necessary steps for the election of a Grand Master.

In compliance with the call, the representatives of thirty-two Lodges met at Edinburgh on the 30th of November 1736, when William Saint Clair tendered the following resignation of his hereditary office:

I, William Saint Clair, of Roslin, Esq., taking into my consideration that the Masons in Scotland did, by several deeds, constitute and appoint trillium and Sir William Saint Clairs of Roslin, my ancestors and their heirs, to be their patrons, protectors judges, or masters, and that my holding or claiming any such jurisdiction, right, or privilege might be prejudicial to the Craft and creation of Masonry, whereof I am a member; and I, being desirous to advance and promote the good and utility of the said Craft of Masonry to the utmost of my power, do therefore hereby, for me and my heirs, renounce quit claim over give, and discharge all right, claim, or pretense that I, or my heirs, had, have, or any ways may have, pretend to, or claim to be, patron, protector, judge, or master of the Masons in Scotland, in virtue of any deed or deeds made and granted by the said Masons, or of any grant or charter made by any of the kings of Scotland to and in favor of the said William and Sir William Saint Clair of Roslin, my predecessors, or any other manner or way whatsoever, for now and ever; and I bind and oblige me and my heirs to warrant this present renunciation and discharge at all hands. And I consent to the registration hereof in the books of council and session, or any other judges' books competent, therein to remain for preservation." (Lawrie's History of Freemasonry, London - 1804 AD, page 148).

The reading of the Preface of Lawries's book, if not the entire book, is highly recommended to anyone who may think that the Masons are a subversive organization. It is evident that they are a benevolent organization that maintains secrecy to protect the secrets of the ancients from those who would destroy them. The entire book can be accessed for free at: (*books.google.com*).

The Sinclair's relationship with the Masons, and their family's part in the colonization of North America, would explain the secrecy that has surrounded both the history of the colonization of the Americas, and the history of the Sinclair Family.

HENRY SINCLAIR IN AMERICA

The controversy over what happened to Sir Henry Sinclair I, who was credited with leading the liberation of Scotland from England, has endured since the time of his announcement to depart for the New World in 1398. For the first time, evidence will be presented which will substantiate his arrival in the Americas. Circa 1397, Henry I drew up his will and turned over the title to everything he owned to his relatives. Sir Henry was a very spiritual man, he informed his family that he was leaving for the New World to convert and baptize the natives. He was never officially heard from again. Feigning ignorance of Henry's whereabouts, history simply wrote him off as dying in 1400 AD.

The Micmac tribe of Nova Scotia tells a story about a king who travelled from an island far across the sea with many soldiers, stayed for a year and left again: this story fits exactly with the Zeno Narratives' of the events. There is also, at Westford in Massachusetts, a rock with a strange design on it. This carving looks like the outline of an armored knight, complete with a shield bearing the crest of the Clan Gunn. This is claimed to be the memorial to Sir James Gunn, who presumably was lost on the expedition. The modern stone nearby reads:

> "*Prince Henry First Sinclair of Orkney Born in Scotland made a voyage of discovery to North America in 1398. After wintering in Nova Scotia, he sailed to Massachusetts and on an inland expedition in 1399 to Prospect Hill to view the surrounding countryside, one of the party died. The punch-hole armorial effigy, which adorns this ledge, is a memorial to this knight.*"

In 1849 a cannon, allegedly dating back to the late 1300s, was dredged from the harbor of Louisburg on Cape Breton Island: exactly the sort of cannon that would have been carried on their ship.

DRUID HILL PARK, MARYLAND

It is not likely that a man of Sinclair's stature would go off on a wild goose chase. It is more likely that there was an established place for him to go. That place is in Baltimore Maryland in an area known as Druid Hill Park. The Baltimore area is known for its strong Scottish heritage.

Baltimore is also very close to what eventually became the capitol of the United States. Surrounded by the city of Baltimore, Druid Hill Park is known to have a long, unbroken, Scottish heritage. Interestingly, the nearby capitol of the United States, Washington, DC, lies on the 111 degree radial that extends from Inspiration Peak. The 111 would imply the number 3, the most sacred number to the Masons.

The name Druid Hill in itself is enough to spark your interest. Research has found, that the names of places that we take for granted today most likely had an associative meaning when they originated. We have found, that there is a reason for this place to be called Druid Hill. The area was once fed by natural springs and contains three pools (Once again the number three.) next to each other which are about 2 feet deep. No one will admit what they think the pools were used for; in fact when the Baltimore Zoo was first constructed they were used as ponds for the seals. They are no longer used for that purpose. They look very much like three baptismal ponds, which would have been perpetually filled by the natural springs in the area. This fits right in with Henry Sinclair's parting words in Scotland; "*I am going to La Merica to baptize the Natives*". (La Merica being the Templar term for the new world. It means; "The Western Star") A portion of Druid Hill Park was later a 15th century cemetery.

Druid Hill Park (West Side)

Druid Hill Park, as seen from the air. Notice the white grave markers on the left of the photo and one of the baptismal ponds, in the center of the photo, with the road going around it.

The same view as the previous one with the orientation of the cemetery stones marked. All the termination points are important Celtic markers. Notice the three markers on the left of the picture which form a triangle used to solve the Newport Tower Mystery. (Close-up in next photo.)

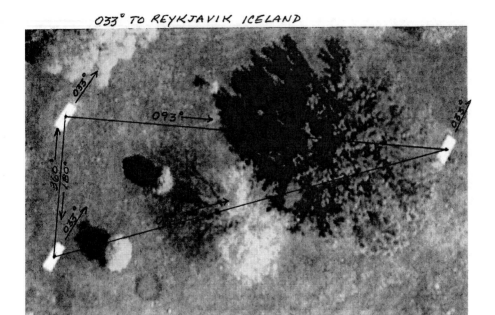

The Druid Hill Triangle

This is a close-up of the three markers which provide the solution to the Newport Tower mystery. Notice that they all point toward Reykjavik Iceland, the home port of the Vikings, and resupply point for the Celts when traveling to the Americas. The angles which make up the triangle are exactly the same as those used in the Newport Tower solution. The men that created this must have been high up in the Celtic hierarchy, in order to have known this secret information. This further confirms this as the home of Henry Sinclair I.

356

Druid Hill Gravestones in 2008

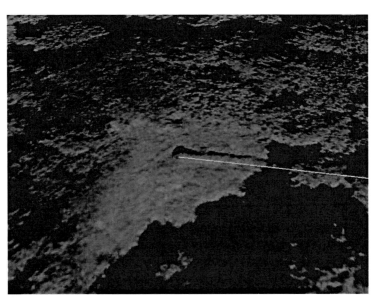

One of the linier mound markers around Druid Hill Park.

This particular line is oriented to 115 degrees and points to the Southern tip of Africa, a common Celtic landmark.

Close-up of one of the three baptismal ponds.

Ground view of one of the three baptismal ponds.

Stairs leading down to the baptismal ponds.

Listed on the National Register of Historic Places, the recorded history of Druid Hill Park began over three centuries ago when the Susquehannock Indians, presumably converted by the Sinclair party and their successors, ceded land that included the park's area and its holdings to the officials of the Baltimore Charter in 1652. History tells us that the original settlers in the Baltimore area did not encounter the distresses of war and famine which early colonists in other locations had encountered. The surrounding native inhabitants were friendly, and had an abundance of food. In 1639 AD a representative government was established. Thus the republican commonwealth of Maryland was founded. The Indians and Europeans lived together in peace and harmony built on mutual respect and cooperation. The royal Indian family asked to be baptized so that they could convert to Christianity. They were converted and their daughter was educated in St. Mary's, then the capitol of Maryland. The land comprising Druid Hill Park was eventually placed in the care of Lord George Buchanan, one of the seven Scotish commissioners responsible for the establishment of Baltimore City, and included 579 of the 745 acres that comprise Druid Hill Park today. Around 1750 AD, the land was sold and handed down to Colonel Nicholas Rogers (1753-1822 AD) also of Scottish descent. In 1858 AD, the descendants of Rogers' family reluctantly sold the property to the city of Baltimore. In 1860 AD, the land was incorporated as a Baltimore municipal park, and became America's third public park.

One of the items in the park is a prominent statue of William Wallace. William Wallace is a hero of Scotish independence and the sovereignty of the Scotish people (The movie Braveheart was modeled after his life.) Wallace was a military leader during the Wars of Scottish Independence waged against the English. He was eventually captured and brutally murdered by the English. Later Sir Henry Sinclair I fought for and won the final independence of Scotland from England.

In 1893 AD, a man named William Wallace Spence began his voyage to America from Edinburgh, Scotland. Edinburgh just happens to be the same city from which Sir Henry Sinclair I began his voyage to America. William Wallace Spence became a supremely successful Baltimore merchant and financier. Spence, a Baltimore City commissioner and philanthropist, commissioned the Royal Academy of Scotland artist, D. W. Stevenson, to duplicate the sculpture of William Wallace on display at the Abby Craig in Sterling, Scotland. He then offered it to the city of Baltimore for display at Druid Hill Park. Both the Sinclair family and the original Wallace family were heroes of the Scotish Revolution. There are only two copies of this statue in existence. The King of Scotland has one, and Druid Hill Park has the other. What does that tell you?

**Statue of William Wallace (Braveheart), Hero of Scotland,
Overlooking Druid Hill Park Lake.**

**Orientation of the William Wallace Statue toward Edinburgh, Scotland,
the previous home of Henry Sinclair I.**

Full Length View of the Promenade at Druid Hill Park

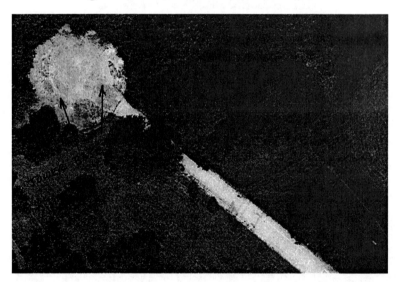

North End of the Promenade, Showing the Location of the Original Stone Tower that was the Sinclair home and defensive structure.

(Notice the lines that cross the promenade for its entire length. They point to an ancient Orkney Island geoglyph, similar to the one on the south end of the promenade.)

The north end of the promenade shows the foundation where the defensive lookout tower was built by the Sinclair party. In the next picture, you will see a tower similar to the one that was built here. The picture is the tower that was built, on the Saint Lawrence Seaway by the Farams, after off loading the Sinclairs at Druid Hill.

The Faram Tower - Maitland, Canada - Built c1410 by the Faram family.
This tower is similar to the one that was built at Druid Hill Park, MD.
(Photo courtesy of Chris Sanfino)

These towers were built as living quarters as well as to be used for observation and defense against hostile natives. The openings for the windows and doors can be seen. Also the remains of the wood supports, to hold an observation deck, can be seen below the door opening. Two similar towers were also built in Sulpher City, Oklahoma. I have photos, but those towers have since been destroyed.

South End of the Promenade, With Geoglyph

Notice the white lines, crossing at intervals the full length of the promenade. They all point to the Orkney Island Geoglyph shown in the next photo. Notice that the two geoglyphs resemble each other.

Endpoints for the bearings displayed in the above photo.

003 Degree Radial - North Entrance to Baffin Bay at Greenland. Used by the Vikings prior to Sinclair coming to America.
041 Degree Radial - Bearings of the stripes running across the Promenade lead to the Prehistoric Stone Circle in the Orkney Islands.
042 Degree Radial - Northern Tip of Scotland, Country of Henry Sinclair I
045 Degree Radial - Edinburgh, Scotland, Home of Henry Sinclair I
083 Degree Radial - Canary Islands. Owned by Scotland's ally, Portugal

089 Degree Radial - The 7000+ year of Golfo de Cintra Geoglyphs. These geoglyphs were discovered by the Faram Foundation in 2008 by following a coded geoglyph from the Nabta Playa site in Southern, Egypt. The bearings included in the Golfo de Cintra geoglyph also point to Newport, Rhode Island USA, Trinidad and Guimar Island in the Canary Islands, which are also mentioned in the Sinclair Geoglyphs. One of the bearings in the Golfo de Cintra Geoglyphs points to the place where the Giza pyramids would be built 4000 years later. Columbus stopped at Trinidad on his second trip to the Americas.

115 Degree Radial - Southern Tip of Africa

113 Degree Radial - Southern side of the Entrance to Delaware Bay, USA

143 Degree Radial - Entrance to the river that now separates Suriname from French Guiana. These two small countries received the only land given to any country on the East Coast of South America by Portugal. They were most likely given as South American Ports for the Dutch and the French.

153 Degree Radial - Trinidad, Island. Mentioned in the Golfo de Cintra Geoglyph, the Sinclair Geoglyph, and visited by Columbus on his second trip to the Americas..

185 Degree Radial - Points to where the equator meets the West coast of South America, in Ecuador.

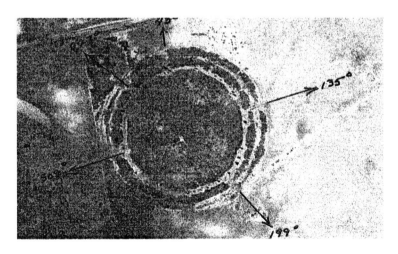

The Prehistoric Stone Geoglyph in the Orkney Islands.

365

The preceding geoglyph was located by following the many lines which cross the Druid Hill Park Promenade, all of which are oriented to 041 degrees. This geoglyph is similar in design the one shown at the south end of the promenade.

THE COLONY of MARYLAND

Sir George Calvert has been called the founder of Maryland. He was knighted by King James of Britain in 1617 AD. Sir Calvert was a member of the East India Company, and also of the London Company, by whom Jamestown Virginia was colonized.

Sir Calvert's son Cecil married Anne, the daughter of the Earl of Arundel, who was a member of the Roman Catholic Church. This union brought him into close contact with distinguished Catholics. He became an advocate for the Spanish match, and on the floor of the House of Commons; he inflamed the resentment of King James against that body by giving him a highly-colored account of their proceedings in the matter. In the summer of 1624 AD, his closeness to the Church of Rome became so contentious that he was forced to step down as Secretary to King James. He later was given a post in Ireland to where he relocated.

The Roman Catholics of England were suffering much persecution at that time from the Puritans on one side, who were daily increasing in strength, and from the Churchmen on the other. Lord Baltimore desired to provide an asylum for Catholics in America. In the spring he sailed for Virginia, arriving at Jamestown in October. The Virginia Company created so much opposition to the Catholic presence, that he was induced to surrender the Jamestown Charter and pursue one for territory north and east of the Potomac River. This area adjoined the Chesapeake Bay, which he had previously visited. Lord Baltimore returned to England and succeeded in obtaining a new charter. Unfortunately,

Lord Baltimore died in London before returning to the New World. His son Cecil received the charter a few months afterward. The land was to be called Maryland, supposedly after Queen Henrietta Mary.

The Maryland charter, drawn up by Lord Baltimore gave greater democratic privileges to the settlers under it than any issued before it, by monopolist or monarch. It took the territory out of the control of the English King, who had no legal rights to the Americas, provided for no taxation and provided for religious tolerance. Prior to this, only the Protestant Scotts had tolerated religious freedom. Presumably, the reason that Lord Baltimore chose that area to colonize, was because it had already been settled by Henry Sinclair and the Farams beginning c1400 AD.

After a hectic voyage, the colonists sailed up the Potomac to the Heron Islands. The natives came to them one after another, and were disarmed of all hostility by having previously met with no violence from previous colonists. On the edge of the forest stood groups of Indian men, women and children, clad in native clothing, to welcome the newly arrived colonists.

At that point, the elected Governor Calvert took formal possession of the territory. The governor then proceeded to lay out a capital city that was dedicated to the Virgin Mary, also a Celtic religious icon. The town was named St. Mary's in order to strengthen the argument that the Baltimore's were of the Orthodox persuasion, even though they called themselves Catholics. The number of geoglyphs around the New World that point to St. Marys, Maryland is significant. In view of the fact that the geoglyphs were executed by Celts it would be inconsistent to think that the markers were pointing to a place named after the Queen of England, but rather a place named after the Virgin Mary, the religious matriarch of the builders of the geoglyphs, the Orthodox Christian Celts.

END CHAPTER

Chapter 12

The Colonizing of America

Before we begin the story of the Celts and the Farams in the Americas, let's review what has led up to this point. Prior to the first millennium AD, the Farums lived in Galicia. It was around 700 AD when they departed for Denmark, ahead of the Muslim invasion of Europe. Their neighbor, ally, and Celtic partner Portugal was conquered by the Muslims, as was Spain, their non Celtic neighbor. Upon leaving Galicia, (Today part of Spain) the Farums returned to their ancient homeland of Zealand Denmark. There they lived from c700 - 1397 AD, both collecting taxes for Denmark and providing liaison for the Templars. It was during this time that they established the city of Farum, Denmark which is located on the harbor named Farum Sound, 12 miles North of Copenhagen. The Farums were deeply involved with the Templar organization while living in Denmark. After the Templars were forced out of Europe, they were transported to both the Americas and Scotland by the Farum fleet. During this time, the Templars assisted in liberating Scotland from England under the leadership of King Robert the Bruce. Due to the political and religious conditions in Denmark, when Scotland became independent, the Faram's moved, with Henry Sinclair to America. This move was both to assist Henry Sinclair in his move to North America, and to defend the new established Templar Territory from being colonized by the non- Celtic Norse.

After hundreds of years of visitation by the Portuguese, Danes, Scotts, Irish and their predecessors, there was a growing population of Celts in North America, New England and the Saint Lawrence Seaway areas. As a result of the Templars leaving Europe, there was now a large and formidable army which needed a home. Prior to the time the Farams were forced out of Galicia, they were closely aligned with Portugal. This alliance continued even after the Templars were forced out of Europe. After the Templar Order was terminated, the Templars were asked by Portugal to assist in eliminating the Muslims from the Iberian Peninsula. Neither Galicia, the Templars, nor Portugal were previously allied with Spain but circumstances dictated that Spain be included in the liberation of the Iberian Peninsula. This was accomplished through the establishment of a new Templar Order, by Portugal, titled "The Military Order of Christ." This title accomplished two objectives, one was to obtain the blessing of the Vatican, and the other was to allow the Templars access to the Iberian Peninsula under a new name. Not only would they assist Portugal and Spain, but also the country of Galicia, which their ancestors had abandoned to the Moors 700 years previously. The battle to liberate the Iberian Peninsula lasted until 1492 AD. This is the same year that Christopher Columbus sailed for the Americas. You will discover in the next chapter, this was no coincidence.

Sometime around 1332 AD, the date of the Searcy Geoglyph, Portugal ceded the eastern half of what is now the United States to the Templars. Research indicates that the territory designated by the Searcy Geoglyph, which was hastily crafted only 30 years before the ceding of the Kensington Runestone 1362 Territory, may have been done to exclude the Norse from colonizing the newly established North American Territory. There is archeological evidence that shows, through Norse Runes and Geoglyphs, that there was a concentrated Nordic presence from Minnesota to Texas and Louisiana, west of the Mississippi River during this time period.

Just prior to the Searcy land grant the Little Ice Age, c1303-1309 AD, and freezing climatic changes would have forced the Greenland and Iceland Norse to travel south to a warmer climate. The fact that the non-Celtic Vikings were originally only given Iceland to colonize c1000 AD, rather than the well known land in North America, can only mean that they were not originally planned to be part of the colonization of North America.

The colonization, by the Norse, of the Celtic Territory east of the Mississippi River was blocked by the ceding of this land, as demonstrated by the Searcy Geoglyph, to the Templars by Portugal. This land grant forced the non-Celtic Norse immigrants to begin colonizing the territory west of the Mississippi river. This territory was just outside the territory designated by the Searcy Geoglyph. The fact that the Norse could have blocked further expansion of the Celts to the west prompted Portugal to cede the territory described by the Kensington Runestone in 1362 AD, to the Templars; however, the Territory described by the Kensington Runestone had not yet been made public. This led other countries to assume that the land west of the Mississippi River was open to colonization.

In 1803 the US coordinated with Napoleon Bonaparte of France to acquire, from Spain, the land known as the Louisiana Purchase. Three months after he acquired the territory, which he promised Spain he would never sell; Napoleon sold the Louisiana Purchase to the US. This again froze the Norse out of being colonizers of the US and owners of land that would have blocked US access to the western United States. It is presumed that this is when the Norse moved north to the safer territory along what is now the Canadian border.

This action by the US, which by today's standards would be considered inappropriate, is just one more reason for historians, who would not want this information known, to try and hide this part of US history. The knowledge, that the original founders of the country did not want the Norse to colonize within the North American Territory, would place a black eye on the face of American history. Or worse, what if there were battles between the US and the Norse? Norsemen who had been close allies of the Sinclairs and Danes in centuries past.

The physical manifestation of the 1362 AD land transfer from Portugal, which included what is now the entire United States, was formally confirmed by the building of the Geoglyphic Pyramids on the island of Tenerife, in the Portuguese Canary Islands, c1822. The Tenerife Geoglyph identifies the 1362 AD boundaries of the North American Territory, as described on the Kensington Runestone, perfectly. It is believed that the Tenerife geoglyph was created, at the late date of 1822 AD, in order to justify the impending Mexican American War; a war which begin in 1846 AD, in order for the US to retrieve the land west of the Louisiana Purchase.

The United States government knew that the Kensington Territory, ceded to the Templars in 1362 AD, extended from the coast of the Atlantic to the Coast of the Pacific. This prompted the proclamation by President Polk, who was the President during the war with Mexico, to proclaim: It is our "Manifest Destiny" that this country extends from the Atlantic to the Pacific

Oceans. By that time, Spain had colonized the western third of what is now the United States, and President Polk wanted it back. After negotiations with Mexico to purchase the land failed, President Polk sent General Zachery Taylor, later President Taylor, to the Rio Grande River to provoke Mexico into a war to recover the lost territory.

Sometime after 1362 AD, after being ceded the North American Territory, all the Portuguese stone towers marking the major North American survey points, were destroyed by some group, who did not wish the complete story in the colonization of the North American Territory known. To this day, some group is still destroying any Celtic geoglyphs, or runic petroglyphs, which are found in the US. (See Appendix D)

Some of the tower bases can still be found, if you know where to look. Many of these stone towers still exist in places outside the United States. The Celts preferred to use, less obvious, geoglyphs as survey markers. Geoglyphs were so difficult to locate they were not discovered by the public until recently.

The Masonic Colonists

During the 15th century, the members of the Freemason Order begin to arrive in America from Europe. The Freemasons, although descended from the Templars, were of a different breed than the warriors that preceded them. These aristocratic late comers were intent on establishing the Masonic Democracy in the US, which we enjoy today. This meant that the Masons had a problem. There predecessors were primarily remnants of what they considered an obsolete, non-capitalistic, spiritually different, lower class of people. The progeny of any previous Celtic colonists (Native Americans) enjoyed an introspective spiritual existence, which included only taking from the land what was needed for their existence. Although admirable, this existence left the Ancient American Colonists vulnerable to attack from forces more powerful and technologically advanced than they were. The Masons knew this and attempted to establish a country that would combine the best attributes of both philosophies. Based on current information, it now appears that the Celts had plans to build the North American Territory into a peaceful and spiritual sanctuary, for their transcendentalist beliefs. Transcendental Meditation, being the oldest form of communion with God on the planet, was passed down through Tibetan Monks, and supposedly taught by Jesus to the Celts. The building up of North American Territory under Protestant and capitalistic ideals turned the early Celtic landowners (Native Americans) against the Masons. The only religious criteria for joining the Masons, is that you believe in God. This goes hand in hand with Transcendentalism. However, there were many other factions that molded this country, outside the Masonic Fraternity, that tended to dilute their philosophies and make the US an imperfect form of Masonic ideals.

There is the distinct possibility that the Native Americans, Celts and Norse may have even joined forces against the new leadership of what would become the United States. This would explain the current archeological conundrum of Celtic and Norse artifacts being found in collocated areas west of the Mississippi River, and in New England. It is certain that the Native American landowners (Celts) in the Eastern US had contempt for the ruling class during the War of Independence. This is based on the treaties and land sales, in which the Native Americans engaged, in favor of the British.

After the Masons replaced the North American Templar organization, and other Europeans begin immigrating, they were now obligated to include religions outside the Masonic Fraternity, in their "Grand Experiment" called Democracy. This transition was not difficult. The Templars and Cistercian Monks were committed to a vow of celibacy, and so within one generation they would have all been deceased.

This timing fits perfectly with the founding of the Masons c1450 AD, just 51 years after Henry Sinclair, the Templars, and the Farams came to America. The Farams would not have suffered this extinction, since they were a succession of married Templar leaders, rather than Templar Knights.

The Eastern American Indians, for lack of a better collective name, came to be called by the US government, the "Mississippian Indian Culture". The term Mississippians was a gross misnomer, since the collection of tribes ranged from Florida to the Mississippi River, and from the Mississippi River to Ohio and other states of the Ohio River Valley. This was an easy way to group all the cultures of early European origin into a single group. The many mound geoglyphs constructed by the group called the Mississippians indicate that they were the descendants of earlier Celtic explorers. These people were living off the land in accordance with their Celtic religious beliefs. The US Government even labeled five of the Mississippian tribes as the "five civilized tribes". These five tribes, along with others, were marched to Oklahoma in 1830, a journey known as "The Trail of Tears". Contributing to this atrocity was the fact that the Native Americans collaborated with the British during the American Revolutionary war. This was most likely done in protest to the now Protestant colonist's attempts to change the way the Native Americans lived. The siding of many of the Native American Celts with the British, against the overpowering Protestant colonizers, may have been what led to their harsh treatment of the Native Americans after the Revolutionary war with Britain.

This was just prior to the United States going to war with Mexico, and the Western Plains Indians. If a war erupted with Mexico, the remnants of these early Celtic colonists, now called Indians, may have been perceived as a threat to this newly formed democracy. The treatment of these early American colonists, by forcing them into a concentration camp called Indian Territory (Oklahoma), sounds like a dress rehearsal for the experience the Japanese Americans endured in WWII.

The rightful claim of the North American Territory, by the Native Americans is exemplified by the various negotiations, and land transfers, which the Native Americans made with the British, during the Revolutionary war. Their disdain for the newly established Protestant and Catholic democracy resulted in the sale of much of the Celtic colonized land in the US to the British. Of course the British lost this land when the Masonic constabulary won the Revolutionary war. Some of the treaties between the Native Americans and the British are outlined here.

The Treaty of Easton

The Treaty of Easton was a colonial agreement in North America signed in October 1758, during the French and Indian War (Seven Years War). Briefly, chiefs of 13 Native American nations, representing tribes of the Iroquois, Lenape-Delaware, Shawnee and others, agreed to be allies of the British colonies during the French and Indian War (Seven Years War), already underway. In return, the British colonizers of Pennsylvania and New

Jersey recognized native rights to hunting grounds, and settlements in the Ohio Valley. They promised not to establish additional settlements west of the Appalachian Mountains.

Negotiations of more than a week were concluded on October 26, 1758, at a ceremony held in Easton, Pennsylvania between the British colonial governors of the provinces of Pennsylvania and New Jersey, and representatives of 13 Indian nations, including the Iroquois, who sent Chiefs of three of their nations to ensure their domination of the Ohio Country region; the eastern and western Lenape (Delaware), represented by two chiefs, the Shawnee and others. More than 500 Native Americans attended the outdoor ceremony, after lengthy negotiations to bring peace to the regions of Pennsylvania, New Jersey and the Ohio Country.

Conrad Weiser served as an interpreter and arbitrator for the British colonial governments. The negotiations were held to hopefully resolve conflicts created by The Walking Purchase of 1737, which had lasting effects on the relationships between the Native Americans and the colonists. Attorney General of Pennsylvania, Benjamin Chew, Esq. attended the negotiations of the Treaty of Easton and documented the proceedings in his *"Journal of a Journey to Easton"*.

The treaty specified that the Native American nations would not fight on the side of the French, against the British, in the current war. In return, Pennsylvania returned large blocks of land which the Iroquois had ceded a few years before; the British colonial governors promised to recognize Iroquois and other tribes' rights to their hunting grounds in the Ohio River valley; and to refrain from establishing colonial settlements west of the Allegheny Mountains after the conclusion of the war. This clause of the treaty contributed to the Crown's subsequent Proclamation of 1763, by which it attempted to reserve territory west of the Appalachians for Native Americans and prohibit European-American advancement into the area. In addition, colonial governor William Denny of Pennsylvania agreed to negotiate directly with the Lenape-Delaware again without Iroquois intervention and marked the agreement by rekindling a "council fire." The conference concluded on October 26, 1758 and in November, Governor Denny announced to the Pennsylvania Assembly that *"a general peace was secured at Easton."*

By the treaty, the Lenape ceded all remaining claims to land within the Province of New Jersey, for the sum of one thousand Spanish dollars. They received payment immediately.

The Treaty of Fort Stanwix

The Treaty of Fort Stanwix was an important treaty between Native Americans and the British Empire. It was signed in 1768 AD at Fort Stanwix, located in present-day Rome, New York. It was negotiated between Sir William Johnson, and representatives of the Six Nations of New York.

The purpose of the conference was to adjust the boundary line between Native American lands, and British colonial settlements set forth in the Royal Proclamation of 1763 AD. The British government hoped a new boundary line might bring an end to the rampant frontier violence which had become costly and troublesome. Indians hoped a new, permanent line might hold back British colonial expansion.

The final treaty was signed with one signatory for each of the Six Nations and in the presence of representatives from New Jersey, Virginia and Pennsylvania, as well as Johnson. The Native American nations present received gifts and cash totaling £10,460 sterling, the highest payment ever made from colonists to Native Americans. The treaty established a Line of Property which extended the earlier proclamation line of the Alleghenies (the divide between the Ohio and coastal watersheds), much farther to the west. The line ran near Fort Pitt and followed the Ohio River as far as the Tennessee River, effectively ceding the Kentucky portion of the Colony of Virginia to the British, as well as most of what is now West Virginia. The lands south and west of the Kanawha had recently been confirmed to the Cherokee by the Treaty of Hard Labor, and during the Fort Stanwix proceedings, the British were astonished to learn that the Six Nations still maintained a nominal claim over much of Kentucky, which they wanted to be added into the consideration. In addition, the Shawnee contested Virginian settlements between the Alleghenies and Ohio until 1774. (The Treaty of Camp Charlotte).

Although the Six Nations of New York had previously recognized English rights southeast of the Ohio River at the 1752 Treaty of Logstown, they continued to claim ownership (by conquest) over all land as far south as the Tennessee River — which they still considered their boundary with the Cherokee and other "Southern" tribes. Although representatives of the Indian nations who actually occupied these lands, primarily the Shawnee and Lenape, were present at the negotiations in 1768, they were not signatories and had no real role in the Iroquois' sale of their homeland. Rather than secure peace, the Fort Stanwix treaty helped set the stage for the next round of hostilities along the Ohio River, which would culminate in Dunmore's War.

The treaty also settled land claims between the Six Nations and the Penn family, the proprietors of Pennsylvania, where the lands acquired in 1768 were called the "New Purchase." Due to disputes about the physical boundaries of the settlement, however, the final treaty line would not be fully agreed upon for another five years.

The final portion of the Line of Property in Pennsylvania, called the Purchase line in that State, was fixed in 1773, by representatives from the Six Nations and Pennsylvania who met at a spot called Canoe Place at the confluence of West Branch of the Susquehanna River, and Cush Cushion Creek, in what is now Cherry Tree, Pennsylvania. The reason for the Treaty of Fort Stanwix was that the press of population growth, and economic development, turned the attention of investors and land speculators to the area west of the Appalachians. In response to demands by settlers and speculators, British authorities were soon pressing the Iroquois and Cherokees for concessions of land in their country. The Treaty of Lochaber, with the Cherokee, followed in 1770 adjusting boundaries established in the Treaty of Hard Labor, whereby the Cherokee withdrew their claim to part of the same country, encompassing the south part of present-day West Virginia. No longer able to play off rival colonial powers, following the British victory in the French and Indian War, Indians were reduced to a choice between compliance and resistance. Weakened by the recent war, they negotiated away parcels of land in exchange for promises of protection from further encroachments. Therefore, in 1768 AD, the Iroquois gave up their claim south of the Ohio, hoping thereby to deflect English settlement away from their own homeland.

The Treaty of Lochaber

Following the Treaty of Fort Stanwix in November of 1768, which established the boundary lines to the north of Virginia, Lord Shelburne in London was anxious to settle disputes along the western frontier in order to avoid more conflict with the Native Americans. This led to the Treaty of Lochaber, which was signed in South Carolina on October 18, 1770 by British representative John Stuart and the Cherokees. Based on the terms of the accord, the Cherokee relinquished all claims to property from the North Carolina and Virginia border, to a point six miles east of Long Island of the Holston River in present-day Kingsport, TN, to the mouth of the Kanawha River at present-day Point Pleasant, West Virginia, in Mason County. The North Carolina-Virginia border at this time was along the 36° 30' parallel in present-day Tennessee. The south fork of the Holston River was agreed to become the southern bounds due to settler's confusion of where the parallel ran. Therefore, "North of the Holston" settlers were considered outside of the Cherokee lands. In this treaty, the Cherokee surrendered their rights to the remaining land in present-day southern West Virginia not included in the Treaty of Hard Labor in October of 1768.

The Treaty of Fort Pitt

Nothing better illustrates the contempt of the Masonic elite, who made up the ruling class of the future United States, than the Treaty of Fort Pitt, and all the other broken treaties between the Native Americans and the US.

The "Treaty of Fort Pitt", also known as "The Treaty with the Delaware", "The Delaware Treaty", or "The Fourth Treaty of Pittsburgh", was signed on September 17, 1778, and was the first written treaty between the new United States of America and any American Indians, the Lenape (Delaware Indians) in this case. Although many informal treaties were held with Native Americans during the American Revolution years of 1775–1783, this was the only one that resulted in a formal document. It was signed at Fort Pitt, Pennsylvania, site of present-day downtown Pittsburgh. It was essentially a formal treaty of alliance.

The treaty gave the United States permission to travel through Delaware territory and called for the Delaware to afford American troops whatever aid they might require in their war against Britain, including the use of their own warriors. The United States was planning to attack the British fort at Detroit, and Lenape friendship was essential for success.

In exchange, the United States promised "articles of clothing, utensils and implements of war, and to build a fort in Delaware country "*for the better security of the old men, women and children ... whilst their warriors are engaged against the common enemy.*" Although not part of the written treaty, the commissioners pointed out the American alliance with France, and intended that the Delaware would become active allies in the war against the British.

According to Daniel Richter in "*Facing East from Indian Country*", the Delaware perceived the agreement as "merely free passage" of revolutionary troops and the building of a protective fort for defending White Settlers. The American leaders intended to use the fort for offensive campaigns and wrote into the treaty that the Delaware would attack their native neighbors.

The treaty also recognized the Delaware as a sovereign nation and guaranteed their territorial rights, even encouraging the other Ohio Country Indian tribes friendly to the United States to form a state headed by the Delaware with representation in Congress. This extraordinary measure had little chance of success, and some suggest that the authors of the treaty were knowingly dishonest and deceitful. Others suggest that it was the Delaware chief White Eyes who proposed the measure, hoping that the Delaware and other tribes might become the fourteenth state of the United States. In any case, it was never acted upon by either the United States or the Delaware.

Within a year, the Delaware were expressing grievances about the treaty. A delegation of Delaware visited Philadelphia in 1779 to explain their dissatisfaction to the Continental Congress, but nothing changed, and peace between the United States and the Delaware Native Americans collapsed. White Eyes, the tribe's most outspoken ally of the United States, died in mysterious circumstances, and the Delaware soon joined the British in the war against the United States.

Signers of the treaty were White Eyes, Captain Pipe (Hopocan), and John Kill Buck (Gelelemend) for the Lenape, and Andrew Lewis and Thomas Lewis for the Americans. Witnesses included Brigadier General Lachlan McIntosh, Colonel Daniel Brodhead, and Colonel William Crawford.

THE FARAMS IN AMERICA

The Faram Tower, Maitland, Canada (c1410)

While researching ancient geoglyphs, I was eventually led to the Faram Tower, in what is now Maitland, Canada. This ancient structure was built on the north shore of the Saint Lawrence Seaway c1410 AD, after the Farams and Sinclairs came to North America. The Saint Lawrence Seaway was a major route for any ship exploring North America. At the time I had no idea that my ancestors had built this historic tower. Further research begin to reveal that my ancestors were the builders of the tower. I was not surprised, since I had learned previously that the Farams were builders of towers, lighthouses and churches for at least two millennia.

The Faram Tower was originally constructed within the North American Territory, just south of the line running from the NW end to the NE end of the Inspiration Peak 1362 mile long radials.

This territory was eventually colonized by the Celts long time ally, France. France's occupation of this territory ended with a British Victory in the Seven Years War, a war that existed between France and England from 1754 to 1763 AD, just before the British tried to take over the 13 colonies that would become the United States.

It was also discovered, that on the grounds surrounding Faram Tower, there exist geoglyphs which point back to the Farams previous homes in Galicia and Zealand, Denmark. This, along with other interconnected evidence in Britain, proves the tower's connection to the Faram family is genuine.

Bearings Emanating Geoglyphs on the Faram Tower Property

In the preceding photo is an aerial view of the property on which the Faram Tower sits. As is repeated in the construction of major geoglyphs, there are other geoglyphs placed around the structure to tell a story. These stories could be outlining a territory, showing where the builder was from, telling of the travels of the individual. In this case, it appears that it is all of the above. Although the bearings seem to point in indiscriminant directions, they are actually well thought out, and show that the builder had a true knowledge of the geography of the world. A close look at the destinations of the bearings will show that they are endpoints, which you have seen many times before. The bearings shown in the photo were obtained using higher magnification than what is shown.

Explanation of important radials in the previous photo:

1. The 067 degree radial not only points to Galicia, but to the very town, Corunna, that the Farams inhabited from before 43BC to c700 AD.

2. The three radials 043, 044, and 045, pointing to Denmark, show a definite affinity for that location. The Farams lived in Denmark from c700 AD to 1397 AD.

3. The 133 degree radial points to the Newport Tower, a key geoglyph in defining the North American Territory which later became the USA.

4. The 177 degree radial points to the SE corner of the territory, Cat Island, given to the Templars by Portugal.

5. The radials that point to the tip of Florida, the tip of South America, the Galapagos Islands, and the Tip of Yucatan, are all very important survey points used by the Celts.

One of the Ancient Tin Smelter Towers in Cornwall, UK

Throughout history, the Farams carried Tin and Copper from Cornwall to all the coasts of Europe. They were very familiar with the construction of the smoke stacks at these mines.

An Ancient Tin Mine in Cornwall, Britain

The construction of the Faram Tower, and others that exist both within and outside of the US, are identical to the towers used in mining in Cornwall, England. The only difference is the addition of doors and windows. This is further confirmation that the Celts were in the Saint Lawrence Valley. Their presence is also indicated by the numerous ancient mining sites that exist in the area.

Radials Pointing to the Faram Tower

The Radials Emanating From Three Traffic Circles in the City of Congleton, UK.

(One redial terminates at the Faram Tower while the other terminates on the island of Tobaga, on the Pacific side of Panama. Tobaga Island, as well as many other islands in both the Atlantic and Pacific, are labeled with the Faram Exploratory Geoglyph.)

The main geoglyph that ties the Farams to the Faram Tower, in Maitland Canada, is in the British town of Congleton, UK. Archaeological digs have shown, that the town was first occupied c10200 BC. The first historical reference to the town occurred in 1282 AD. The Farams built the first church in this town and laid out the first streets. As you can see, one of the radials emanating from the traffic circles, which are frequently used as geoglyphs around the world, points to the Faram Tower. This pretty well clinches the Faram involvement with the origin of the tower. Other radials associated with the Faram Tower, shown below, show the intense calculations which were done before deciding where to place the tower.

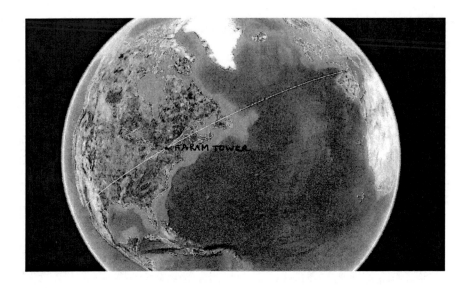

**The radial extending from the tip of Baja, passing through Faram
Tower, and ending on the western border between France and Spain.**

A radial originating at one of the main reference points for the North
American Territory, the tip of Baja, extends to the border between France and
Spain. France was a major influence in the history of the Danes, Scotts and
Templars which settled North America. At the time the Tower was constructed,
the Templars were fighting for Spain and Portugal, against the Muslims. The
termination point on the border of France and Spain is also the home of the
Basque culture which, in 1540 AD, initiated the replacement for the Catholic
Cistercian/Templar Order, now known as the Catholic Jesuit Order.

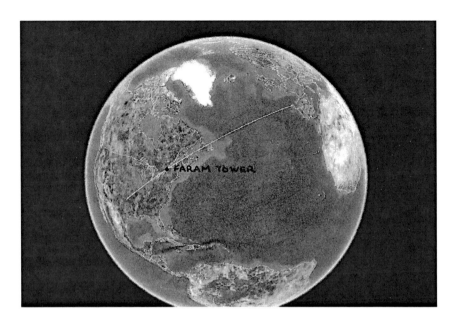

The radial extending from Sulpher City, OK geoglyph to Galicia

During the Celtic exploration of the Americas, the Sulpher City Geoglyphs were constructed on the southern 1362 mile radial emanating from Inspiration Peak. The Sulpher City geoglyphs were constructed by the Celtic colonist, in an attempt to include Mesoamerica in the North American territory. Although Mesoamerica was part of the original North American Land Claim, it had not been included in the land grant from Portugal in 1362 AD. The Sulpher City geoglyphs were an attempt to once again include Mexico in the North American Territory. This action was thwarted by Spain's invasion of Mexico in 1519 AD.

Sulpher City is the only major geoglyph that is not mentioned in the geoglyphs of antiquity prior to its construction. This means that it was most likely an after thought that followed the important geoglyphs that preceded it. Even with that being the case, it was positioned so that one of the radials emanating from the Sulpher City Geoglyph passed over Faram Tower while terminating at the north tip of Galicia, the Farams previous home over 700 years earlier.

During the "Trail of Tears" relocation of Eastern Native Americans to Oklahoma, the Chickasaw tribe demanded that they be relocated to the Sulpher City, Oklahoma area. It was necessary for the US Government to purchase the Sulpher City land from the Choctaw, who had already been moved there by the US, in order for it to be available to the Chickasaw Tribe. This shows an affinity by one of the "Civilized Tribes", the Chickasaw, toward the many Celtic Geoglyphs that existed there. This is just one more reason to believe that the tribes known as the "Five Civilized Tribes" were early European settlers. This combined with the geoglyphic properties of the Mississippian Indian mound cultures and geoglyphs proves this point.

The Cape Cod Geoglyph

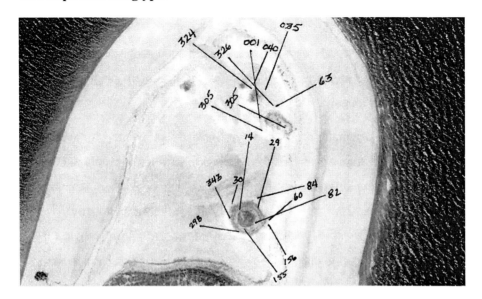

The two 305 degree radials running from Cape Cod to Faram Tower

Endpoints for the bearings displayed in the previous photo.

001 Degree Radial - North Entrance to Baffin Bay Greenland
014 Degree Radial - Disco Bay Greenland (Home of Eric the Red)
030 Degree Radial - West Tip of Iceland
035 Degree Radial - Reykjavik, Iceland
040 Degree Radial - West Tip of Newfoundland
060 Degree Radial - South Tip of Nova Scotia
082 Degree Radial - The Azores
087 Degree Radial - Northernmost Island in the Canary Islands
155 Degree Radial - Bermuda
298 Degree Radial - NW Corner of the USA
305 Degree Radial - Faram Tower, Maitland, Canada
324 Degree Radial - Entrance to Nelson River, Hudson Bay (Viking route to the center of North America)
326 Degree Radial - Montreal, Canada
330 Degree Radial - North West Entrance to NW Passage
343 Degree Radial - Southern Tip of Ireland

The preceding geoglyph was, most likely, placed by the Faram family. The fact that the two 305 degree radials, which point to Faram Tower, are stand alone geoglyphs is significant. In addition to the two circles that make up the northern 305 degree radial, there is also a raised mound geoglyph next to it, which makes up the southern 305 degree radial. The southern geoglyph cannot be seen using this magnification.

Obviously, the originator of this geoglyph wanted the Faram tower to be recognized. The Faram Tower was the headquarters for the Farams and Templars, while exploring and securing the area along the northern boundary of the North American Territory. This information is validated by both the Medicine Hat Geoglyph (*Google keywords: Medicine Hat Geoglyph*), and the Faram family distribution map along the Stonehenge boundary, shown later in the chapter. The most important radial in any geoglyph is the 090 degree radial. In the Medicine Hat geoglyph, which was originally in the North American Territory, is now in Canada. The 090 degree radial points directly to Faram Tower.

Radials Emanating from the Faram Tower

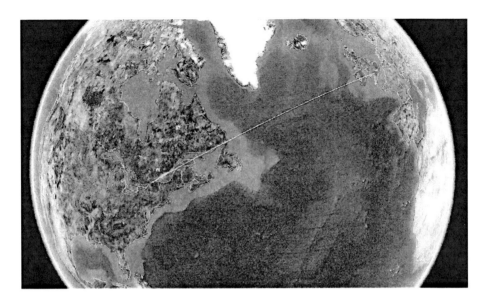

The Implied Radial Running From the Faram Tower to Stonehenge

(What better way to proclaim the Farams Celtic heritage than by situating the Faram Tower at a location where running a line through Belle Island, an island also pointed out by the Stonehenge Geoglyph, points back to Stonehenge?)

Faram Tower was the headquarters for the Templars and Farams working along the northern border of the original North American Territory. I am certain that you are beginning to see these survey markers were not placed indiscriminately around the world, but were carefully thought out before they were placed. This is true of all major geoglyphs. This must be done for the geoglyph to deliver the message that it was intended to send.

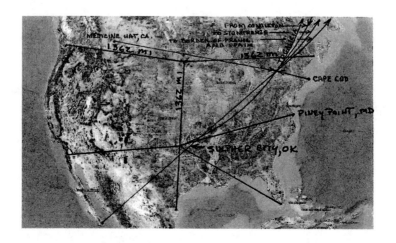

This is a Compilation of the radials pointing to, or running through, the Faram Tower. Many geoglyphs on the Oklahoma Indian Reservations point to Faram Tower also (Not shown), indicating a Celtic relationship.

THE REVOLUTIONARY WAR

The French Celtic sympathizers, with an early knowledge of the existence of North America through their Templar connections, settled what is now known as Southeast Canada. This territory was just north of the original boundaries of the North American Territory and just south of the territory outlined by the Stonehenge geoglyph.

After the existence of the Americas was made public, by the voyage of Columbus, British expeditions explored, and later settled, along the Atlantic coast. It should be remembered, that all the land north of the Southern Stonehenge boundary was now considered British property. In 1775 AD, The American Revolutionary War, often called the War of Independence, but in reality a war to fend off British invaders, began as a war between the Kingdom of Great Britain and the Thirteen Colonies. This gradually grew into a world war between Britain on one side and the newly formed United States, France, Netherlands and Spain on the other. In 1776 AD, the United States declared

396

their independence as a separate country, through the document known as "The Declaration of Independence". The Revolutionary War ended in 1783. The main result was an American victory, and European recognition of the independence of the United States. It is no coincidence that the same countries that played an important part in the previous history of the Celts and Templars were also US allies during the Revolutionary War.

The US Territory According to the Treaty of Paris c1783 AD.

The northern US border originally consisted of the land south of a line drawn between the ends of the NW and NE 1362 mile long radials emanating from Inspiration Peak. After the war with British, in 1783, the Treaty of Paris moved the Northern boundary of the US to the south. The 45th parallel was established as the border between Lower Canada (Quebec) and New York State (including what is now Vermont). The St. Lawrence River and the Great Lakes became the boundary between Upper Canada and the United States.

397

Westward expansion, of both the British Territory and the United States Territory, saw the boundary extended west along the 49th parallel from the Northwest Angle at Lake of the Woods to the Rocky Mountains, under the Convention of 1818. This convention terminated British claims south of that latitude, which was part of Rupert's Land, a territory in British North America. The treaty also terminated U.S. claims to land north of that line in the watershed of the Missouri River, which was part of the Louisiana Purchase of 1803. This transaction resulted in the US giving up the northern part of the drainages of the Milk River, the Poplar River, and Big Muddy Creek.

Disputes over the interpretation of the border treaties, as well as mistakes in surveying the boundaries, required additional negotiations resulting in the Webster-Ashburton Treaty of 1842. The treaty resolved the dispute known as the Aroostook War over the boundary between Maine on the one hand, and New Brunswick and the Province of Canada the other. The border along the boundary waters in present day Ontario and Minnesota, between Lake Superior and the Northwest Angle, was also redefined.

In 1844 a boundary dispute, during U.S. President James K. Polk's administration, led to a call for the northern boundary of the U.S. west of the Rockies to be latitude 54° 40' north (Where the current southern tip of Alaska ends.), but Britain wanted a border that followed the Columbia River to the Pacific Ocean. The dispute was resolved in a compromise, called The Oregon Treaty of 1846. This treaty extended the 49th parallel as the boundary through the Rockies. You should find it meaningful, that even though the entire northern boundary of the original North American Territory changed due to war, negotiations and treaties, the northern boundary of the United States still retains the same end points as the original territory as described by Inspiration Peak territorial boundary.

A Cruel Twist of Fate, or Choice?

Dispersal of the First, Historically Recorded, Farams in North America.

The black dots, on the previous map, show the final dispersal pattern of early Faram families after their arrival in North America. The Farams, in all but one of these locations, no longer exist. The Farams were the leaders of the Celtic Warrior Class, while the Sinclairs were leaders of the Celtic Royal Class. Based on the dispersal pattern, and other information, the Farams at some point, spread out just south of the original North American Territorial border, the curved line.

Interestingly, one of the Faram families was located on a river running from the Ottawa River to Georgian Bay. The Georgian Bay is the large body of water just north of, and connected to, Lake Huron. Of all the known routes leading to the Great Lakes, it appears that the Faram family, and their troops may have been guarding the shortest route to the Great Lakes coming from the North Atlantic, through the Saint Lawrence Seaway. I am not aware of this route being mentioned in any academic discussions of routes to the Great Lakes. This location is the marker just north of Georgian Bay. By blocking all the routes to North America, through the Saint Lawrence Seaway, the Norse would have been forced to find another route to the interior of North America. That route was located by entering the Nelson River on the western shore of Hudson Bay. Interestingly, this route leads to Minnesota and the western shores of Lake Superior, the current location of most of the Scandinavian heritage in the United States.

In 1783, after the Revolutionary War, a treaty between Britain and the United States was drawn up. The "Treaty of Paris" ended the war and recognized the sovereignty of the United States over the territory bounded roughly by, what is now Canada to the north, Florida to the south, and the Mississippi River to the west.

As can be clearly seen in the previous photo, that boundary change left the Farams, who had established themselves along the northern border of the US, in the newly negotiated British territory. Whether this was planned or was a cruel twist of fate upon the Faram's is not clear. Knowing that the Farams were knowledgeable about things that were happening in the upper echelons of the government, it is my belief that they chose to locate in what would become British territory. After all, the Farams had businesses in the British Isles. They may have also been displeased with the radical changes that they saw in the philosophy of the newly established Government of the United States.

The country for which the Celtic Warriors had such disdain (Britain), and the country for which they had given so much the USA, had negotiated them into being British subjects and separated from the country for which they had fought so hard. Since Scotland, by decree, was now a Protestant Country, the Farams may have opted to become British citizens. This would explain the Farams operation of their lumber-mill, in Fishlake, England, just a few miles south of the Scottish border.

From this point on, the Faram name begins to disappear from what was now Canada. The Faram name does not reappear in the United States Census, or immigration records, until many years later through the immigration of Farams from England. The many geoglyphs we have studied, all over the world, have led us to many "modified Faram Crests" along both the east and west coasts of South America. I suspect that exploration was one of the Faram solutions to their displacement by the Treaty of Paris.

The borders, though modified, represented by the Kensington Runestone, were finally realized, through the "Treaty of Hidalgo", after the Mexican American War. This would explain the large population of Norse in Minnesota. There is ample evidence to show that the Norse moved south, along the area west of the Mississippi River, after they learned in 1332 AD, that they were not welcome in the Templar Territory east of the Mississippi River. If the Masons were intent on moving the Norse out of the area west of the Mississippi river prior to 1803, the Louisiana Purchase gave them the public authority, which they had previously lacked, to ensure that their path to the west coast would not be blocked. Any colonists that may have traveled further west, after the Louisiana Purchase, would have again fallen under US control, after the Mexican American War pushed the US boundaries to the Pacific Ocean.

The portion, of what is now the United States west of the Mississippi River, had already been ceded to the Templars in 1362 AD, as attested to by the Kensington Runestone and Inspiration Peak. Even though the American colonists knew they had title to the lands west of the Mississippi they could not reveal this to the British, during negotiations for the Treaty of Paris, because their benefactor, Portugal, was also an ally of Britain, the country which the US had just defeated in a war.

The fact that the Treaty of Paris was the only public document, outlining the boundaries of the US, suggested to the world that the territory west of the Mississippi river was open for colonization by other countries. This prompted Spain, France, and the disenfranchised Norse to begin claiming, and colonizing the territory west of the Mississippi river. Up to this point, it appears that only Portugal, the original claimants to all of the Americas, and the US knew that the US held claim to the western portion of what is now the USA. This is, most likely what prompted Portugal to build the Tenerife geoglyphs c1822 AD confirming the right of the US to these western territories. If the US was going to challenge Mexico for the western portion of the United States, they needed a clear claim as to what territory Portugal had given them.

As you gathered from reading the Chapter titled "The Sinclairs in America", the Sinclairs disappeared from American history also. The original Templar colonists may have been set on establishing a Monarchy in the North American Territory mirroring the one in Scotland; however, the influx of European Masons, prior to the Revolutionary War, wanted a totally new nation based on their Protestant beliefs and democracy. This transition would have been blessed by the Sinclair family which followed Henry Sinclair I. This is best illustrated by the life of William Channing (Biography follows) whose statue adorns Touro Park, the location of the Newport Tower in Newport, Rhode Island. Ironically, Newport is the very site where these stories began 7000 years ago, with a radial pointing from the Egyptian Golfo de Cintra Geoglyph, to what later became Newport, Rhode Island USA.

Did Sir Henry I have a hand in establishing Democracy in North America? It is most likely that Sir Henry was more interested in his spiritual beliefs than his Royal position. As a result, the influential Masonic elite that followed him would have been able to undermine any attempt at a Monarchy, and establish what would become the most powerful democracy on earth.

It should be remembered that, most cultures of this time period maintained extreme prejudices against any people that were from another culture or social status. The people that came to North America after the Templars were no longer Templars; they were elite Masons combined with other cultures. Even though the Masons had originated from the Templars, the Masons may have no longer held the same ideals.

WILLIAM ELLERY CHANNING

The Channing Statue in Touro Park, Newport, RI

William Ellery Channing (April 7, 1780 – October 2, 1842 AD) was the foremost Unitarian preacher in the United States in the early nineteenth century. William is credited with bridging the gap between Celtic Orthodox Transcendentalism and European Protestantism, with a religion known as Unitarianism. He was known for his articulate and impassioned sermons and public speeches, and as a prominent thinker in the liberal theology of the day. Channing's religion and thought were among the chief influences on the early New England Transcendentalists (Celts), though he never embraced their views, which he saw as extreme.

Channing was born in Newport, Rhode Island, a grandson of William Ellery, **a signer of the US Declaration of Independence.** Channing became a New England liberal, rejecting the Calvinist doctrines of total depravity and divine election which were brought to America by British Protestants. Channing enrolled at Harvard College at a troubled time, particularly because of the recent French Revolution. Society was passing through a most critical stage. The French Revolution had diseased the imagination, and unsettled the understanding of men everywhere. The old foundations of social order, loyalty, tradition, habit, reverence for antiquity, were everywhere shaken, if not subverted. The authority of the past was gone. He graduated first in his class in 1798 and was elected commencement speaker; however, the faculty at Harvard prohibited him from mentioning the Revolution and other political issues.

Channing as a Theologian

As time passed and more immigrants came to America, they brought with them their protestant religions. The Celts had originally settled the country while worshiping under Orthodox Christianity (A combination of Transcendentalism and Christianity), as their primary method of communication with God. In Europe there had since been a similar movement, away from Catholicism and toward Protestantism. Although the Lutheran faith prevailed in Europe, the Calvinist and Presbyterian faiths were the faiths brought to the US by the Scotts. Protestantism, although showing contempt for the Catholic ethics, brought much of the Catholic doctrine with it.

At the time of Channing's theological transition, Calvinism was the primary religion in New England. In opposition to traditional American Calvinist orthodoxy, Channing preferred a gentle, loving relationship with God. He opposed Calvinism for *"... proclaiming a God who is to be dreaded. We are told that God is a loving God. We are told to love and imitate God. But would a loving God do things that we would consider most cruel in any human parent, ...were he brings his children into life totally depraved (of wisdom) and then pursues them with endless punishment"*. Channing was caught between the Celtic transcendentalist beliefs in a loving God and living off the land, and the capitalistic, protestant version of Catholicism brought to America by the Calvinists.

Calvinism (also called the Reformed Tradition or the Reformed Faith) is a major branch of Western Christianity, that follows the Theological tradition and Christian practices of John Calvin and other Reformation era theologians. Calvinists broke with the Roman Catholic Church, but differed with Lutherans on the real presence of Christ in the Lord's Supper, theories of worship, and the use of God's law for believers.

Presbyterianism is a branch of Protestant Christianity that adheres to the Calvinist theological tradition, but whose congregations are organized according to Presbyterian polity. Presbyterian theology typically emphasizes the sovereignty of God, the authority of the scriptures, and the necessity of grace through faith in Jesus.

Presbyterianism originated primarily in Scotland, where Scotland ensured a Presbyterian Church government in the acts of Union in 1707. Most Presbyterians found in England can trace a Scottish connection. The Presbyterian denominations were taken to North America, primarily by Scotts and Scott-Irish immigrants. The Presbyterian denominations in Scotland hold to the theology of Calvin and his immediate successors, although there is a range of theological viewpoints within contemporary Presbyterianism.

Transcendentalism is the modern noun used to describe the ancient Tibetan belief that man can better communicate with God, as an individual, through meditation. This ancient practice was reintroduced into modern society in the 1830's and 1840's, in the Eastern region of the United States. This was done as a protest to the general state of culture and society, in particular the state of Unitarian intellectualism being taught at Harvard University Divinity School. Unitarianism was the same religious compromise developed by William Ellery Channing.

Among the Transcendentalists' core beliefs is the inherent goodness of both people and nature. Transcendentalists believed that society and its institutions, particularly organized religion and political parties, had ultimately corrupted the purity of the individual. Transcendentalists believe in the power and rights of the individual, rather than the collective power of political parties and organized religion. The major figures in the movement were: Ralph Waldo Emerson, Henry David Thoreau, John Muir, Margaret Fuller, Amos and Louisa May Alcott and Walt Whitman.

Most people are not aware that the principles that the 19th century Transcendentalist were trying to revive, were the same principles for which the Celts and the Templars had fought so hard to retain through their Orthodox Christianity. Transcendentalism (Enlightenment through meditation.), while not being a religion, was part of the fundamental teachings of Jesus. It was not until the Catholic Church, with their need to control the individual, revised the teachings of Jesus, and required communication with God through the Church. The teachings of Jesus did not require a religion. It surely did not require adherence to the ridged doctrine of any church, or the giving of offerings in order for the individual to be in the favor of God. The Catholic Church went so far as to require individuals to communicate with God through a priest in the confessional, before they could have their sins pardoned.

In order to get a glimpse into the way a transcendental way of life would work, all one has to do is research the well documented spirituality, sharing of community wealth, and tendency to live off the land, all practices which the early American Celts had brought with them, or had taught others, after coming to America from Europe. The religious beliefs and symbols, which the early Celts brought with them, permeate the American Indian cultures. Unfortunately, these early Celtic cultures did not fit into the progressive, capitalistic and Protestant ideas of immigrants that came to North America during the 15th century and later.

Channing's struggle to rationalize Calvinism, over Transcendentalism, continued through the two years that he lived in Richmond working as a tutor. He came to his definitive faith only through much spiritual turmoil and difficulty. In 1803 Channing was called as pastor of the Federal Street Church in Boston, where he remained for the rest of his life. He lived through the increasing tension between religious liberals and conservatives, and took a moderate position, rejecting the extremes of both groups. Nevertheless, he became the primary spokesman and interpreter of Unitarianism when he preached the ordination sermon of Jared Sparks in Baltimore in 1819; it was entitled "Unitarian Christianity". In that address he explicated the distinctive tenets of the Unitarian movement. Other important tenets were the belief in human goodness, and the subjection of theological ideas to the light of reason.

In 1828, he gave another famous ordination sermon, entitled "Likeness to God". The idea of the human potential to be like God, (Also a Celtic belief) which Channing advocated as grounded firmly in scripture, and was seen as heretical by the Calvinist religious establishment of his day. It is in this address which Channing first advocates the possibility for revelation through reason, rather than solely from scripture. Revelation through meditation is an ancient practice, and a practice of the Jesuit Order of the Catholic Church, of which the newly elected Pope Francis is a member.

Even at the end of his life, he adhered to the non-Socinian belief in the preexistence of Jesus: "*I have always inclined to the doctrine of the preexistence of Christ (Reincarnation being another Celtic belief), though I am not insensible to the weight of your objections*" (Boston, March 31, 1832)

What the Unitarian movement amounted to was a non-violent repetition of the Catholic Churches suppression of Transcendentalism, that was imposed upon the Nazarenes 1500 years earlier. For some reason, whether it is monetary or spiritual, modern religion cannot grasp the concept of an individual communicating directly with God. For whatever reason, organized religion must place themselves between the two. Is this because there is no monetary enrichment to organized religion by instructing an individual how to be responsible for their own spiritual enlightenment? Some might say a church community is necessary in order to bring people to God. If this is so, would it not be better for those truly seeking enlightenment to be introduced to God, and then be released to increase their spiritual knowledge.

Channing's Later Years

Channing had an enormous influence over the religious (and social) life of New England, and America, in the nineteenth century. Towards the end of his life, Channing embraced immediate abolitionism. His evolving view of abolitionism was fostered by the success of British abolition in the British West Indies in 1834, and the absence of the expected social and economic upheaval in the post-emancipated Caribbean.

Channing wrote extensively about the emerging new national literature of the United States. He wrote that national literature is "*the expression of a nation's mind in writing*" and "*the concentration of intellect for the purpose of spreading itself abroad and multiplying its energy.*" The Catholic Jesuit Order also places a priority on higher education, and has instituted more colleges than any other Order in the Catholic Church. Channing died in Old

Bennington, Vermont, where a cenotaph is placed in his memory. He is buried in Mount Auburn Cemetery, Cambridge, Massachusetts.

Legacy

A Statue of Channing is located on the edge of the Boston, MA Public Garden, across the street from the Arlington Street Church where he served. There is another facing Channing Memorial Church, built in Newport, Rhode Island in 1880 to commemorate the 100th anniversary of his birth. The same year, a younger Unitarian minister in Newport, RI, Charles Timothy Brooks, published a biography, *"William Ellery Channing, A Centennial Memory"*. In 1885 "The Channing School for Girls" opened in London, primarily for the daughters of Unitarian ministers.

Channing had a profound impact on the Transcendentalism movement (Celtic Beliefs), though he never officially subscribed to its views; however, two of Channing's nephews, Ellery Channing (1818–1901) and William Henry Channing (1810–1884), became prominent members of the movement. Channing is memorialized for his attempt to bridge the gap between Transcendentalism and the Protestantism that was present in the early days of the colonization of the United States. Transcendentalism is once again gaining in popularity as a disciplined individual's method of direct communication with God, without the politics and other shortcomings of organized religion.

It is clear that Channing represented the culmination of a transition from the Celtic Transcendentalist Monarchy, to a Unitarian Protestant Democracy. This is why his statue was placed in Touro Park in Newport,

Rhode Island, one of the strongholds of the elite that transformed this country into a Democracy. It also explains why the Celtic role in American History has been erased from the history books.

THE JAMESTOWN COLONY

Jamestown, historically speaking, was the first documented settlement in the United States. This historical inaccuracy has been allowed to stand, as it takes the spotlight off the Celts settling the Americas, and places it with the more palatable British colonization. The Jamestown settlement was initiated by the Virginia Company out of England, with an Englishman named John Smith as the head of the expedition. Jamestown had a very difficult time surviving due to weather, malnutrition, Indians and disease. In 1610, what was left of the settlers boarded their ships and began their journey back to England. They were met at the entrance to the James River by two ships named the Patience and the Deliverance. The new contingent was led by Sir Thomas Gates, who became their new governor. He convinced the colonists to remain, and with new leadership the colonists survived. In 1611 AD Sir Thomas Dale became the Governor of the colony. He introduced strict discipline with a code of laws called *'Laws, Divine, Moral and Martial'*. Penalties for disobedience were severe.

In 1612 AD, a man named John Rolfe began growing tobacco in the area. In 1614 AD, the first Virginian tobacco was sold in England. Exports of tobacco soon became the mainstay of the Virginian economy. Gradually the colony expanded. In 1618 AD, the Virginia Company offered 50 acres of land to anyone from England who could pay for the cost of their voyage across the Atlantic. If they could not pay, they could become indentured servants. When they arrived, they had to work for the company for several years to pay back the cost of their passage. Also, in 1619 AD the first representative government in North America was created, when the House of Burgesses met. (Burgess is an old English word. A burgage was a plot of land in a town on which a house was built.).

In 1624 AD, the Virginia Company was dissolved, and the English Crown took over the colony. This is one of the first intrusions of British colonialism into the North American Territory. Future intrusions would lead to the war between the United States and England. By 1660 AD, the population of Virginia was 27,000. By 1710 AD, it had risen to 78,000. However, in 1699 AD, the seat of government of Virginia was moved from Jamestown to Middle Plantation (Williamsburg). Afterwards Jamestown went into decline.

Norfolk, Virginia

In 1619 AD, the Governor for the Virginia Colony, Sir George Yeardley, established four incorporations, termed cities, for the developed portion of the colony. These formed the basis for colonial representative government in the newly minted House of Burgesses. What would later become Norfolk, Virginia was put under the Elizabeth City incorporation.

Norfolk grew in the late 1600s when a "Half Moone" fort was constructed, and 50 acres were acquired in exchange for 10,000 pounds of tobacco. The House of Burgesses established the "Towne of Lower Norfolk County" in 1680. In 1691, a final county subdivision took place when Lower Norfolk County split to form Norfolk County (present day Norfolk, Chesapeake, and parts of Portsmouth) and Princess Anne County (present day Virginia

Beach). Norfolk was incorporated in 1705 AD and in 1736 AD, George II granted Norfolk a royal charter as a borough.

It is documented, in the book of Virginia Land Patents (1623-1666 AD), that the name Faram appears in 1637 involving the transference of land to new colonists in what would become Norfolk, Virginia. Those documents pertain to land in the new colony just 50 miles from Jamestown. This would mean that, just as in previous historical events involving the early colonists, the Farams were at the forefront of the event. It would be my guess that the Farams, being ship owners, were somehow involved in the transportation of the colonists to Virginia, and decided to also get involved in land sales. At about this time the Farams were also involved in the timber business in England, and may have been transporting the timber from the clearing of land in Norfolk back to Britain. In addition, in 1657 AD, Maryland State archives document that a Cottain Faram arrived as an immigrant from Scotland. Maryland is known for its early contingent of Scottish immigrants.

For the next hundred years or so, the Farams were involved in the logging business, at a town named Fishlake, on the eastern border between Scotland and England. Most of the trees in England had been depleted over the past centuries, for firewood and houses, and there was a big demand for wood products.

By 1775 AD, Norfolk developed into what contemporary observers argued was the most prosperous city in Virginia. It was an important port for exporting goods to the British Isles and beyond. In part because of its merchants' numerous trading ties with other parts of the British Empire, Norfolk served as a strong base of British Loyalist support during the early part of the American Revolution. After fleeing the colonial capitol of Williamsburg, Lord Dunmore, the Royal Governor of Virginia, tried to reestablish control of the colony from Norfolk. Dunmore secured small victories at Norfolk but was forced into exile by the American rebels, commanded by Colonel Woodford. His departure brought an end to more than 168 years of British colonial rule in Virginia. It is not recorded how many years of Celtic influence was connected with the area, prior to the British colonization.

At this critical time, it was necessary for the Farams to make the decision to align with the colonists or return to England. Even though they had strong ties to the new world, the relatives and businesses of the original Farams were in Scotland and England. My branch of the Farams chose to return to England. By loosing their free access to the massive resources of the Americas their fortune began to dwindle.

1760 AD finds John Faram Sr. in London getting married to Ann Ashton. His son, John Jr., was born nine months later. Based on what followed, it would be a good guess that he was in London to be educated as a land surveyor. The revolutionary war between the Colonies and England most likely had something to do with my ancestral grandfathers' change of trade, from shipping and logging, to land surveyor. John Jr. was associated with, and most likely worked for, George Stevenson, considered by many as the father of modern railroading. John Faram Jr. had nine children while moving around in the counties of Lancashire, Manchester, Cheshire and Staffordshire. As a surveyor, he would have been buying up right of way for the first commercial railroad in the world, The Liverpool and Manchester Railway. The railroad carried its first load of paying passengers on the 15th of September, 1830. John Jr. must have dedicated himself to seeing the railroad finished as he died just 12 days later at the age of 70.

One of John Faram's nine children was named Samuel. Samuel is the line from which this author descended. Samuel without a doubt followed in the steps of the great Faram tradition of Celtic Orthodoxy. Thanks to his father, Samuel was a wealthy man. He lived in close proximity to the Wedgewoods of pottery fame, in the town of Etruria, Staffordshire, England. Samuel assisted in establishing the town of Astbury, now named Congleton, and was responsible for building the Church of Saint James in that city. (This is the city where the traffic circle geoglyphs point to Faram Tower, on the Saint Lawrence Seaway, in what is now Canada.) The church is still in operation and retains its Orthodox Christian identity.

Samuels's son Francis remained in the railroad business and was engaged in the business of building locomotives. The son of Francis, Arthur Frank Faram, was involved in the selling of locomotives. When Arthur Frank's father died he took his inheritance and in 1901 moved to Fort Worth, Texas, USA where his sister, Anne Wallace, was already living. When he arrived he had with him a large, about 8 feet long, exact duplicate and working model of an English steam locomotive. After a lukewarm period of locomotive sales the locomotive was set up at the Fort Worth Zoo to carry children around the zoo. Being an exact replica steam engine, it was soon realized that it was too difficult to operate on a regular basis and a less complicated engine replaced it. The original locomotive was last seen, fully restored, in the Fort Worth Museum of Science and Industry, obstensively belonging to one of the curator's brother. All the Farams in the world are related and descended from the Farums that moved to Scotland from Denmark and changed their name to Faram.

Arthur Frank Faram
31 Dec 1855 – 28 Nov 1930

Arthur Stanley Faram
24 Aug 1894 – 9 Jun 1962

Arthur Joseph Faram
5 Nov 1919 – 01 Sept 1983

Arthur Donald Faram
Born 1942

NATIVE AMERICAN RELOCATION

After the Revolutionary war, and prior to the Mexican-American War, most of the tribes that lived east of the Mississippi River were relocated to Oklahoma (Indian Territory) as the result of the "U.S. Indian Removal Act of 1830".

This treatment most likely was in retaliation for the Native Americans (Early Celtic colonists) siding with the British during the Revolutionary War. Another reason may have been that the government was afraid that the Native Americans would side with the Spanish in the pending Mexican-American War. Many of the relocated tribes constructed geoglyphs, in Oklahoma, to restate their claim to the lands from which they had been driven.

AN OKLAHOMA GEOGLYPH

A Geoglyph on an "Indian" Reservation in Oklahoma
(Location withheld)

417

This geoglyph is one of the most impressive found in the United States. The simplicity of design is combined with the highest level of skill and functionality. The geoglyph is located, as are many, on the reservation of one of the tribes that were relocated from east of the Mississippi River to Oklahoma. This geoglyph, as do the others on Oklahoma reservations, prove that the so called Mississippian Tribes that were relocated to Oklahoma were of Celtic descent. These Oklahoma geoglyphs cry out to the people of later generations to remember that the Celtic people were here, and able to define their travels, long before the Masons arrived and decided that the original Celtic colonists were in the way of progress. The following four photos show the complexity in the design of this geoglyph. The geoglyph is stating that the territory east of the Mississippi River, in reality, belongs to these disenfranchised Celtic descendants. They also include some of their places of origin in Europe to substantiate their claims. Please notice that the places named as end points in this geoglyph have been seen many times before.

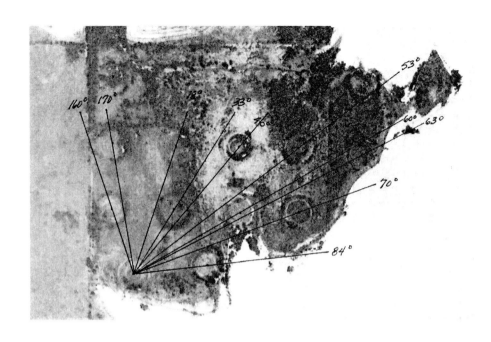

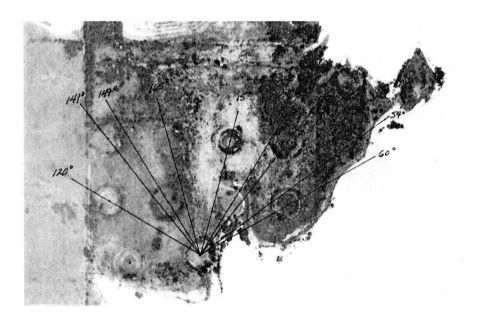

419

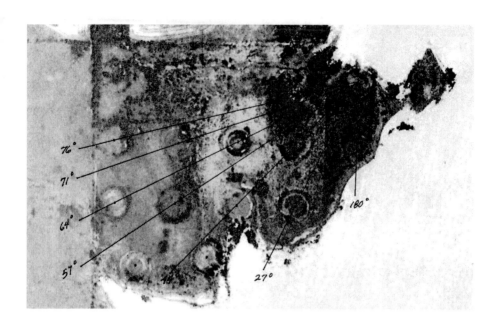

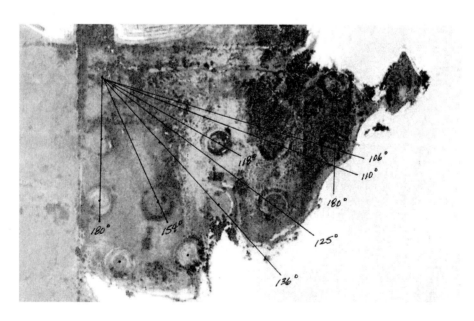

Endpoints for the bearings displayed in the above photos.

015 Degree Radial – East Tip of Southampton Island, Hudson Bay
018 Degree Radial – West Tip of Lake Superior
027 Degree Radial – Tip of Meta Incognita Peninsula, Canada. Entrance to Hudson Bay.
031 Degree Radial – South Tip of Iceland
037 Degree Radial – North Tip of Scotland
040 Degree Radial – Intersection of the Three Largest Great Lakes
044 Degree Radial – Entrance to Lake Melville, Canada
053 Degree Radial – Closest Point in Galicia, Iberia
057 Degree Radial – Faram Tower, Maitland Canada
060 Degree Radial – End of the NE 1362 Mile Long Radial From IP
063 Degree Radial – Southern Tip of Portugal
054 Degree Radial – Corunna, Galicia
064 Degree Radial – Southern Tip of Nova Scotia
070 Degree Radial – Canary Islands (Owned by Portugal)
071 Degree Radial – North Tip of Sandy Hook Peninsula, NJ
076 Degree Radial – Cape May Point, NJ, Entrance to Delaware Bay
084 Degree Radial – The City of Dakar, The Westernmost Point in Africa
106 Degree Radial – Old Entrance to Savanna River, GA
120 Degree Radial – Confluence of the Arkansas, White and Mississippi Rivers
125 Degree Radial – Southern Tip of Florida
136 Degree Radial – Entrance to Lake Pontchatrain, LA
141 Degree Radial – Mississippi Delta
149 Degree Radial – North Tip of Marsh Island, Iberia, LA, Vermillion Bay
154 Degree Radial – Chichin Itza, Yucatan (Geoglyph that designates Mesoamerican Territory.)
165 Degree Radial – North Tip of Galveston, Bay
170 Degree Radial – West Tip of Galveston Bay, Texas
180 Degree Radial – Orientation Radial and Location of Geoglyphs in Matagorda, Texas

END OF CHAPTER

Chapter 13

The Columbus Secrets

Christopher Columbus, 1451-1506 AD

The name Christopher Columbus is the Anglicization of the Latin Christophorus Columbus. His name in Italian is Cristoforo Colombo, and in Spanish Cristóbal Colón. After reading this chapter, I am certain you will agree that the story of Columbus is not at all what we have been told. This chapter is not written to infer that Columbus did not travel to America; there is plenty of historical evidence to establish that fact. This Chapter will validate that by the time Columbus made his voyage, the Templars and Celts owned the North American territory mentioned throughout this book, and that Spain had knowledge of this fact. This chapter will also prove that Spain had plans to conquer Mesoamerica even before Columbus began his voyage. Based on this information, the story that Cortez invaded Mesoamerica on his own, without permission from Spain is most likely not true.

THE QUEST FOR SUPPORT

In 1485 AD, Columbus presented his plans to John II, King of Portugal to cross the Atlantic. He proposed that the king equip three sturdy ships and grant Columbus one year's time to sail out into the Atlantic, search for a western route to the Orient, and return. Columbus also requested that he be made "Great Admiral of the Ocean", appointed governor of any and all lands he discovered, and given one-tenth of all revenue from those lands. The king submitted Columbus's proposal to his experts, who rejected it. It was their considered opinion that Columbus's estimation of a travel distance of 2,400 miles (3,860 km) was, in fact, far too low. The true reason for the denial was that Portugal did not want their colonies in South America discovered, until after the current war against the Muslims was over.

In 1488 AD, Columbus appealed to the court of Portugal once again, and once again, John II invited him to an audience. King John again showed no interest in Columbus's far-fetched project. Columbus traveled from Portugal to both Genoa and Venice, but he did not receive encouragement from either. Columbus had also dispatched his brother Bartholomew to the court of Henry VII of England, to inquire whether the English crown might sponsor his expedition, but also without success.

Columbus then sought an audience with the monarchs Ferdinand II of Aragon and Isabella I of Castile, who had united many kingdoms in the Iberian Peninsula by marrying, and now, by ruling together. On 1 May 1486, Columbus received permission to see Queen Isabella. Columbus presented his plans to the Queen, who, in turn, referred it to a committee. After the passing of much time, the experts of Spain, like their counterparts in Portugal, replied that Columbus had grossly underestimated the distance to Asia. They pronounced the idea impractical and advised their Royal Highnesses to pass on the proposed venture.

However, to keep Columbus from taking his ideas elsewhere, the Spanish Monarchs gave him an annual allowance of 12,000 maravedis and, in 1489 AD, furnished him with a letter ordering all cities and towns under their domain to provide him food and lodging at no cost. This was a full 6 years prior to the departure of Columbus for the New World. In reality this was a contingency plan by the Vatican, Spanish and Portuguese. They now knew that Columbus was very serious about crossing the Atlantic. If he was successful he would have discovered the Portuguese, Mayan, Aztec and Masonic colonies already in the Americas. The Portuguese and Spain needed a tactic to delay his departure until they had finished their war against the Moors (Muslims). Once the war was over they could divert their resources to protecting their interests in the Americas.

On January 2, 1492, the last Muslim leader, Muhammad XII, known as Boabdil to the Spanish, surrendered complete control of Granada, to Ferdinand

and Isabella, Los Reyes Católicos ("The Catholic Monarchs"). The re-conquest (Reconquista) of Iberia was complete.

On the evening of August 3, 1492 AD, Columbus departed from Palos de la Frontera with three ships: a larger carrack, the Santa María (A Galician ship), and two smaller caravels, the Pinta (Meaning painted), and the Santa Clara, nicknamed the Niña (Meaning little girl) after her owner, Juan Niño of Moguer. The monarchs forced the Palos inhabitants to contribute to the expedition. The Santa María was owned by Juan de la Cosa and captained by Columbus. The Pinta and the Niña were piloted by the Pinzón brothers (Martín Alonso and Vicente Yáñez). The ship the Santa Maria was not only a Galician ship, owned by Juan de la Cosa, but Juan is also responsible for printing the now famous map called the "Juan de la Cosa Map". The map was printed c1500 and shows 25 ancient geoglyphic survey markers that currently exist on the North and South American Continent. These geoglyphs would have taken centuries to explore and construct. Could both the North and South American Continents have been explored from coast to coast in the 8 years between the voyage of Columbus and the printing of the map? I think you already know the answer. (*"Ancient Signposts"* - The Faram Foundation, Amazon.com 2011)

THE PINZON BROTHERS

The Pinzón brothers were Spanish sailors, explorers and fishermen, natives of Palos de la Frontera, Huelva, Spain. All three were Marisco Muslims according to Christian scholar Jerald Dirks. Martín Alonso, Francisco Martín and Vicente Yañez Pinzon, participated in Christopher Columbus's first expedition to the New World and in other voyages of discovery and exploration in the late 15th and early 16th centuries.

The brothers were sailors of great prestige along the previously held Muslim coast of Huelva. Huelva is located in Spain near the border with Portugal. Thanks to their many commercial voyages and voyages along the coast, they were famous, well off, and well respected in the maritime community. The strategic position of Huelva was established by the historic Atlantic port of Palos, from which expeditions had set forth to the African coasts as well as the wars against Portugal, organized on many occasions, by the Pinzon family.

Martín Alonso and Vicente Yáñez, captains of the caravels La Pinta and La Niña are the best known of the brothers, but the third brother, the lesser-known Francisco Martín, was aboard the Pinta as its master.

Although they sometimes quarreled with Columbus, on several occasions the Pinzón brothers were instrumental in preventing mutiny against him, particularly during the first voyage. On 6 October, Martín intervened, in a dispute between Columbus and his crew, by proposing an altered course (which Columbus eventually accepted) and thus calming the simmering unrest. A few days later, on the night of 9 October 1492 AD, the brothers were forced to intercede once again, and this time they proposed the compromise that if no land was sighted during the next three days, the expedition would return to Spain. On the third day, land was in fact sighted by Juan Rodriguez Bermejo (also known as Rodrigo de Triana). Could it be a coincidence that the Pinzon brothers knew exactly what correction to make in order to land on the first island outside the SE corner of the Templar Territory, a territory ceded to the Templars by Portugal, Spain's ally? Could it have been a coincidence that the Pinzon brother knew exactly when they would sight land? It is clear that either the Pinzon brothers, or Juan de la Cosa, had already been to the Americas many times. Juan being a Galician (The starting point of our story about the Farums.) was most likely the one with the navigation knowledge to the Americas. Not only did Juan de la Cosa travel with many famous explorers, but his name implies that he may have had some secret navigation device that we no longer know about. As I mentioned before, people of that time were named after something peculiar to that person. Juan de la Cosa is Spanish for "John of the Thing". I have always wondered what "The Thing" referred to.

Why would the Monarchs of Spain, and the King of Portugal, choose three Muslim brothers to accompany Columbus to the Americas? After all, hadn't the two countries just spent 700 years getting rid of Muslim control and weren't the Pinzon brothers the architects of wars against Portugal? The obvious answer is that they had many reasons to persecute the Pinzons, but instead used this, and the Pinzons knowledge of the Americas, against them in directing Columbus to the uncolonized and unclaimed parts of the Americas. (Actually, the Caribbean had already been claimed by the Mayans, as indicated by the Chichin Itza Pyramid geoglyphs, but that is another story.)

THE FIRST VOYAGE of CHRISTOPHER COLUMBUS

After departure, Columbus first sailed to the Canary Islands which belonged to Castile (An eastern extension of Galicia), where he restocked the provisions and made repairs. After stopping over in Gran Canaria, he departed from San Sebastián de La Gomera on 6 September, for what turned out to be a five-week voyage across the ocean. A lookout on the Pinta, Rodrigo de Triana (also known as Juan Rodríguez Bermeo), spotted land about 2:00 on the morning of 12 October, and immediately alerted Columbus by firing a small cannon. Columbus later maintained that he himself had already seen a light on the land a few hours earlier, thereby claiming for himself the lifetime pension promised by Ferdinand and Isabella to the first person to sight land.

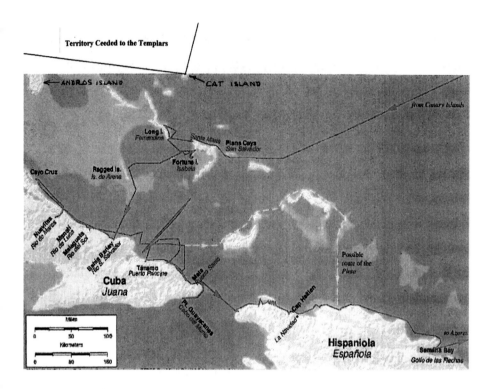

The map shows labels including:
Territory Ceeded to the Templars, ANDROS ISLAND, CAT ISLAND, from Canary Islands, Long I. Fernandina, Santa Maria, Plana Cays San Salvador, Fortune I. Isabela, Cayo Cruz, Ragged Is. Is. de Arena, Nuevitas Rio de Mares, Manati Rio de Luna, Matanzas Rio del Sol, Bahia Bariay Rio & Salvador, Tanamo Puerto Principe, Mata Gento Carino, Cuba Juana, Pt. Guayacanes Cabo del Monte, La Navidad, Cap Haitien, Possible route of the Pinta, Hispaniola Española, Samana Bay, Golfo de las Flechas, to Azores

Scale: Miles 0 — 50 — 100; Kilometers 0 — 80 — 160

The First Voyage of Columbus

(Please note that the preceding map, and documentation from the voyage, verifies that the Pinta left the other two ships at some point near Cuba. Also notice the jagged lines on the route that exist between Hispaniola and the Island of Tortue. This information is vital to the following story.)

While performing research on Columbus, I ran across a story that I had never heard before. Until the writing of this chapter I just placed it in the back of my mind because of the lack of validation. Now that I have obtained a definitive map of the first voyage of Columbus, and Wikipedia has updated their information, I am inclined to believe that the story is true. The story asserted that one of the ships, the Pinta, captained by one of the Pinzon brothers, mysteriously departed the convoy at Cuba and was not seen again until 45 days later, after Columbus had supposedly began his trip home without the Pinta.

428

The story indicated that the Pinta mysteriously joined Columbus near an island off the coast of Hispaniola (Haiti).

The story also said that when the Pinta arrived back in Spain it was loaded with a cargo of Gold. This is not hard to believe after reading that Montezuma, 27 years later, sent Hernan Cortez, while an official in Cuba, a circular piece of gold three feet wide. This was accompanied by a circular piece of silver three feet wide, along with much more gold. This was payment to keep Spain from invading Mesoamerica. Why did Montezuma think Spain was going to invade Mexico? This question is answered by one of the Geoglyphs that Columbus and the Pinzon brothers placed during their first voyage to the Americas. All that payment of gold did was intensify the appetite of Cortez who, supposedly against orders from Spain, invaded Mesoamerica in 1519 AD. Thus began the quest for gold, and the Spanish Inquisition in the Americas.

It should be noted that the Spanish Inquisition was sponsored by the Vatican, and that a priest accompanied every Spanish expedition in order to protect the interests of the Church. An exception to the harsh treatment of the natives was the Catholic Jesuit Order, who protected the American Indians from slavery whenever possible.

THE "EXPLORATION"

Columbus explored the northeast coast of Cuba, where he landed on 28 October. On 22 November, Martín Alonso Pinzón took the Pinta on an unauthorized expedition to places unknown. Columbus, for his part, continued to the western tip of Hispaniola, where he landed on 5 December at what is now Mole-Saint-Nikolas Bay.

There, the Santa María *"allegedly"* ran aground on Christmas Day 1492 AD, 20 days after it arrived, and had to be abandoned. The native Chief in the area, Guacanagari, gave Columbus permission to leave some of his men behind. Columbus left 39 men behind and founded the settlement of La Navidad, Haiti. When he departed Haiti he sailed along its northern coast, with a single ship, until he encountered the Pinta on 6 January 1493." (Wikipedia - Keyword Christopher Columbus.)

Did the Santa Maria really run aground or was it left behind by the Pinzon Brothers, with a crew of 39 men, to collect more gold after Columbus returned to Spain? Based on the documented information, a picture is emerging of what transpired during the Columbus expedition. From the documentation available, and the history of Columbus in later life, it appears that he was but a pawn in a plan by Spain to gather gold and occupy Mesoamerica.

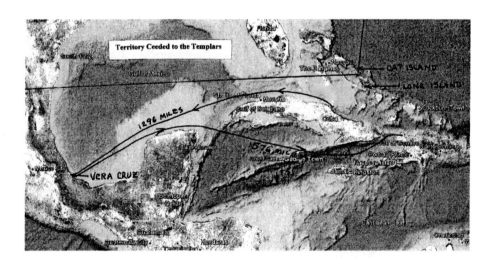

Presumed Route of the Pinta During its Absence

The preceding map depicts the probable route of the Pinta, prior to rejoining Columbus at Hispaniola. The fact that the two ships were able to locate each other at all in such a vast ocean is inconceivable. The only way that this could have happened was for the Pinzon brothers to have known the area, and have agreed to meet at an easily recognized point, such as between the island of Tortue and the Island of Hispaniola (Haiti). The Pinta was missing from 22 November, 1492 until 6 January, 1493, a period of 45 days. Allowing for a speed of only 5 knots the Pinta could have traveled 5400 miles during that period of time.

It is most likely that the Pinta traveled to Vera Cruz, Mexico to obtain gold for Spain. If this is true, it would have been logical for the Pinta to have left the other two ships at the northernmost point in the voyage, while off the coast of Cuba. The distance from that point to Vera Cruz is 1296 miles. The distance from Vera Cruz to Hispaniola is 1576 miles. Based on this mileage, the sailing time from Cuba to Vera Cruz and back to Hispaniola would be approximately 24 days. Based on the 45 days that the Pinta was absent, this leaves 21 days unaccounted for. Assuming that the Pinta did go to Vera Cruz, which this author has many reasons to believe, a portion of the 21 days would have been used in resupply, negotiations and loading. During our research it was learned that Vera Cruz, Mexico and Lisbon, Portugal are two of the oldest cities in the Atlantic. I find it interesting that both countries play a part in this story.

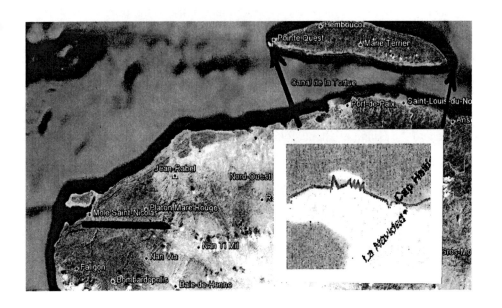

Mole-Saint-Nicolas, Haiti

The Pinzon brothers most likely had agreed to meet between the Island of Tortue and Hispaniola. The Pinta most likely passed by the bay where Columbus was waiting, and proceeded to the agreed meeting place. When the captain of the Pinta found no one waiting, he would have dropped anchor at the east end of the island and waited for Columbus and his brother.

The preceding photo is provided to show two things. The bay where Columbus was waiting, and the zigzag pattern (Called tacking in nautical terminology.) taken by the Nina after leaving the bay. Tacking like this in such confined quarters is very dangerous unless you already know the depth of the water. This type of maneuver would be used if there were limited visibility, such as a light fog, and you were looking for another ship. The visibility to the horizon from the deck of a ship is 12 miles. The distance between the two land masses here is only four miles. This would preclude the need for tacking unless the visibility was diminished and you were looking for another ship. It should also be noticed that as soon as the two ships joined up, there is no more tacking and they began their voyage home.

THE COLUMBUS GEOGLYPHS

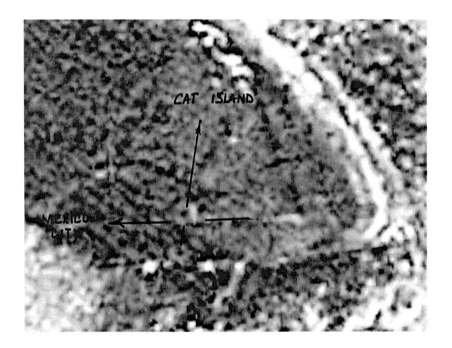

Geoglyph#1 Constructed by the Columbus Expedition
(The location is not disclosed to protect the site.)

The preceding geoglyph shows one of many geoglyphs that Columbus placed in the Caribbean to claim the territory for Spain. The radial extending to Mexico City is based on the white line on the right side of the photo. The geoglyph also shows a line projecting to the SE corner of the Templar territory. Using the standard protocol of running a line through the center of the two circles, located at the bottom left of the photo; the line terminates precisely, at Cat Island. Cat Island is the southeast corner of the territory given to the Templars by Portugal.

This proves, along with a second Columbus geoglyph shown below, that Spain knew about, and had plans to colonize, the Caribbean and Mesoamerica, prior to the sailing of Columbus on his first voyage.

This is but another validation of the origins of the United States of America, which has been the subject of this book. Only two of the many radials depicted in the previous geoglyph are shown, in order to confirm Spain's intentions.

Geoglyph#2 Constructed by the Columbus Expedition
(The location is not disclosed to protect the site.)

434

Geoglyph #2 is a more defined geoglyph, which is located more than 250 miles away from Geoglyph#1. Each side of these stone structures constitutes a bearing pointing to a place that meets the protocols of the ancients, and outlines the new territory claimed by Spain. This geoglyph, as are all geoglyphs, is confirmed as legitimate, by one of the bearings pointing to a cardinal point of the compass, in this case 360 degrees. The final verification stems from the fact that one of the radials points directly to Geoglyph #1.

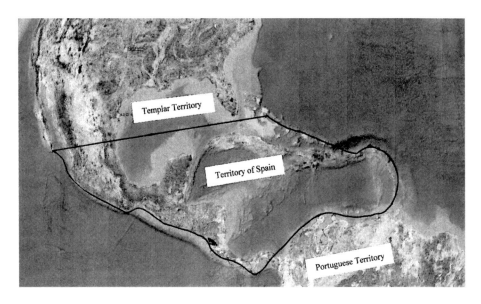

**The Territory Claimed by Spain on the First Voyage
of Columbus, as defined by Geoglyphs #1 and #2**

Based on the Information now available, it would appear that Spain had two objectives when they sent Columbus to the "New World". One was to geoglyphicly establish their claim to the Caribbean and the surrounding territory. The second, was to bring back gold to Spain to help eliminate the deficit that they had acquired during the 700 year long war against the Moors. The Portuguese, most likely, did not participate in this adventure since they already had substantial colonization in eastern South America (Brazil) by this time. Spain had other motives. They were now aware of the vast horde of gold brought back to Spain, by the Pinzon brothers, from the Aztecs. Spain, and the Vatican, wanted more gold and all the land that they could conquer. If you will notice, on the following map, none of the voyages of Columbus encroach upon the territory ceded to the Templars by Portugal, or on Brazil, which was colonized by Portugal.

The Vatican also had motives to participate in the planning of this expedition. During the 700 year war with the Muslims, the influence of the Catholic Church had been decimated. The Vatican's control had also been compromised, by the split of Europe into two camps consisting of Eastern Europe and Western Europe. The Orthodox Churches prevailed in the Eastern half of Europe, and the Western half was involved in a dispute for control of the Church, between the Vatican and the royal families of France. Both Spain and the Vatican needed to restore their wealth and prestige. To protect the Vatican's interests, a priest accompanied each expedition that the Conquistadores made to the Americas.

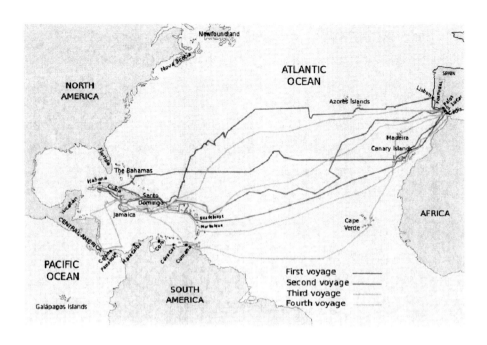

The Four Voyages of Columbus

Between 1492 AD and 1503 AD, Columbus completed four round-trip voyages between Spain and the Americas, all of them under the sponsorship of the Crown of Spain. These voyages marked the beginning of the massive exploitation, and colonization of Central and South America, and are thus of enormous significance in Western history. Columbus always insisted, in the face of mounting evidence to the contrary, that the lands that he visited during those voyages were part of the Asian continent, as previously described by Marco Polo and other European travelers. Columbus's refusal to accept that the lands he had visited, and thought he claimed for Spain, were not part of Asia might explain, in part, why the American continents were named after the Templar term "La Merica" (**The Western Star**) and not after Columbus. The lack of knowledge by Columbus, of where he had been, further confirms that

437

the Pinzon Brothers, and Juan de la Cosa, were the driving force during the expedition, and were responsible for the building of the geoglyphs.

Coincidentally, in 1850 there was a Freemason Order instituted named "**The Order of the Eastern Star**" which was initiated by a Freemason named Rob Morris in Boston, MA, an East Coast city in "La Merica". Rob Morris was a Freemason Official. The order was a fraternal order open to both men and women; however, the members are required to be either a Master Mason or a member of his family.

It was never intended that Columbus be crowned the discoverer of the Americas. It wasn't until years later that the United States decided that they `would not contest myths that Columbus discovered America. Columbus was sent to the Americas to establish Spain and Portugal's claim to the Caribbean. Neither Columbus, nor Spain had their eye on North America. North America had already been ceded to the Templars, in return for their help in ridding the Iberian Peninsula of the Muslims.

> *"Columbus Day was the brainchild of New York state senator Timothy Sullivan, an archetypal Tammany Hall man who greased the wheels of New York City's notoriously corrupt political machine during the late 19th century and early 20th century. His bill to set Columbus Day aside passed by a vote of 86 to 35 in 1909, and the initial reaction from those hardworking Americans of yore wasn't great. People labeled it superfluous and called for its repeal."*
>
> *Sullivan's power was so great there is no doubt he could accomplish the fete of getting this bill through Congress. Sullivan began life selling newspapers as a young boy from Ireland. During his rise to fame he was deeply involved in the criminal element in New York. Once he achieved his political success he protected the people with whom he had risen to power.*

Sullivan served in the NY State Assembly, the NY Senate and the US Congress.

Sullivan forced the bill on reluctant New York lawmakers and they in turn forced it on other States, an objector wrote of the day; "Its occurrence interferes sadly with the conduct of business in the season which should be the busiest, but once we have a holiday we must keep it. Luckily there are no other new holidays in sight at present." (The Origins of Columbus Day, Katy Steinmetz, Times Online - Monday, Oct. 11, 2010)

END CHAPTER

Conclusion

Well, what do you think? I know there has been a barrage of technical data thrown at you, and some of it may have been confusing or downright unbelievable. In order to get the full impact of the book you must have accepted the premise that Geoglyphology is a legitimate and ancient science. Although the origin and time period in which the science originated would be an important part of the story, that part of the puzzle has yet to be determined. What is important is that you have understood and accepted the physical information set down before you. I have attempted, whenever possible, to provide the reader with physical, geometric and photographic proof of the facts presented here. That is why there are so many photos. The premise that ancient people understood and used such complicated mathematics is staggering to the mind of anyone.

There has been speculation, that it was extra terrestrials which assisted the people down through time, in plotting these gigantic puzzles. To date I have not accepted this hypothesis. There is ample proof, that precedes this data, that shows that the great majority of the world used and understood astronomy, in some cases better than we do today. There is now ample proof, contrary to what we have been taught, that the ancients have traveled the world accumulating knowledge for thousands of years.

Take a look back at what our modern culture has achieved in just the past 200 years. There is now proof that ancient, and intelligent, civilizations existed

440

thousands of years before we have been told. When you consider the information that could have been developed over thousands of years, about magnetic deviation, the locations of the stars and planets, coupled with the fact that the people traveled the world and may have had very accurate maps, it then becomes clear that the ancients could have accomplished the calculations involved in the science of Geoglyphology.

Our research shows that Geoglyphology was also being used as late as colonial times in the design of forts, and even the streets of Washington, DC USA. This would indicate that the founders of the US were aware of this science. This would seem to preclude persons using the help of extra terrestrials in figuring out these complicated puzzles.

You may have found it interesting, that the subjects covered in this book are primarily the same subjects that have been shrouded in secrecy from the time the Vikings sailed from Norway c1000 AD, until the voyage of Columbus in 1492 AD.

A few of the subjects that have been left out of the history books, and seem to be taboo, are;

- The Greenlanders move to the North American Territory after they were frozen out of Greenland and Iceland.

- The fate of the Templars after they were run out of Europe

- The history of the United States prior to Columbus

- The many voyages by the people of Europe, to the Americas, which are recorded in known documents in Europe but have not made their way into the history books.

- The many artifacts, structures and influences involving pre-Columbian cultures in North America, which prove that Europeans were here long before Columbus.

- The almost paranoid fear of Archaeologists to acknowledge, or even to investigate, that any pre-Columbian European object found in North America is authentic.

The secrecy which surrounds these subjects, unfortunately, coincides with the Masons changing their name from the Templars and their move to North America. Could it be that the Masons claimed the North American Territory for themselves, to the detriment of the many cultures, which came before them?

So, for the readers who had trouble following the mountain of information that was presented here, I am going to do a short, pictorial, recap of the main points that were presented in the book. The Geoglyphs presented will be just the important history making geoglyphs, in chronological order, with a brief description as to what they are, and why they are important to history.

It is my hope that through this book, and others that may follow, we can all discover the truth of our national heritage

THE GEOGLYPHS

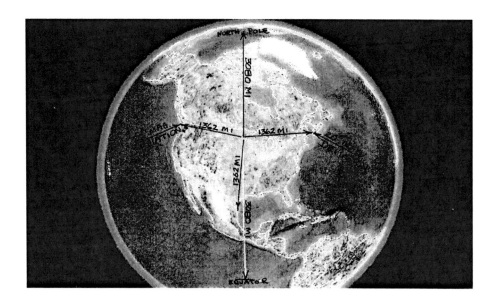

The Original Inspiration Peak Territory (pre-3100 BC)

Well this is where the North American Territory started, at the Inspiration Peak Geoglyph. This geoglyph is only dated back to c3100 BC, because that is the date of the only authenticated geoglyph, Stonehenge, which points to it. It is my opinion that it could be dated at c5000 BC, or earlier. The reason being, that the Caral Peru Geoglyph, which identifies the entire continent of South America, is dated as being at least 7000 years old.

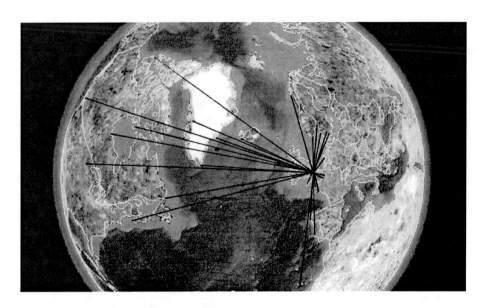

The Stonehenge Boundaries (c3100 BC)

Stonehenge is known to have been built by the Celts that lived in the southern plains of Britain. This in itself shows the vastness of the territory of which the Celts had knowledge. The North American Territory, mentioned in the previous geoglyph was divided up several times. The Stonehenge geoglyph seems to be the first division of the North American Territory. This amendment included what is now Canada in the Territory of the ancient Celts. In order to accomplish this, and the other geoglyphic partitions of land, the ancients would have had to have been traveling the world. In all my research I have not found one issue that could not be explained by world travel, excellent maps, the knowledge of magnetic deviation, and an understanding of astronomy.

Tiniteqilaq, Greenland Geoglyph Boundaries (c1100 AD)

The Tiniteqilaq geoglyph, by its very nature, was constructed by either the Celts or Vikings after the Vikings departure from Europe. It would have been necessary for these boundary changes to have had the approval of the Celts, when it was constructed. Not only have the boundaries been extended down to include Newport, RI USA, but the eastern boundaries of the territory described by Stonehenge have been moved to the west to only include the areas which we now think of as having been Celtic.

The Searcy Geoglyph Boundaries (c1332)

The Search Geoglyph is the only known ancient and historically important,
geoglyph that has an unbroken family provenance since its conception.
According to the family testimony, 20,000 acres of this territory were deeded to
Benjamin Searcy, c1332 AD, by the King of Portugal. This was a time when
the Templars were fighting alongside Portugal and Spain to liberate the Iberian
Peninsula from the Muslims. At the time the land was ceded to the Searcys a
geoglyph was constructed which outland the area, now the eastern United
States, east of the Mississippi River. Since Portugal held claim to both North
and South America, and had survey markers to prove it, it would follow that
they ceded this land to the Templars for their assistance in Iberia. The Searcys
say that at one time there were four corner posts on their land which contained
runic writing. Those markers have since disappeared.

446

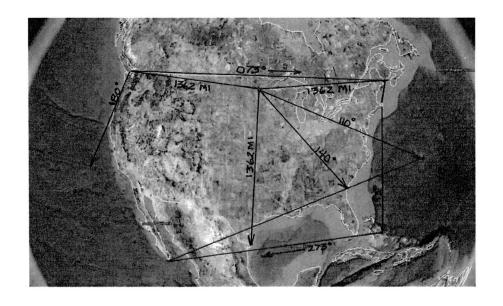

The Inspiration Peak, Kensington Runestone, Newport Tower Boundaries The 2nd territory, after the Searcy geoglyph, awarded to the Templars by Portugal c1362 AD)

Just as the Searcy Geoglyph outlined a territory east of the Mississippi c1332, this territory consists of the boundaries outlined by the combination of the Newport Tower, the Kensington Runestone and Inspiration Peak. The date 1362 is inscribed on the Kensington Runestone which is presumably the date that this second parcel of land was ceded to the Templars by Portugal. This would fit nicely with the date of 1473 AD, the carbon dated date of the first construction of the Newport Tower. The Newport Tower points directly to both the Kensington Runestone and Inspiration Peak. This also would be consistent with the date of 1562 AD, the earliest date possible for the second inscription on the Kensington Runestone, the inscription which defines the territory.

The United States Territory According to the Treaty of Paris (1778 AD)

I find it beyond the realm of circumstance, that the land that was negotiated for with the British, after the United States war of Independence, is identical to the Searcy Geoglyph boundaries in Vicksburg, MS USA, which was established c1332 AD. Why the US kept the land west of the Mississippi River, which Portugal ceded to them in 1362 AD, a secret during the Treaty of Paris negotiations remains uncertain; however, it is believed the information was suppressed to protect Portugal, who was the mutual ally of both the US and Britain.

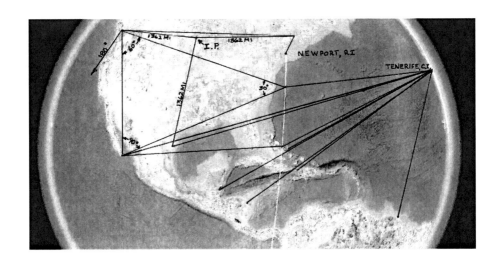

The Tenerife, Canary Island Geoglyph Boundaries (c1822 AD)

Because the USA had not revealed, in any public document, that in 1362 AD they had been given the land west of the Mississippi River by Portugal, a re-affirmation of the US territory ceded to them by Portugal was necessary. This reaffirmation came in the form of another geoglyph called the Guimar Pyramids, on the Island of Tenerife, in the Portuguese owned Canary Islands.

With Spain beginning to colonize the western lands given to the US in 1362 AD by the Portuguese, as preserved on the Kensington Runestone, the US needed validation for their plan to reclaim the land. The Tenerife geoglyph provided this validation. The US attempted to purchase the land from Mexico but that failed. This led to the Mexican American War. As you can see the radials generated by the Tenerife Geoglyphs, constructed in the first half of the 19th century, meet and confirm the territory which was ceded to the Templars by Portugal in 1362.

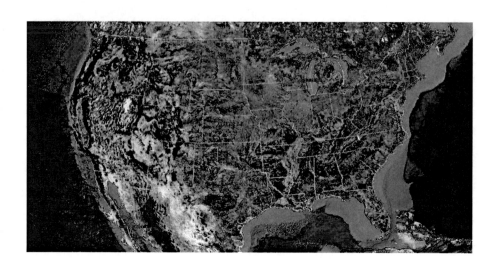

The United States of America (c1848 AD)

Once the Tenerife Geoglyph confirmed the territory rightfully belonging to the United States, the United States went to war with Mexico in 1846 AD. After the War, through "The Treaty of Hidalgo", the US gained the land north of the current southern border of the United States and forfeited that land south of the current border. The northern border of the US was decided after numerous negotiations, and treaties, between the US and Britain. After many years, England granted Canada their independence.

END CHAPTER

DNA Haplogroup R1b

A Haplogroup identifies DNA traits which identify locations where your ancient ancestors lived. As history has stated, the Celtic Culture originally migrated through the Slavic states to wind up in Western Europe. That fits perfectly with my research which showed that the Farums were tracked back to Galicia on the Iberian Peninsula. The Galicians moved to Denmark c700 AD, where our branch founded the city of Farum, Denmark. Many reasons converged at the end of the 14th century that caused the entire Farum clan to move to Scotland and Ireland. Only one family that moved to Scotland changed their name to Faram. This change made it easy to follow their lineage from that point on. Of course, the numbers of persons in this Haplogroup will increase as more people are tested. The location of the persons that appeared on this test confirms my research by showing up not only in the countries where my research had revealed that they had lived, but also in numbers proportionate to the length of time that they lived there.

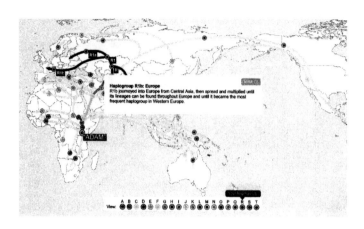

The Faram Haplogroup R1b

(The Celts are represented by the black lines)

YDNA

YDNA tracks the male DNA in any given family. It is through the mutations in any given family's DNA markers that they, and their predecessors, can be identified. The countries where these mutations show up, give an indication as to where those people's ancestors have lived in the past. To my amazement, and gratification, the YDNA hits on my DNA tests show only the locations which I had already identified through my family history and research. Now that you have read the book you can see why this was necessary. Had I not provided such confirmation it would be difficult for a reader to believe that any family could be involved in so much history. As you can see in the previous

chart, the Slavic Haplogroup migration ends where our R1b Celtic story starts, just north of Galicia.

YDNA Distribution of Arthur Faram

Listed below are the countries in which my 12 Marker DNA appeared in more than one percent of the population which was tested prior to 4/15/2013. The 25 Marker and 37 Marker results contain "all" of the countries that were listed in their categories. (Source: Family Tree DNA –

http://www.familytreedna.com/)

12 MARKER – Exact Match

Canada *

France

Ireland

Portugal

Puerto Rico

Scotland

Spain (Including Galicia, Basque and the Azores)

United States

- For context purposes Canada was included, even though it showed only a 0.3% total.

YDNA Distribution of Arthur Faram (Cont.)

25 MARKER -1

England

Portugal

25 MARKER -2

Belgium

Denmark

England

France

Germany

Ireland

Portugal

Puerto Rico

Scotland

Spain

Switzerland

United States

Wales

37 MARKER -4

Germany

Prussia

Portugal

Azores

Scotland

Spain (Galicia)

END OF APPENDIX "A"

APPENDIX B

Carbon Dating the Newport Tower

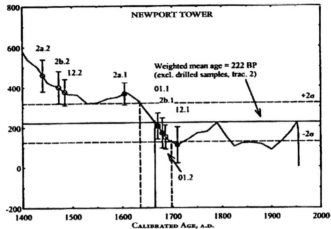

Position	Height above ground (cm)	Sample Depth (cm)	Sample No.	Lab. No. AAR-	Fraction of total sample (%)	Carbonate concentration (%)	^{14}C Age (BP)	$\delta^{13}C$(‰) PDB
TOWER:								
Flue above fireplace	550	Surface	X.1	1284.1	45	42	205±65	-12.3
			X.2	1284.2	55		150±60	-11.5
Pillar 7	120	7-42	2a.1	1352.1	20	21	365±55	-12.9
			2a.2	1352.2	80		460±80	-9.4
			2b.1	1352.3	50	17	170±75	-10.7
			2b.2	1352.4	50		400±80	-9.7
			32.1	1504.1	83	2.0	No meas.	-10.8
			32.2	1504.2	77		No meas.	
			3b.1	1504.3	40	1.7	No meas.	-11.3
			3b.2	1504.4	60		No meas.	-10.4
Fireplace	430	10-20w	8.1	1353.1	57	5.8	(-110±70)*	-12*
			8.2	1353.2	43		(130±70)*	-11.6
Pillar 6	20	10-25	12.1	1286.1	37	52	110±90	-13.4
			12.2	1286.2	63		375±65	-9.7
Pillar 8	250	Plaster	Bulk (conv.)	Hel-3181			290±110	-6.4
Excavated 1949			Ox bone	1280			25±60	-19.7
WANTON-LYMAN-HAZARD HOUSE:								
Basement	30	Surface	H 23.1	1287.1	52	70	80±100	-16.3
			H 23.2	1287.2	48		160±60	-11.3

* Excluded due to low carbonate content

FIGURES 3 AND 4. HEINEMEIER AND JUNGNER CALIBRATION CURVES AND DATA TABLE.

Presented Above is The Heinemeier and Junger Report

Since 1996, when the team of Heinemeier and Junger performed carbon dating using samples from the Newport Tower, their data has been considered flawed by some researchers. However, it is this researcher's opinion that neither their data nor their techniques were flawed. The outcome of the Heinemeier and Junger report was confusing because it developed not one, but two, closely grouped sets of data. Rob Carter summed it up when he wrote:

"Other researchers working on this technique for dating stone structures in South America report success at dating pre-Columbian mortared walls. There were no serious inconsistencies between the carbon dates and other corroborating evidence. What made their work [Heinemeier and Junger] different?"

The results were not flawed, but led us to overlook the obvious. There are two camps of thought on the date of the Newport Tower. First, there are the Templar enthusiasts who contend that the tower was constructed in the 15th Century. Second, there are the Colonist Enthusiasts that claim that the tower was constructed in the 17th Century. I believe they are both correct. Is it not possible that the tower was built in the 15th Century, partially destroyed, and then rebuilt from the remains in the 17th Century? All signs point in that direction. This line of reasoning is especially compelling when it is considered that the Kensington Runestone, by necessity, was updated sometime after 1559 AD.

1. The Heinemeier and Junger report shows two close groupings, one in the 15th Century and the other in the 17th Century.

2. The H & J Report contains so much data that a very important fact has been overlooked.

Their data is not arbitrary because each of the three samples that were used in their graph consistently contained both a 15th Century date and a 17th Century date. (The researchers were careful not to include samples which were flawed by low carbon content or from a possibly contaminated surface source.)

This can only lead to one logical conclusion. The tower was built in approximately 1463, the average of the three 15th Century dates presented in the data, and then rebuilt in approximately 1663, the average of the 17th Century data, using material from the old structure. Curiously, the average dates of construction are exactly 200 years apart.

Sample....................Date

2a1...........................1610
2a2...........................1440

2b1...........................1670
2b2...........................1470

12-1..........................1710
12-2..........................1480

END OF APPENDIX "B"

APPENDIX C

Magnetic Deviation

Magnetic Deviation and It's Affect on Navigating a Compass Heading

GEOMAGNETIC MAPS (dish size list or tuning page)
(to Western Hemisphere, Eastern Hemisphere, Footprints by Dish Size)

The most important geomagnetic fact to remember, the earth's magnetic field is neither uniform, stationary, nor perfectly aligned with the planet's poles. True north can be determined with a compass reading plus/minus (as appropriate) the location's magnetic deviation. Magnetic deviation (also called magnetic declination, magnetic variation, or compass variation) is the angle between the north compass (magnetic) heading and the heading to true (geographic) north. For absolute accuracy, you can call your local airport control tower to find the magnetic correction value for your area; this value can also be found on local maps though many maps ommit this value. The following maps are also called isogonic maps. North America, South America, Europe, Middle East, Orient/New Guinea, Australia/New Zealand, Global

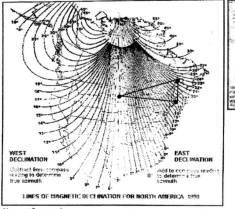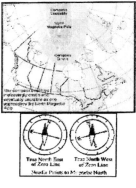

(top of page)

Source: http://www.geo-orbit.org

Magnetic Deviation Chart for North America

The previous chart depicts the North American Continent, and shows the amount of Magnetic Deviation at any given point in the United States. On that chart, the Newport Triangle has been overlaid in its proper position. Notice that the Newport Triangle progresses from 5 degrees West deviation to 15 degrees East deviation, passing through the 0 degree line of deviation. That means that while progressing from the West side of the triangle to the East side, you will pick up a 20 degree error. That error is demonstrated on the diagram that follows.

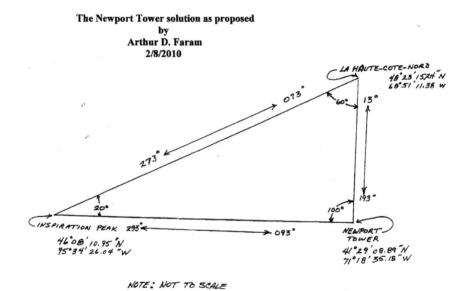

The Newport Tower solution as proposed
by
Arthur D. Faram
2/8/2010

NOTE: NOT TO SCALE

The Newport Triangle

Notice that the magnetic headings, obtained from the point of origination, from East to West and from West to East are exactly 20 degrees off from what they should be. The opposite heading on any true course should be exactly 180 degrees from each other. These magnetic headings are 20 degrees off as the result of the magnetic deviation along that line. That deviation does not exist in a true course plotted by celestial navigation or GPS. How the ancient mariners did it is a mystery, but their calculations are either directly on target or only a few hundred feet off, sometimes on courses extending over thousands of miles.

END OF APPENDIX "C"

APPENDIX D

Destroyed Geoglyphs

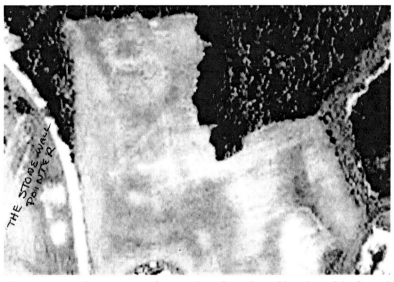

The Kensington Runestone Campsite, One Day North, with Geoglyphs
(Before)

After

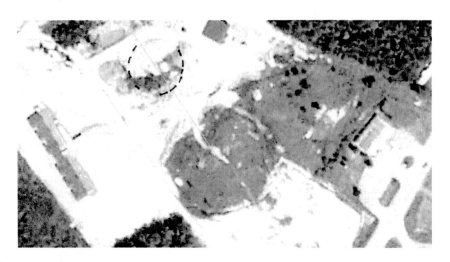

**The 1362 Mile Radial, Northeast Endpoint, and Associated Geoglyph
(Before)**

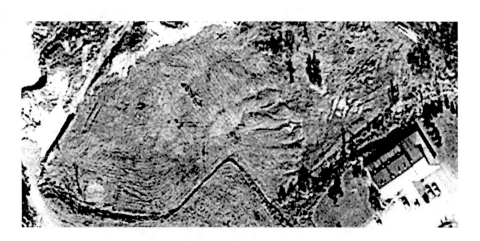

(After)

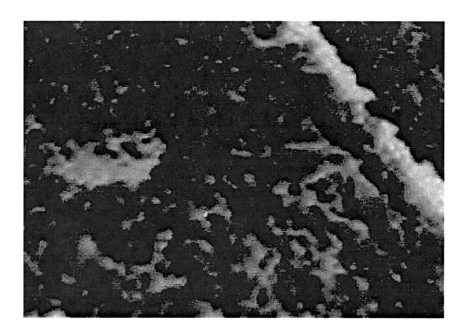

The Sulpher City Towers on the Left with a Line Geoglyph on the Right (Before)

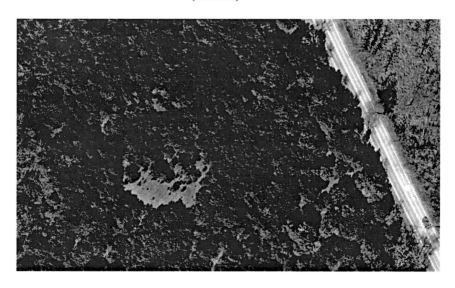

(After)

These are the stones which made up the line geoglyph in the previous two photos. They were photographed while they were waiting to be disposed of. The geoglyph used to be behind the tree in the center of the photo.

What used to be a Sulpher City Geoglyph (Left) with the stone pointers that used to surround it laying alongside the road waiting to be picked up for disposal. (Right)

A Geoglyph Near Vicksburg, Mississippi
(Before)

(After)

Sources

A Commentary on "Sources".

Now that we are living in the computer age, and since most data that we use are retrieved from the Internet, it seems redundant to list a number of books, which can't be updated, as sources. The data that resides on information related websites, such as Wikipedia, and Academic websites has been reviewed by the webmasters, the public, and can be updated. Most of the time there are numerous choices on the same topic which allow immediate access to differing ideas. If you are so inclined, each subject in Wikipedia has a book resource at the bottom of the page,. All significant information in this book, or information that cannot be retrieved from a reliable internet source, has the source annotated within the text of the book. This provides a quick and convenient way to access references without searching through hundreds of, possibly irrelevant, and outdated books.

The information age is moving so fast that by the time a book is published it is sometimes out of date; therefore, the sources for our research include internet resources unless the information originates from an offline source.
Since there is so much information in this book, which is just being revealed, or has been archived for many years, it was necessary to provide a more convenient way to research the information. I am hoping that this format will initiate a change to a more relevant way to provide source information.

Sources:

Wikipedia (Using the appropriate keyword, under the Creative Commons License. http://www.creativecommons.org/compatablelicenses)

Google (Using the appropriate keyword.)

Google Earth (Using the ruler function.)

The Faram Foundation Archives (Verified through history resources)

Faram Family Oral History (Verified through history resources)

Familytreedna.com

Ancestry.com

Imbedded references, within the text

Keywords: the search keyword, used in the above media, should be the subject which you wish to confirm, or for which you desire more information.

CPSIA information can be obtained at www.ICGtesting.com
Printed in the USA
LVOW05s1636290913

354605LV00013BB/884/P